AMERICAN
ENDURANCE

AMERICAN ENDURANCE

BUFFALO BILL, the Great COWBOY RACE of 1893, and the Vanishing WILD WEST

Richard A. Serrano

Smithsonian Books
Washington, DC

This book may be purchased for educational, business, or sales promotional use. For information, please write: Special Markets Department, Smithsonian Books, P.O. Box 37012, MRC 513, Washington, DC 20013.

Published by Smithsonian Books
Director: Carolyn Gleason
Managing Editor: Christina Wiginton
Production Editor: Laura Harger
Editor: Duke Johns
Designer: Nancy Bratton
Map: Bill Nelson

Library of Congress Cataloging-in-Publication Data
Serrano, Richard A.
American endurance : Buffalo Bill, the Great Cowboy Race of 1893, and the vanishing Wild West / by Richard A. Serrano.
Description: Washington, DC : Smithsonian Books, 2016. |
    Includes bibliographical references and index.
Identifiers: LCCN 2015047567 | ISBN 9781588345752
Subjects: LCSH: Endurance riding (Horsemanship)—West (U.S.)—
    History—19th century. | Horse racing—West (U.S.)—History—
    19th century. | Cross-country (Horsemanship)—West (U.S.)—
    History—19th century. | Cowboys—West (U.S.)—History—19th century. |
    Buffalo Bill, 1846–1917. | World's Columbian Exposition
    (1893 : Chicago, Ill.) | West (U.S.)—History—1890–1945.
Classification: LCC SF296.E5 S47 2016 | DDC 798.40978—dc23
LC record available at http://lccn.loc.gov/2015047567

Manufactured in the United States of America
21 20 19 18 17 16   5 4 3 2 1

For Michael, Ben, Elise, and Alexander
My buckaroos

Daring, laughter, endurance—these were what I saw
upon the countenances of the cow-boys.

Owen Wister, *The Virginian: A Horseman of the Plains,* 1902

Contents

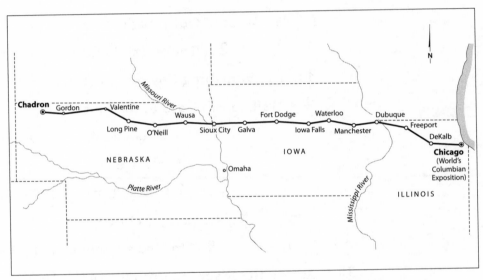

Route of the Great Cowboy Race from Chadron, Nebraska, to Chicago, 1893

The West of Our Imagination | 1

Of all the riders in the Great Cowboy Race of 1893, none was better known or more widely feared than the notorious outlaw Doc Middleton. Some cowboys still rode the range and herded cattle; he stole horses. Many more were starting to settle down and raise families; he lived by the gun. He had been hunted for years by sheriffs' posses, scrambling along the Niobrara River basin.

He rode through the tiny town of Chadron, Nebraska, several days ahead of the race. In the afternoons, he trotted his horse up and down Second Street, exercising it, keeping the brown gelding lean and limber. The men peered at him from the saloon and shop windows. The ladies dashed outside and plucked strands from the horse's tail. Souvenirs, they said; keepsakes.

The race began near dusk on a June afternoon in 1893, with a pistol shot fired from the balcony of the new Blaine Hotel. But Doc at first held back. Under his wide-brimmed hat, his eyes followed the other eight riders as they vanished in a whirl of hooves and dust.

"Boys," he told the Chadron crowd, his beard so long it nearly hid his holsters. "I'm behind now. But I may be ahead." With a cowboy holler, he galloped off.

John Berry rode, too. He normally worked as an engineer and surveyor, and unlike Doc Middleton, he was far from being any wild cowboy. He helped lay the right-of-way for the Fremont, Elkhorn, and Missouri Valley Railroad, pushing one track at a time through the Nebraska Panhandle. He had helped plat the town of Chadron, too. When gossip around town turned serious about a thousand-mile cowboy race from Chadron to Chicago and the World's Columbian Exposition, Berry helped map the route.

1

For that, the Chadron race committee had ordered him disqualified. But Berry rode anyway—under protest. When he reached the finish line at the thousand-mile tree marker at Buffalo Bill Cody's Wild West show next to the fair in Chicago, he nearly fell off his horse. He was caked in dust, and his clothes were shredded. "I rode the last 150 miles in twenty-four hours," he gasped. "Sore? Well, I should say I was.... I am so sleepy I can't talk. I have had no sleep for ten days to amount to anything."

For two weeks he had raced his chestnut stallion (named Poison) through the Nebraska Sand Hills, across Iowa cornfields, and into Illinois, often just hoofbeats ahead of county deputies, humane society and animal rights protesters, and two governors who pledged to shut down the race and arrest any rider who abused his horse.

The Great Cowboy Race of 1893 tested a particularly American virtue: endurance. It was launched at the close of the Western frontier and near the start of the twentieth century. Nine men rode leaning over their horses, hats slapping in the wind, defiant symbols of the vanishing Wild West. For two weeks they thundered toward the noisy, crowded, cobblestone metropolis of Chicago and the dazzling White City of the World's Columbian Exposition.

In Chicago, cable cars and electric trolleys were fast replacing horses. The exposition was focused on the future, a future that would not include cowboys. It previewed the wonders of the world that was to come, while the West looked back at the cowboy past.

The American frontier was born of adversity; hard times rocked its cradle. The epic push to settle the vast swaths of grassland and uphill country past the Missouri River had taken muscle, courage, and ingenuity. Days filled with hard labor were followed by lonely twilight in dugouts far from families back east or across the broad Atlantic. Isolation shrouded the Plains, and in some locations the threat of Indian attacks lurked over the next ridge.

Yet there persisted an innate drive to break the land and hammer down stakes, to launch rough-and-tumble pop-up towns on either side of the Rockies, to toughen the frontier resolve, and to carry the country into that new and modern American century.

Chadron sprouted up just south of the purple badlands; Wounded Knee lay just a day's ride away in southwestern South Dakota. The town was begun near the White River and Chadron Creek. It was founded by an Irish widow named Fannie O'Linn. She set up a trading store, got herself appointed postmistress, and brought in a livery stable. The saloons followed her. But when a new railroad line swung six miles out from the O'Linn settlement, people simply picked up their homesteads and moved in closer to the new depot. Thus was born the city of Chadron, another fragile Western outpost clinging to survival.

Some summers, swarms of grasshoppers devoured the wheat and corn stalks, the feed lots, and the rare tree or bush on the flat, endless landscape. Wooden cattle fences and farm machinery were swallowed whole. The hoppers would burrow deep inside a man's beard and eat his hat to pieces. Desperate pioneers set fire to their fields, hoping to block the hordes of insects. The bugs flew around them.

In winter the land hardened and froze. During the 1886–87 season, thousands of range cattle perished in icy creek beds and along fallen fence lines in what cowboys called the "Great Die-Up." The next winter, young students were buried in head-high snowdrifts, trying in vain to slog their little legs home. Historians have called it the "Children's Blizzard." Hundreds of lives were swept away by the wind, the snow, and the below-zero temperatures.

In another fierce winter storm, a young cowboy named Billy "the Bear" Iaeger lost his way. For days he dug and searched for an abandoned barn, a silo, or a sod house, anywhere to shelter from the blowing snow. Frostbite claimed his feet and fingers. But Billy endured. In Chadron, he became a saloon keeper, police judge, city clerk, and a town leader. His old friend William "Buffalo Bill" Cody occasionally bought him new "artificials" from St. Louis, and soon Billy was gliding around town with a fresh set of legs. When the cowboy race was starting to look like a sure thing and Cody wanted it to head straight to his Wild West show in Chicago, Billy the Bear naturally was appointed to the race committee.

Buffalo Bill was a born promoter. The famous scout and buckskin hunter had just returned in early 1893 from a triumphant tour of England, where he stunned packed audiences with his authentic cowboys and Indians chasing each other around a sand and gravel track, and with his own skilled sharpshooting from a speeding horse.

He met and entertained the queens of England and Holland. He won the hearts of the world.

Returning home, Cody wanted his Wild West show to share in the glory and profits of the Chicago World's Columbian Exposition. Where else did he belong, if not to the world? But the fair said no. Cody represented the past, the old Western world; the fair would be about the future. So Buffalo Bill leased a large tract of land next to the fairgrounds and soon was rivaling the fair itself. That summer of 1893 would be the showman's best run ever.

To drum up business, he also donated a sizable hunk toward the prize money for the Great Cowboy Race. In return, Chadron marked off the thousand miles from the balcony of the Blaine Hotel to Cody's tent door in Chicago. The Indian fighter with a record number of buffalo kills would himself be at the finish line. And he would personally award the winner a glittering, gold-laden Colt revolver. All eyes would be trained on the galloping cowboys and, naturally, Buffalo Bill.

Something else was happening that summer in Chicago. A little-known historian from Wisconsin, Frederick Jackson Turner, addressed a gathering of the American Historical Association and delivered his new thesis, "The Significance of the Frontier in American History." Just three years earlier, the U.S. Census Bureau had proclaimed the frontier no more, saying that America's quest for new Western land had run thin and the search for new expansion was over. Turner proclaimed that while the American spirit was driven by new adventures, the westward wanderlust had at last spent itself. Within the boundaries of the United States, there were no more frontiers to claim, no new lands to conquer.

President Lincoln had begun the movement with land grants during the Civil War. Wagon trains pushed over the old scout trails. Telegraph cables and railroad lines stitched the country together. Telephone poles shot up, and the dangling phone wires, some cut by Indians desperate to preserve their own way of life, marked a new way west.

The buffalo slaughter was nearly complete. All that remained were scavengers scooping up the bones whitening in the sun on the High

Plains. Most Plains Indian peoples, their primary source of food and blankets disappearing, laid down their weapons.

The December 1890 massacre at Wounded Knee, the last of the great Indian War engagements, came less than three years before the cowboy race. The Chadron newspapers dispatched their reporters to record the slaughter, and they wired home stories of frozen Lakota corpses on the Pine Ridge tundra and the eerie prolonged echo of the Lakota Ghost Dance.

The great Sioux chief Red Cloud, who once ruled the lush Platte River Valley, surrendered to life on the Pine Ridge Indian Reservation. Occasionally he ventured down to Chadron in full headdress for Fourth of July celebrations. But he was a shadow of what he once had been. From a platform erected in the shade of the Dawes County Courthouse, the broken chief shared a few words with the Western immigrants who had brought white ways to a red world. "I was always cheated, and so were my people," he told them. "I don't like to make a fuss about this, for I want to be friends to you all. This land is mine. I want you to be my friends, and we will live as friends in the future."

Army Captain Charles King, who helped lead the U.S. troops and went on to glorify their adventures in dozens of Western novels, remembered the Indian Wars well. "It is all a memory now," he later told a gathering of veterans. "But what a memory to cherish!"

The romance, the thrill, the daring, the stubbornness, the sheer adventure of the Wild West—all of it was ending. Like the cowboys sputtering to keep ahead in the Great Race, enduring saddle sores, leg blisters, raw knuckles and chapped faces, the searing summer heat, the drenching summer rain, little food, little water, tired and shredded and exhausted, like John Berry nearly falling off his horse, the Old West too was weathering away.

Several state humane society inspectors followed the cowboys and reported their findings across the telegraph wires and new phone lines. Others chased them on bicycles, on boats, on mules, in carriages, and on foot. In small towns along the route, people stood for hours, anxious for a hint of hooves or a whiff of dust. Boys climbed trees to keep a lookout.

A newspaperman spotted some of the cowboys sleeping in the back of a rolling buggy, trying to rest up while beating the others to Chicago. Other racers secretly shipped their horses by train to get ahead. Some carried wire cutters to snip shortcuts through fenced pastures. Many rode at night; it was cooler then, and the low-hanging lantern moon lit their way. Two competitors stopped at a small-town Iowa circus and for laughs bucked around the arena on a trick mule.

But much of the riding and racing were done alone, on long stretches through the interior plains of the United States, pushing farther away from the cowboys' beloved Western range. Mandatory stops at local inspection stations slowed them down, as did brief moments for a meal, a bed, and a barn. Then in a burst they would be gone again, another day's ride, to another town over another hilltop.

Far away in Chicago, the city was in an uproar. The Illinois governor had pardoned several anarchists, igniting calls for his ouster. Clerics and city fathers brawled over whether to close the fair on Sundays. A financial panic cleaved the downtown business district. A serial killer was at work. And Carter Harrison, the beloved mayor of Chicago, who had done so much to keep the White City glowing and the fair a success, was soon to be assassinated by an out-of-luck office seeker.

In Chadron, news of the Great Cowboy Race sometimes rode in with a passing stranger. Otherwise the anxious crowds gathered at the local newspaper offices, and for two long weeks people hungered for updates. Who was ahead? Who had dropped out? And where the devil were they?

The Harsh Land | 2

Two years before the cowboys came racing through the Nebraska Sand Hills, two young sisters started for home on a late Sunday afternoon in May. Tillie and Retta Haumann, part of a German immigrant family, strolled hand in hand through the spring wildflowers, the primroses, and the native prairie grasses. The quilt of gold and yellow-green spread before their feet, perfect for trying out their new shoes.

A coal miner in the old country, Carl August Haumann and his family had sailed in 1883 to the United States and settled first in Illinois. Eight years later, they pushed on to rural, untamed Thomas County in north central Nebraska. The closest town, Thedford, was just four years old, founded by immigrants on new railroad tracks that lanced through the heart of the hills.

The Haumanns were expanding rapidly, too. Carl and his wife, Henrietta, first stepped off the depot with ten children; four more would be born in Nebraska. They would become the largest family in the county, noted for the vast orchards their father and the boys tended on their homestead six miles north of town.

On that Sunday in May 1891, Tillie, eight, and Retta, four, journeyed to visit an older sister a mile and a half away. Around four in the afternoon, they started to return home. By nightfall they had not arrived, nor in the morning. Neighbor men set aside their plows and planting and scoured the wind-scooped hills and hollows, calling the girls' names. By sundown Monday, all they had picked up were a few signs of feet and hands and knees, small prints in the sand and grass. Over and around the hills, the men poked and prodded. By Wednesday morning they could tell that the girls had slept close to each other. Sometimes Tillie had carried her younger sister, it appeared.

Once the girls spied a prairie fire in the distance. Tillie told Retta to wait while she climbed a hill to scan the countryside. Through the shimmering blue haze, she could see another hill and then another, a mirage of sand hills. Down below, Retta decided to catch up with Tillie by circling around that first hill. And so the girls were separated.

Wednesday afternoon the men stumbled upon Retta, walking alone and carrying one of her new shoes, the sole worn off. The men rushed over the surrounding hills, but four more days would pass before they came upon Tillie. She had spread her apron next to a spray of rose bushes after wandering seventy-five miles and a whole county east across the Sand Hills. She had been gone a week, and there she lay down and died.

They lifted her body onto a railway hand car and carried her home. Her devastated family hardly recognized their first child born in the new country. Her pale skin was darkened from exposure, and her little legs were blistered from thickets and brush. Only her new shoes gave Tillie away.

The West and the prairie: the people, the droughts, the winters, the fires, the plagues, the sweat and the toil, and every evening the cinnamon sunsets. Embracing and evil. Charming and deadly. One moment youth flashes in all its boundless energy; next comes a sudden, searing loss, followed by anguish, followed by despair. Against all this the High Plains roll on and on, flat and endless, silent and unresponsive, their strength in their vastness.

Two other daughters of old Nebraska would endure the hardships of Western frontier life and eventually rejoice in the indomitable spirit of the pioneers.

State historian and writer Mari Sandoz would call Nebraska "the land that is yet to be found." Her father, "Old Jules," years earlier had pioneered much of the region and for a while scratched out a living selling rolled-up maps for $25 to those hunting new sections of free land. As a young girl, Mari spread the maps out on their dusty cabin floor and, ignoring her baby brother's cries, imagined the strips of buckbrush and hackberry leaves, the "Big Muddy" Missouri River and the watery Platte, the Wildcat Range and the Pine Ridge. In her mind's eye, she saw the hearty cattle and the heaving oxen, the men windburned and footsore, the sad-eyed women glancing backward as the wagons jostled and pulled them deeper into the frontier West.

"It was this gradual climb toward the Continental Divide, with water and grass all the way westward—the direction the white man seems to move over the globe—that made the state the world's great path of empire," Mari Sandoz wrote. The weary migrants, she observed, "began to spill off like golden grain sifting from a creaking wagon, leaving little settlements to sprout up all along from the Missouri westward, always headed into the sunset."

What they often found was a country too fickle to hold down, too broad to understand—an odd May blizzard or an October afternoon that "can be so lovely it stops the heart," Sandoz wrote. Germans, Irish, Swiss—all were tough before they arrived, tougher if they stayed. Find one man alone in the uncut wilderness, hammering up a fence and putting down roots, and he will be squinting at the sky. Find two or more together, spading a dugout or patching a "soddie," or sod house, and they will be jabbering about the weather. Find them five years later, and they will never leave.

In the 1890s, those drought and depression years, Sandoz's father had known an old Pawnee rainmaker who for $10 swore he could command an inch of precipitation to fall on unquenched pastures. For $20 he promised a soaker. No one was wealthy, but Old Jules and his neighbors counted out twenty one-dollar bills and for good luck tossed in a jug of whiskey. The Pawnee danced, sang, and cavorted, and sure enough the skies opened. The happy farmers cheered until the rain turned to hail and the hail pounded their crops into the ground.

Still the settlers kept coming. "One young woman drove the cattle of a relative all the way from Wisconsin to Nebraska, afoot," Sandoz wrote. "And in my childhood I knew a man and wife, immigrants from Prague, who had pushed a wheelbarrow with their few household goods clear across Nebraska to our region for a homestead." The first Bohemian to settle in the Nebraska Territory would walk routinely to St. Joseph, Missouri, and back for groceries, a substantial round trip that took him twice across the Missouri River.

More and more wagons pushed farther west, and the Indians' livelihood eventually gave way. There were too many white men to hold back, too few Indians to resist them. Sandoz recalled an old Sioux who used to plant and dig up potatoes and in his last years

An immigrant family pauses on their journey west through Nebraska's Loup River Valley, 1886. (Library of Congress)

would sit and marvel at the modern conveniences immigrants lugged over the prairie. "All his family had died of the coughing sickness because, he said, they had slept in a cornered log shack," Sandoz wrote. "He would never cross our doorstep but often sat outside on the woodblock for hours, visiting over his pipe."

The wagon ruts delivered the settlers deep into the brush and tall grass, tired, sore, lonely, and often scared. Yet life could be enchanting. "Nowhere are the songs of the meadowlarks finer, the wild flowers and the sunsets more magnificent, than on the higher reaches of the state," Sandoz wrote.

The author Willa Cather and her family left Virginia for a new home in Nebraska in 1883; she was nineteen by the summer the cowboys came barreling through from the Panhandle to the Chicago lakefront. And like the Haumann girls, Cather lost herself in new surroundings. "I knew every farm, every tree, every field in the region around my home, and they all called out to me," she once said. "My deepest feelings were rooted in this country."

Much of the state was grass and dirt, and homes and farms were three or four miles apart. Wagons were drawn by heavy workhorses, barns raised with the muscle of neighboring men. In the spring, homesteaders put their shoulders to the plow and broke the virgin ground into chunks.

In an essay titled "Nebraska: The End of the First Cycle," Cather told of pioneers gathered in an eastern Nebraska log cabin to witness the installation of a new telegraph machine. When the gadget began to click, the men removed their hats, "as if they were in church." The first wire to flash west across the Missouri River into Nebraska was not a market report; there would be plenty of those to come. First to arrive was instead a line of poetry: "Westward the course of empire takes its way."

To Cather, "the old West was like that." For her, writing one of her early novels, *O Pioneers!*, "was like taking a ride through a familiar country on a horse that knew the way." Thirty years after leaving the West, Cather, in her New York apartment, could still recall her first day out there. She and her family loaded up on an April morning and drove across the tallgrass prairie to her grandfather's ranch near the Kansas–Nebraska line. "I was sitting on the hay in the bottom of a Studebaker wagon, holding on to the side of the wagon box to steady myself," she remembered. "The roads were mostly faint trails over the bunch grass in those days. The land was open range and there was almost no fencing. As we drove further and further out into the country, I felt a good deal as if we had come to the end of everything."

In time she learned to adore the soft side of the hard West. The wild plum jam, picked and mashed and canned. Quilts embroidered with state flowers. The black soil, the bronze prairie, the opal sky. A hundred miles in every direction the golden wheat strands swaying, as if sweeping off to Russia. All around her Cather listened to the Bohemian accents and with her pen created the velvety brown eyes of her future heroine, Ántonia Shimerda. From a child's perspective, the land was bursting with life—young like Willa, vast swaths of it still unlearned and untouched.

"Whenever I crossed the Missouri River coming into Nebraska," she said in her later years, "the very smell of the soil tore me to pieces. I was always being pulled back into Nebraska." She remembered the fat prairie chickens, the quail hidden in the high grass, and the wild ducks paddling around the lagoons. From those lagoons the first settlers toted water on their backs to their homesteads.

Men, women, young families, and old pioneers were "warm, mercurial, impressionable, restless, and over-fond of novelty and change," Cather said.

The West was not always so cherished. For decades it was scorned by Easterners as the "Great American Desert." With little rain or too many downpours, thin topsoil or hard clay, and the Rockies' peaks a barrier to progress, it seemed nothing would come of the vast region. For many, the useful West ended at the Missouri River bluffs, and not a footfall farther.

Even as far back as 1838, when Senator Daniel Webster of Massachusetts had opposed a measure to fund a mail route between Independence, Missouri, and the Columbia River Gorge, the vast Western expanse appeared to be a ghost preserve for migrant Indian tribes to squabble over. "What use have we for such a country?" Webster asked.

President Lincoln opened the land when he signed the Homestead Act of 1862. Then the settler planted his boots on it, dug his shovels in, built a home, and raised a barn. He hoped his crops would take root and strain for the sky. Then maybe he could earn enough folding money to buy fence rails. He had horses to feed and cattle to shelter. He dowsed for water below the earth and prayed for rain from above. Often high mortgages and farm supply loans threatened to close down his place. But if he stayed for five years, if he improved it and reaped a life from the harsh land, then that quarter section of 160 acres would be his.

Settlements in Nebraska grew by 324 percent in the 1860s and 135 percent in the '80s. Where once there had been no white population, now one million filled its farthest reaches. By 1890 more than three million people had elbowed into Nebraska, Kansas, and North and South Dakota.

The best spots were seized near rivers or streams or along hillsides that sheltered settlers against the wind. Still more trains followed of white-top wagons carrying more settlers, farmers, and ranchers pouring in.

"You must make up your mind to rough it," cautioned a pioneers' guide from 1870. "You must cultivate the habit of sleeping in any kind of surroundings, on a board and without a pillow, indoors or out. I have been to sleep on horseback. You must be prepared to cook your own dinner, darn your own socks if you wear them, and think yourself fortunate if you are not reduced to the position of a man I knew, who lay in bed while his wife mended his own pair of trousers."

The guide also warned, "Learn to ride as soon as you possibly can; a man or boy who cannot ride is, in a new country, about as valuable as a clerk who cannot write in a city office." Those who took the stage-coach were told, "Never shoot on the road as the noise might frighten the horses. Don't discuss politics or religion. Don't grease your hair, because travel is dusty."

A hearty bunch they were, struggling with stubborn oxen, broken wheels, rutted tracks, fleas and manure, sudden lightning bursts, high-water creeks, and, all too often, isolation, loneliness, and boredom.

George Washington Franklin arrived in Nebraska in the fall of 1885 from too-crowded Iowa, slogging two weeks over the rug-ged trails. A year later Thomas Jefferson Huntzinger wagoned from Akron, Ohio, to Independence, Kansas, then walked the rest of the way to Colorado. He established a claim there, then hurried on a train back to Missouri, where he hitched up a team and a double-box wagon. Then he drove back.

In 1887, Wallace Hoze Wilcock cleared Illinois and headed for eastern Colorado. He dropped off his wife and two babies in Nebraska and pushed on alone to Colorado. There he staked his claim. But by the time he returned to Nebraska, collected his family, and made it back to his new home in Colorado, sixty other homesteaders had already crowded in.

Towns sprang up like wild prairie mushrooms. Soddies were scooped out of the dirt, the hillsides, and the river beds, their walls braced with cheesecloth to hold back the winter frost. Men mixed lime and sand to shore up the rafters. Black-and-white newspaper pages, once read, were pasted in like wallpaper, then read again standing up. Newspaper sheets also doubled as winter blankets.

When someone fell sick, often the cures were warm manure for snakebite, warm urine for earache, and roasted mouse for measles. Warts? Toss a bean into the well over your left shoulder. Rheumatism? Carry a potato in your pocket. If a prairie photographer swung by, the family gathered outside, Ma or Grandma in the only chair, Pa and the rest of the family standing erect and stone-faced beside the others. None of them smiled. A dog might wag its tail. Sometimes a pig rutted.

But the families persevered; they endured. By 1877, the community of Antelope County, Nebraska, had grown in eleven years to 1,500 people, two flour mills, two sawmills, six post offices, nine stores, five lawyers, three preachers, and that most precious commodity of all, a town doctor. Tiny Haigler, Nebraska, was a mere frontier village in 1885, about thirty settlers trying to hang on as more adventurous immigrants rolled past them searching for greener pastures. In a few years' time, Haigler sported a brand-new school building, a two-story city hall, two churches, two hotels, and a pair of dueling money lenders.

Just getting "out there" was tough enough. On June 5, 1864, George Edwin Bushnell wrote in his traveling diary from south central Nebraska: "(Sun.) Saw 2 Antelopes, and yesterday morning saw an Elk. Passed three ranches to-day, passed 47 wagons, and traveled 40 mi. and camped on The Platte bottom, 40 mi. from Ft. Kearney."

June 13: "(Mon.) Passed 5 Indian graves, about 7 ft. from the ground on scaffolds. Near the Junction House, we passed 262 wagons today."

June 22: "(Wed.) Saw the peaks of the Rocky Mountains 130 mi. distant."

In 1874, Cora A. Beels rode west with her family. She was seventeen and her parents were divided about the journey. They rode by rail to Wisner, Nebraska, then continued in a lumber wagon another thirty miles to Norfolk. "A tire came off of one of the wagon wheels, and all the rest of the way my father walked beside that wheel keeping the tire pounded on with a stick," she recalled years later. "So our progress was very slow. And with every added mile the spirit of our gentle mother sank still lower."

At Norfolk, in northeast Nebraska, the Beelses' first home was a one-room board shack with two small windows and a loft. "Our kitchen was a large dry-goods box, set on end before the door," Beels said. "The cooking was done on a gasoline stove." Hungry Indians knocked at their door seeking ginger cookies and other handouts. Prairie fires lit up the sky; one blazed for three nights. June floods roared through the Norfolk valley, swamping the grain fields, the rainwater rising above the baseboards of pioneer huts. Yet despite the uncertain journey and the tensions between her determined father and unhappy mother, Beels at eighty-four remained proud of what they had endured. "The blood of pioneers flows in my veins," she said.

In 1878, Lucy Alice Ide and her husband, Chester, crossed the plains in a prairie schooner. They launched from Wisconsin and joined a wagon train of forty-one migrants bound for the Washington Territory. The journey spanned four months and thirteen days. One man fell sick en route, bleeding from his lungs. He left the wagons and continued by rail.

When the wagons reached Nebraska, and thunder and lightning brought an all-night rain, Ide wrote in her diary, "If this is the style of Nebraska, I do not care to stop here long." Farther across the state, the caravan stopped for church and a Sunday sermon. "It does us good for it has been four weeks since we heard the last one," she wrote.

On Plum Creek in central Nebraska, the Ides visited the local jailhouse. "There was a lady confined in the jail for the murder of her husband, and two men in for murder. The lady looked very sad—did not look as though she was guilty; she had her little girl with her."

They continued despite more storms and more horses spooked by thunder; one horse became so agitated it tore away with a "wild snort." Ide wrote, "We just got in order, our wagons chained together and then firmly staked down.... We got to bed without our supper. Only a bite of bread and dried beef." Her spirits sank. "I have not a very good opinion of Nebraska so far," she confided.

They passed four horse carcasses lying on the roadside, felled by lightning. The caravan maneuvered around twenty-five telegraph poles knocked down by high bursts of wind. Seven cattle toppled over dead, struck by railcars. Each morning Ide searched the new day's horizon. "Still nothing but cattle and ponies as far as you can see in any direction," she wrote. "The same dead level prairie." And then at last, "we saw for the first time those cloud-capped, snow-covered, ever-to-be remembered, Rocky Mountains."

Emily Towell rode with forty other covered-wagon families from Missouri to Idaho in 1881. She was fifty-two years old, her husband Alexander sixty-six. "The parting from our relatives and dear ones was very sad and heart rending," she wrote in her diary. "There were many tears shed as last fond farewells and goodbyes were said. Our hearts were heavey [sic] and laden...." They crossed up through Iowa, dipped into Omaha, and plunged onto the Nebraska plains. Sometimes they followed the railway tracks as trains sped past them. "The passengers had a great deal of fun waving," she recalled. "They motioned with their hands, pointing westward."

Near Plum Creek, Frank McCloud, the infant son of some traveling companions, died. The group camped long enough to bury the boy and rest the horses, one "so lame that it was impossible to go further." Another time a mare frightened by a train galloped into barbed wire. Near Sidney in the Nebraska Panhandle, a jolt in one of the wagons set off a burst of gunfire. Two children were killed and their mother and another child wounded.

In an 1894 essay published in the *Outlook*, journalist Charles Moreau Harger wrote that "there is no poetry in living from necessity in a wagon or a one-roomed house." Out on the Nebraska plain, a schoolteacher lamented how she too often stayed the night in the sod homes of her students. "I slept upon the floor," she wrote in her diary. "And festive bedbugs held high carnival over my weary frame." A Nebraska frontiersman mailed a letter to his nervous wife back in Michigan, reassuring her that she would like the new cabin he was building, but maybe not all the dreariness around it. "If we find any peace or happiness on this earth," he pledged to her, "I suppose 99% of it will be within our own home."

Charles Morgan, in eastern Colorado, remembered homesteaders scooping up buffalo chips and other animal dung, carting it home in wheelbarrows for winter fuel. A recently arrived pioneer woman would don gloves to gather the dung. She later would skip the gloves but remember to wash her hands. Before long she never wore gloves or washed at all. Mothers cut up their few dresses and sewed clothes for their children. They scrubbed the clothes in cold-water buckets, without soap. The little ones lay naked under the covers, waiting for the summer wind to dry their clothes.

In one family, the oldest child died the same day another was born. Neighbor women sewed a burial gown while their husbands hammered and planed a casket; the child went to her rest like a "sweet little doll." In Kit Carson County, Colorado, Martha Gilmore Lundy headed up a community drive to plot the first local cemetery. A farmer offered an acre of land; others chipped in money to string a barbed wire fence to keep out the hungry coyotes.

Relentless boredom and routine wore many settlers down. Sameness could cover hundreds of square miles. Jules Haumont of Custer County, Nebraska, in an "old settler" talk years later, said the look of the gray, barren land was what he remembered most. "There were no houses to be seen, no groves, no trees."

In his 1870s diary, Henry H. Raymond described killing time by shooting at telegraph poles in south central Kansas. "Hit it from 60 yards," Raymond wrote. "A beautiful day." For food he hunted wild game, but his aim did not always ring true. "Drove up river, almost to Huntington, went to the lake," he wrote in his broken lettering. "Saw no game, turned for Dodge. Stoped and eat snack where we camped. Cleaned out gun and pistol . . . killed duck but could not get it."

The West was filled with close calls. Matilda Peterson was frying doughnuts in eastern Nebraska when an Indian known as "No-Flesh" and members of his band appeared at her door. The smell of the doughnuts had drawn them; now they crowded inside the cabin and around her stove. A startled Mrs. Peterson dropped one of her doughnuts, and it rolled onto the floor. No-Flesh picked it up, smelled the pastry, and popped it in his mouth. He liked it, so Mrs. Peterson nervously kept frying. Eventually her husband returned home and persuaded the Indians to leave. But No-Flesh returned several days later. He wanted to trade his wife for Mrs. Peterson.

Summer grasshoppers plagued the Plains. Walking to dinner one evening, a Niobrara River Valley man named Herman Westermann heard "a terrible noise" screeching up from behind. It sounded like a hailstorm rather than the cloud of hoppers it was. But the locusts swirled just ten feet above the ground, "moving north against a strong wind." For two hours he lay in the dirt waiting them out, hoping they would pass him over. They did. But along their way the grasshoppers chomped up whole pastures of wheat, potatoes, and onions.

In southeast Kansas, "they came in untold millions," reported the *Wichita City Eagle*, "in clouds upon clouds, until their fluttering wings looked like a sweeping snowstorm in the heavens, until their dark bodies covered everything green upon the earth." The hoppers covered the ground six inches deep. They chewed into cottonwood trees so fiercely that the limbs splintered and the branches snapped. They ate through curtains and devoured clotheslines. They loved salt and swarmed over farmers, their tools, and machinery, hungry for a drop of sweat. They dove for a man's eyes and ears and flew into his mouth. Farmers tried to "fire them out" by setting their fields ablaze. In Custer County, Nebraska, in 1876, the Finch family planted sixty acres of corn. The ears were just about showing when the farm boys heard a cracking and a snapping, and the roar of grasshoppers was upon them. An uncle tried to beat them back with a willow bush. By his count, he killed several thousand.

Winter blizzards were far worse, none more devastating than the fierce storm of 1888. It froze northern Nebraska and the southern rim of the Dakota Territory. A Canadian front bore down on January 12 and gripped the region for hours. The morning began unseasonably mild and then turned deadly cold. "At recess, during the forenoon, we were all out playing in our shirt sleeves, without hats or mittens," recalled O. W. Coursey, a schoolboy in Dakota. "Suddenly we looked up and saw something rolling toward us with great fury from the northwest.... It looked like a long string of big bales of cotton." In Nebraska, Valentine and North Platte dropped to thirty-five degrees below zero. Wind chills hovered at forty below. Men driving work teams could not see their horses. Snowdrifts buried the roads and the woods. The landscape turned crystal blue.

At four in the afternoon, the schools' closing time, hundreds of students and their teachers stayed shivering in their rooms, confused and uncertain. Some tried to make it for home but disappeared. Others turned back to the schoolhouses. But the doors splintered, the window glass shattered, and the roofs blew off.

Lois Royce, a young teacher in Plainview, Nebraska, had sent six students home earlier in the day, around noon. That left three others, one six-year-old and two nine-year-olds. They huddled in the schoolroom and soon ran low on dry wood to keep warm. Miss Royce led the children toward her boardinghouse at a farm about two hundred yards away. They became hopelessly lost. Bt dawn, after cuddling next to their teacher for any breath of warm air, the students were dead. The teacher's feet and hands were frozen. Yet she dug and clawed her way another quarter of a mile for help. Both her feet were amputated, and part of a hand.

What forever would be remembered as the "Children's Blizzard" claimed hundreds of lives. It took weeks, sometimes months, for the snow and the ice to melt and the earth to reveal another frozen body. Many of the little figures were discovered facedown. Many were never found at all.

The Old West could be cold and crude, uncooperative and ugly. The Scottish author Robert Louis Stevenson said Nebraska "seemed miles in length ... a world almost alone without feature; an empty sky, an empty earth."

Settlers often were alone in those far Western reaches.

April 19, 1877: "Maybe you think I am lonesome living all by myself on the prairie," wrote Howard Ruede, a young Pennsylvania German who ventured to Kansas and mailed passels of letters home, hoping to encourage his family to join him. "Today the wind is north, but not very cold. Such a day as this I wish for a paper from home, if not a letter.... It takes a whole week for a letter to come out here.... Last night I dreamed I was at home with you, but woke up to find that my overcoat had slipped off of me. It was pretty cold, too. Families coming out here should bring no luggage but clothes and bedding and a clock."

November 14, 1885: George Washington Franklin jotted in his diary, "Made and hung door.... Grouse came in house I shut door & picked it up alive in the dark, killed dressed & salted it for morning." Franklin slapped together a sod house, two sod barns, a livestock pen, and an orchard in Perkins County, Nebraska. Over the long years of roughing it alone, even after modern times had caught up with the West, he never owned a telephone, installed running water, or put in a bathtub.

September 15, 1891: "I never saw so many rats," Emma Robertson of North Bend, Nebraska, wrote to her Aunt Belle back in Iowa. "After a rain, the rat tracks are as thick as pig tracks in the hog yard. They took all the sweet corn and are working on the field corn." Seventy-six rats were hunted down by dogs and killed one evening; another night twenty-one were caught in a single trap. "When they raised the barn," she wrote Aunt Belle, "you ought to have seen them run."

The East Coast marveled at what the West was struggling against. "They are all provided with ponies," Frank H. Spearman wrote in *Harper's New Monthly Magazine* after a swing out west in 1888. "They think nothing of a horseback ride of 15 or 20 miles, either for business or pleasure."

For those who stayed and dug in, life would "prove up." At the time of the great blizzard of 1888, nearly all of the free land in the Great Plains had been claimed and settled. Farms were spreading along the river runs, pushing against the Continental Divide, spilling onto the California back slopes. In the small towns, church steeples lifted up and saloon doors swung open. After the winter snows, the summer locusts, and the long droughts, telegraph wires and telephone lines that had been knocked down or eaten in half were restrung. Train cars toppled by heavy snows were righted. Spring would come. They would plant again.

Frank Grady was born to settlers from Wisconsin. He could look back at the long arc of his life and recall how his parents "got this place" in tiny Raymond, Nebraska, in 1883, ten years before the Great Cowboy Race. "And here I have been ever since, except for a short period or two when I got wind in my whiskers and had to travel about a bit and see other places," he reflected in a 1941 oral history, when he was sixty-five years old. "But I always came back to Nebraska, a darn good place to come back to, yes sirree!"

Grady could still hear the thin railroad whistle and see the strong men relocating the post office in Raymond. He recalled how the wholesalers in Lincoln shipped in beans, salt, and crackers. He remembered all of his teachers: Miss Stetson, "who used to knock the dickens out of me," and Bessie Jolley, Bertie Woods, and Edith Bowman, "pretty nice women, I'd say." He followed the farmers around on market day and the shop owners too, especially J. W. Kerns, a lumber dealer and politician from Auburn, Nebraska, who fascinated all the boys. "He used to pull up the window and spit a gob of tobacco juice clean down to Main Street."

Grady had known a country "still mainly governed by the hard law of nature, and they say nature in the raw is never mild. The country was pretty wild, but freedom was everywhere. Nebraska was born in freedom and here was reaped a full harvest of liberty."

With freedom comes change, and by 1893, the year of the racing cowboys, the Old West was dying out. Frank Grady accepted that. Most Westerners did. The search for change was why they had trudged out here and had endured such hardships to seed a new life in an old wilderness, one where little German immigrant girls no longer got lost in the beauty of the western Sand Hills. "The world has to grow," Grady said. "It cannot stand still."

The Vanishing Cowboy West | 3

In the old days, the Elkhorn Valley Hotel anchored the corner of Third and Main streets in Norfolk, Nebraska. The square-shaped building became a landmark, spacious enough to also accommodate the county courthouse, a schoolroom, a dry-goods counter, and a theater. A literary society held readings upstairs, next to the overflow guest suites.

Cora Beels's father opened the hotel in 1875. She had come out west with her parents after they lost everything in a fire in Indiana. With each turn of the wagon wheels westward, her mother's spirits had sunk, but her father was itching to start anew. He was a preacher; he felt the call to save souls. They stopped in Norfolk in northeastern Nebraska, and a year later he purchased the hotel for extra income. "The town was a tiny hamlet, clustered around a well," recalled Beels, who became a schoolteacher and never left.

The Beels family soon became acquainted with "Relax" Hale, his gang of cowboys, and their weekly Saturday night romps into town. "They would ride their horses at breakneck speed up and down Main Street with revolvers in each hand, shooting rapidly from side to side," Cora remembered. All business in Norfolk would shudder to a stop. Doors swung closed, curtains lowered, lamps dimmed.

A clerk named Morris Meyer ran the dry-goods store in the downstairs of the hotel. Upstairs, Hale and his cowboys took over the extra guest rooms. "Mr. Meyer was deathly afraid of them," Cora said. "They took particular delight in shooting through the floor into his store while he would frantically pile bolts of goods on the counter for a barricade and hide himself under the counter. Another amusement they enjoyed was to shoot at their beds 'til they set them on fire, and then throw them into the street and watch them burn. The upper floors of that old building were pitted with shots from their guns."

⊷⊢⊏◇⊐⊣⊶

The sound of the name Relax Hale tore like prairie lightning through any town trying to keep the peace in the middle of open country. Just as treacherous were the cowboy desperadoes nicknamed "Lazy Dick," "Itchy Jake," "Six Shooter Bob," and "Windy Jack."

As far back as 1879, cowboys were "shooting off firearms indiscriminately on our streets," reported the *Oakdale (NE) Pen and Plow*. "During the past winter the report of guns and revolvers and the whizzing of bullets sent on foolish errands became so common in the town that no one thought of protesting against it." In some burgs, residents wielded wooden sticks to fight back. In Winfield, Kansas, townspeople stormed a bar over a "misunderstanding" between the brewer and a cowboy customer. For a while in Chanute, Kansas, thirteen saloons clogged the small business strip, and the gamblers' cry of "Keno!" jolted people awake all night. In 1875, a posse of Civil War veterans put a stop to cowboys thundering down the streets of Kearney, Nebraska, and shooting up local businesses by cornering the ruffians in a guard shack. The posse escorted them back to town for trial for shooting one of the veterans. That, they said, was the "last cowboy raid of Kearney."

Between 1875 and 1885, Dodge City, Kansas, reigned as the hot-gun "Cowboy Capital of the World." Exhausted city fathers finally imposed a law against any more Texas cattle snorting up their city streets, the herds bringing not only a halo of range flies, but also the roar of Colt revolvers shattering whiskey bottles.

In 1885 in Kansas City, Missouri, a cowboy named Fred Horne, tall and built, was hauled into criminal court for opening fire on the fairgrounds and wounding one poor man in the face. In the courtroom, he stood up and slowly fingered his gun belt. "Yer honor," he said, "I don't want any row in court, but I ..." The judge dived under his desk, and spectators fled for the exits. "There! There!" pleaded the court clerk. "Please don't talk that way." Horne walked out of court a free man.

"Curly Bill" Brocius, when riled up, could shoot the stoppers off liquor decanters from twenty paces without cracking the glass. Even when drinking, he could steady his trigger finger and knock the hats off nervous freighters and drummers hustling through town. "He was a hero of his kind, and boasted of his own private graveyard," Ben C. Truman wrote for the *Overland Monthly* magazine in an essay titled "The Passing of the Cowboy." No one knew where Curly really hailed from, though some said he almost had gotten himself hung down in Silver City, New Mexico. Six states and territories had placed a price on his head, and whenever he was reported dead he reappeared again, sometimes for another seven or eight years. He may or may not have been killed by Wyatt Earp in a shootout at Iron Springs, Arizona.

"Russian Bill" Tattenbaum claimed to be an heir to an Old World nobleman. He sported a notched pistol and, according to Truman, "led a reckless, dissipated life and once, while practicing at a soldier's bootheel, shot the latter in the leg." One night he stormed into tiny Shakespeare, New Mexico, and announced, "I have just buried my twentieth man." A vigilante committee hung Russian Bill that same night. "He begged and cried for mercy," wrote Truman, "and died like a coward."

Sandy King rode west out of Erie, New York. Along the way his reputation grew with one murder after another, five in all. When his time came to climb the thirteen steps, a cord of rope fastened around his neck, the gunslinger boldly called for a shot of whiskey; then he spoke his last words. "I might reform, my friends, but possibly not. You had better stretch me up as the best thing to do." He paused and asked for a chaser. "Now, boys, I'm ready," said Sandy. "The devil wants us all, and I'd better lead the way. My mother is up in heaven. Of course, I shall never see her. But I will see you all again. Pull away!"

David Love, the young son of a Scottish sheepherder on Wyoming's Sweetwater River, would tell how a cowboy turned up at the family ranch with his finger all but torn off from being wrenched by roping. Love's mother, a Wellesley graduate who had chosen the beauty of the Cowboy State over city life, boiled water, sterilized scissors, and snipped off the tendons. She let the dead finger fall sizzling into the hot coals of a fire box, then sewed a flap of skin over the stump. Giving the cowboy a sweet smile, she said, "In a month, you'll never know the difference." The cowboy saddled up, and little

David watched him drift off over the far ridge, wearing, like many he had seen, one of the "eight-inch-wide heavy belts to keep their kidneys in place during prolonged hard rides."

Charles M. Russell, the Montana artist who depicted Old West scenes and landscapes on canvas and cowboys on horseback in bronze sculptures, liked to quote a brief exchange from his childhood:

"Ma, do cowboys eat grass?"

"No, dear. They're part human."

Long days of driving cattle, exhausted nights under the stars, hats stained in sweat, dirt coating the neck—all were enough to land cowboys on a city's streets for a weekend tear. When they galloped through town shouting and shooting, they could be just as frightening as a band of outlaws. In truth, though, the cowboy's lot was mostly hard work, long hours, and lonely outposts far from human contact.

Nebraska native Charley O'Kieffe was farming around the time of the 1893 Great Cowboy Race, much of it on Sheridan County acreage in the Panhandle, and he had lived through his share of trail-bitten cowboys. At the age of seventy-seven and retired in Minneapolis, he set down his reminiscences with a preliminary note to the reader: "You will find little of romance, no heroes either real or made up, no hired gun-slingers, no hell-raisin' but safe cowpunchers." In his *Western Story* autobiography, he wrote that "among the scores of cowpunchers that I knew personally between 1884 and 1898, none were crack shots although they all could shoot straight enough when the need arose, such as for the purpose of chasing off some sneaky coyote or ending the sufferings of a horse who had broken his leg and could not be saved. And of course a rattlesnake was always an inviting target. Most of these boys were good horsemen, handy with the rope for legitimate uses, and all capable of doing the daily tasks on the average ranch. None were even fair singers, most of them not even able to carry a tune."

Up on the film screen, the cowboy figure was steeped in whiskey, blood, and murder. But to those who rode with him in the waning years of the West, there was something nostalgic in the saddle-sore, dust-grimed, bowlegged cowman. Though increasingly rare, he alone,

one journalist wrote, "dwelt under his tent—the sky," where "the cowboy is a good natured, rollicking, whole-souled fellow, quick to do a kindness and as quick to resent an insult. In all his glory, he was king of the West, clad in his green shirt, red handkerchief, wide-brimmed sombrero, and arsenal of weapons, his chaps, spurs, saddle and gloves."

Marshall W. Fishwick, writing in *Western Folklore* magazine in the 1950s, a time when the few cowboys left in the country mostly roamed Hollywood's back lots, recalled a gallant time when they were "tall, tanned, sinewy [men] quite at home in the great outdoors … weather-beaten and rough…. Never far away is his horse, Old Paint."

Some cowboys rode alone or pushed north in small groups. Nelson Story and a few cowhands steered a thousand head of cattle from Fort Worth, Texas, up to Montana in 1866. The drive took them through Indian country and outlands controlled only by Army posts. "But what school boy knows these early cowboys' names?" asked Fishwick. "What politician ever eulogizes them?"

In June 1883, J. T. Botkin and his brother Ed, along with seventeen trail herders, escorted a line of cattle southwest on the old Adobe Walls Trail from Comanche County, Kansas, to a railhead on the Canadian River in what would become Oklahoma. The big herds were thinning out by then, as were the cattle drives, so this journey marked something of a last hurrah, J. T. wrote, for "when cowboys were cowboys." He scribbled down his recollections:

They knew how to raise cattle, how to gather them in the spring, how to brand them and to market the beef. There were men in that outfit who could ride anything that wore hair and traveled on four feet, and that too with a clean saddle and without having to pull leather.

Our cook was an old hand and always had a few dry limbs put away in his wagon. He saved the axle grease boxes and bacon rinds to burn. The cook boiled the coffee, fried the bacon and managed to half way cook a little corn.

At Old Kiowa there was a saloon and the boys began to licker up. At Medicine Lodge there were several saloons and they lickered up some more. As I remember the outfit stayed a day or two at the Lodge. At that time, Medicine Lodge was strictly a cow town. Everybody was interested in cattle, and so when the outfit arrived the boys were given the freedom of the city and told to "go to it," and they went. They ran horse races on Main Street. At night they built bonfires and tried to see who could ride his horse nearest the fire. They shot holes in the atmosphere while Elm Creek, the Medicine River valleys and the surrounding hills reverberated with the sound of their unearthly whooping and yelling.

The cowboy typically climbed into $15 or $25 boots, sported a $20 hat, and settled into a $40 Cheyenne saddle. Good times or bad, thick or thin, failing or flush, he pocketed about $30 a month, small compensation for a hard life. But his overhead was low: a horse, a saddle, and a blanket to wrap around his shoulders when the fireflies lit the night. The last sound he heard falling asleep was another cowboy sitting sentry, often humming to soothe the cattle. Chow was typically boiled beef, yellow soda bread, tough bacon, blackened beans, and Arbuckle coffee. The coffee was sold from the PO Ranch in Wyoming, and each package came with a stick of peppermint candy and a couple of coupons. A cowboy who drank enough Arbuckle could redeem the coupons for handkerchiefs, razors, scissors, and a wedding ring.

Especially valuable to the cowboy were his socks. Clean socks kept the sweat off his feet and the perspiration from filling his boots, especially with all his weight dug into the stirrups. "When a man rolled out of bed at a quarter to three in the morning and didn't get back to the wagon until between seven and nine at night," commented cowboy George Edward "Ed" Lemmon, "he didn't feel much like hunting a mud puddle and washing out a pair of socks."

Slang reinforced the cowboy aura. A cow wandering off or hunting trouble was "on the pick." A horse snorting and yanking its head was called a "snuffer." A horse unusually strong could be counted a "rim-rocker." Riding a fast horse would leave a cowboy feeling "two points liter 'n a straw hat." A night herder was a "night hawk." Someone careless did not show "cow sense." A fool did not know "dung from honey." Vomiting out on the trail was "airing the paunch." When he headed at last for home, the cowpoke "hit the flats." Women were "she-stuff." Pretty women were "fancy she-stuff." Hard liquor? "A family disturbance."

"The usual ride was sixteen hours per day," recalled L. M. Cox, a Texas cowman who had herded cattle in the 1880s. "I have known cowboys to ride 100 miles per day. No union hours for them. It was from daylight until dark with work, and hard work at that." The cowboy's first love was his mount, Cox said. "My own horse would tell his age by pawing on the ground. And I have been criticized for saying that he could tell marks and brands, but I know he could."

Second to win his heart was the quiet of the prairie. "No cowpuncher ever talked much. Ride further and talk less, few words and fast action," Cox said. Eyes and ears were kept as sharp as a hunting knife. And a good horse was a friend to all. "It lifts a man above himself," it was said on the range.

Few things ever really scared a cowboy; one may have been having to walk. "Great Scott!" an old cow puncher told the journalist Julian Ralph. "What we call riding is to take your horse across country wherever a horse can go—down gullies, up bluffs and just as it happens. A good cowboy rider is unconscious that he is riding. A man who is conscious that he is on horseback ain't a good rider. You want to get on your horse and let your legs flop around loose from the knees down; and you must let your body sit loose, except where it joins the horse and is part of him."

Ed Richards thought nothing of riding twenty to thirty miles to escort a girl to a dance, then see her home before breakfast. Many considered him the best all-round cowboy in northwest Nebraska; he could throw a rope and tie a steer and wear out a bucking horse.

Ed Lemmon worked fifty-three years as a cowhand, bushwhacker, and ranch foreman. He rode many of the great cattle drives from Texas up north through Nebraska and beyond. In 1871, his horse fell on him, crushing his right leg. A year later, he broke the leg again. In the saddle, he carried six-shooters and a Winchester rifle. He lived to the age of eighty-eight. He could remember so much about his youth and his cowboying, and the excitement in 1893 over the cowboys racing from Chadron to Chicago. "The big race turned out to be more of a success than its promoters ever dreamed of," he said. "But even so it was not all on the square, for there are tricks to all trades."

He counted Buffalo Bill and the Sioux chief Red Cloud as friends. Up in the northwest pocket of South Dakota, home also to the "world's largest petrified wood park," they named a town for Ed Lemmon. He wrote later of Mexican bullfighters, cowboy cockfights, gambling dens, and parlor houses of ill repute. The ladies of the evening were called "scarlet poppies," he said. One named Connie was dubbed "the Cowboy Queen." Over the years, she entertained so many squiring partners around Miles City, Montana, that she dazzled paying customers in a $250 dress embroidered with all of their different ranch brands. "They said there wasn't an outfit in the Yellowstone down to the Platte and over in the Dakota too that couldn't find its brand on that dress," Lemmon wrote.

Cowboys and their relentless parade of cattle helped push the Plains Indians onto reservations. And that made way for wagonloads of new technology, new jobs, and new residents. Said durable Cora Beels of Norfolk, Nebraska: "I have seen [my] town pass from the days of candles and oil lamps to electric lights, from stoves to furnaces, bathtubs, Frigidaires, and all the conveniences of modern living."

By June 1893 and the start of the Great Cowboy Race, the open range was swinging shut. To those in town or out on the farm, the cowboy image now seemed more authentic in Buffalo Bill's Wild West arena than on the prairie. Once the cowboy had ridden, slept, and taken his chow outdoors. He had lassoed the wilderness. His freedom had seemed as vast as the untamed country. Now his time chasing stray cattle was fading; the cowboy's heyday, from the end of the Civil War to the start of the 1890s, was drawing down.

"The age of the pioneer and settler is past," noted William S. Cowherd, mayor of Kansas City, Missouri, speaking at the World's Columbian Exposition on the same day that the first of the cowboys came racing into Chicago. "The pioneer wrested the state from the wilderness and filled it with happy homes, schools and churches, and then sat down contented to let the world wag on as it would."

Stakes were claimed, tents pitched, and towns platted, and the gravel roads gave way to wooden sidewalks. The townspeople had outlasted the rowdy cowboys, beat them down, rustled them out. Ranches became farms; farms became spreads; statehood replaced territories.

"They are the ruin of the country," complained an old trail driver from Texas in 1884, frustrated with the farmers. "They have everlastingly, eternally, now and forever, destroyed the best grazing land in the world. The range country, sir, was never intended for raising farm truck. It was intended for cattle and horses, and was the best stock-raising land on earth until they got to turning over the sod, improving the country, as they call it. Lord forgive them for such improvements!

It makes me sick to think of it. I am sick enough to need two doctors, a druggery, and a mineral spring, when I think of onions and Irish potatoes growing where mustang ponies should be exercising, and where four-year-old steers should be getting ripe for market."

Julian Ralph lamented in 1892 in *Harper's Weekly* that "rum, cards and women are the epitaphs in the cowboy's graveyard." He once spotted several sad cowboys lolling around a Montana railroad depot in big flat-brimmed hats, a line of horses hitched to the rail outside. They had nowhere else to go on their bronchos (the common spelling then for western-bred horses).

Two other cowboys showed up in New York in May 1893, hunting for work with "anything that has to do with horses," reported the *New York Sun*. But, the *Sun* stressed, "there isn't any wild West any more. Those people who saw it ten or a dozen years ago saw a little of the wildness and they saw the last. No cowboy thinks of shooting his way through the streets of a Western town for fun in these days. He'd be arrested mighty quick if he tried it."

A new modern world was emerging, one that largely would not include the working cowboy. The transcontinental railroad belted the country. Hordes of white immigrants flooded the frontier, and smallpox traveled with them, devastating the northern Plains and many of the still resisting Indian tribes. Congress stopped making treaties with Indian nations; now they simply pushed them aside.

The Hunkpapa Lakota holy man named Sitting Bull surrendered in 1881. The white man had all but exterminated the buffalo herds, which had fed, clothed, and sheltered his people. The Major Crimes Act of 1885 extended federal jurisdiction over crimes committed on the reservations. Two years later, Congress passed the Dawes Allotment Act, which encouraged Indians to embrace U.S. citizenship.

In December 1890, Sitting Bull was murdered in sudden gunfire on the Standing Rock Reservation, shot down by one of his own, a Lakota reservation police officer. On Pine Ridge two weeks later, amid the fury and shrieks of the Ghost Dance (prophesying a day when the white man would vanish and the buffalo return), soldiers fired into crowds of reservation Lakotas. The bodies of more than two hundred men, women, and children froze in the snow at Wounded Knee Creek; fifty-one more were wounded. The Indian Wars were over.

"Look at me, I am poor and naked," the once great but now contrite Sioux chief Red Cloud had told an audience of white faces at New York's Cooper Institute in 1870. "We do not want riches, but we want to train our children right. Riches would do us no good. We could not take them with us to the other world." No, he said; "we do not want riches; we want peace and love."

To Fourth of July revelers in 1889 at the Nebraska Panhandle town of Chadron, on land once belonging to his vast tribal range, an angry Red Cloud said, "The white people would take all the good land from me, and I would have nothing but bad lands where I would starve to death."

Asked on a train how many white men he had fought and killed, a flippant Red Cloud dismissed the question. "I have been in eighty battles," he said. Confined to the Pine Ridge Reservation, a disparaged Red Cloud told a white visitor, "You see this barren waste. Think of it! I, who used to own rich soil in a well-watered country so extensive that I could not ride through it in a week on my fastest pony, am put down here."

Almost ninety and nearly blind, a dying Red Cloud would gingerly walk the mile and a half each day to the Pine Ridge Reservation post office, looking for some good news to arrive, hoping that the white man had abandoned the West and the old Sioux lands had been restored. He would sit and wait on a wooden bench outside. Joined by a friend, he spun out much of his life's story. But the weary chief spoke primarily of his youth and the gone glory of the Sioux before he had led them hopelessly against the encroaching white masses. Everything else, he acknowledged, was "past."

The meat, clothing, and shelter the buffalo had brought to native peoples were disappearing; soon all that remained were the bones. In 1876, I. G. Baker and Company, in Fort Benton on the northern Missouri River, shipped 75,000 buffalo robes. That fell to 20,000 four years later and to 5,000 by 1883. A year later, it sent none at all. Figures kept by trader Joseph Ullman, headquartered in Chicago and St. Paul, were equally dim. 1882: 40,000 hides and 10,000 robes were shipped. 1884: Less than 2,500 hides, many of them holdovers from the previous year hoping for a better market. A few robes were carried over as well. 1885: Few or no hides.

There had been a time when the red man and white man alike had believed that the great herds would roam the Plains forever. None could imagine the overkill pouring from the barrels of rifles, many belonging to sportsmen leaning out of passenger train windows. "Man never could have exterminated them," one old trapper had once thought. Now, he realized, "they went back into the earth from whence they came."

George Bird Grinnell, in an article for *Scribner's Magazine* in September 1892 titled "The Last of the Buffalo," recalled how years earlier "an Indian once said to me, in the expressive sign language of which all old frontiersmen have some knowledge, 'The country was one robe.'" Now, Grinnell wrote, "the swelling hosts which yesterday covered the Plains today are but a dream."

A pipe-smoking, Yale-educated anthropologist and naturalist, Grinnell discovered that C. J. Jones in Garden City, Kansas, owned one of the last domesticated buffalo herds in the country. He once had managed 250 head; soon he was reduced to fifty, with another eighty trailed down from Manitoba, Canada. Now his fences held a mere forty-five head, fifteen of them breeding cows.

In all, Grinnell concluded, it had taken less than six years to slaughter all the buffalo in Kansas, Nebraska, the Indian Territory, and northern Texas. Some herds feeding on the western plains of Texas "had a brief respite" until white hunters found them, too. "On the great plains is still found the buffalo skull half buried in the soil and crumbling to decay," wrote Grinnell. "The deep trails once trodden by the marching hosts are grass-grown now, and fast filling up. When these most enduring relics of a vanished race shall have passed away, there will be found, in all the limitless domain once darkened by their feeding herds, not one trace of the American buffalo."

Army Colonel J. H. McLaughlin recalled encountering an eighty-year-old Indian warrior "who was determined to kill his last buffalo with his bow and arrows, which he finally did, making the buffalo look like a porcupine with his quills sticking therefrom." With that hunt, McLaughlin declared, "it seemed the slaughter was almost fully completed."

The last white man to claim the last buffalo in Nebraska was A. N. Ward of Milford. He put it at October 1881, when he was hunting black-tailed deer in McPherson County. "I saw this buffalo, which proved to be a two-year-old heifer, coming out of the shallows where it had been for water," Ward said. "I made a capital shot, killing the heifer stone dead at 150 yards with a bullet back of the left fore-shoulder."

The decimation of the herds left the High Plains littered with buffalo bones bleaching under the searing summer sun, and those brought out the hunters, too. One scavenging company reported that between 1884 and 1891 it had carted off the skulls, skeletons, hoofs, and decaying cartilage from some 5.9 million carcasses. The bones filled boxcars to the rim and were shipped to processing plants in Detroit, Philadelphia, and Baltimore. There they could draw $18 to $27 a ton. They were crushed and reduced to paints, dyes, cosmetics, lubricants for iron and steel, even white sugar and sugarcane juice when boiled down. The industry boomed but briefly, and frontier families hard hit by droughts, snowstorms, and the economic panics of the 1890s scoured the creek beds and flats with carts and wagons, hunting for relics of the dinosaurs of the Old West.

The first telegraph poles had been planted in the Nebraska Territory in early 1861, the wood and the wires shipped out from Ohio. With bonuses offered if jobs were completed ahead of schedule, immigrant laborers feverishly strung their way to the Mormon capital in Utah, their giant rivets bolting down the earth. Soon California would be wired in. "Allow me to greet you," foreman Edward Creighton telegraphed his wife from the Great Salt Lake. He promised her (and he was right) that the "two oceans will be united." The wireless telegraph followed, next the radio telephone, and then the radio itself.

By 1893, five railway links spanned the country. That same year, not only did long-distance "telephoning" become possible, but suggestions were also made for how callers could make sure they were heard. Speak loudly, they were encouraged. Shout.

The first automobile was assembled in 1894, and a year later a number of inventors were improving on the horseless carriage. They were crude and expensive, and every young man coveted one. They soon flew right past the horse.

"While I like horses in a certain way, I do not enjoy caring for them," wrote Amos Ives Root of Medina, Ohio, a beekeeper and

A covered wagon with jackrabbit mules confronts the future—an automobile—on the trail near Big Springs in the Nebraska Panhandle, 1912. (National Archives)

tinkerer with just about anything that moved—clocks, widgets, and eventually his Oldsmobile Runabout. When the auto came along, his horse-riding days were finished.

Indeed, Root epitomized the American male's rush from four legs to four wheels. "I do not like the smell of the stables, I do not like to be obliged to clean a horse every morning and I do not like to hitch one up in winter," Root noted in his journal. "I dislike plodding around in the snow, handling an icy harness," he wrote. "Perhaps I might have a warm stable—one that is always warm, like my auto-house; but I should not enjoy it even then. It takes time to hitch up a horse; but the auto is ready to start off in an instant. It is never tired; it gets there quicker than any horse can possibly do."

All these developments spelled an epitaph for the cowboy. "You may stand ankle deep in the short grass of the uninhabited wilderness," said one settler who witnessed the crush of new farmsteads. "Next month a train will glide over the waste and stop at some point where the railroad has decided to locate a town. Men, women and children will jump out, and their chattel will tumble out after them. From that moment the building begins."

In 1885, at the National Cattle and Horse Growers Association convention in St. Louis, Professor E. H. Moore of Colorado warned that "it is plain to see that the days of ranges are numbered. As the Indian gave way to the pioneer, so must the cowboy go before the settler, and the rancher take the place of the ranger, until eight million acres of land now roamed for cattle shall teem with villages and model farms for the cultivation of refined cattle cared for—not by cowboys with revolvers—but by cowboys with brains." A year later, in San Angelo in central Texas, the local *Enterprise* newspaper lamented "the decayed cowboy," announcing that "his glory has departed" and wishing him a fond adieu: "Festive cuss, farewell!"

In 1887, the famed Civil War and Indian fighter General William Tecumseh Sherman wrote to his friend Buffalo Bill Cody at his Fifth Avenue Hotel in New York, where Cody was staying between Wild West shows, and spoke fondly of the days of cowboys and Indians and attacks upon the Deadwood stagecoaches. "Such things did occur in our days, but may never again," he told Cody. He recalled the 9.5 million head of buffalo between the Missouri River and the Rocky Mountains just twenty years earlier, all now killed "for their meat, their skins and bones.... This seems like desecration, cruelty and murder, yet they have been replaced by twice as many cattle.... There were about 165,000 Pawnees, Sioux, Cheyennes, Kiowas and Arapahoes who depended on these buffaloes for their yearly food. They too are gone, and have been replaced by twice or thrice as many white men and women, who have made the earth to blossom as the rose, and who can be counted, taxed and governed by the laws of nature and civilization.... This change has been salutary, and will go on to the end," Sherman wrote. Of the Old West, he noted with a sad finality: "This drama must end; days, years and centuries follow fast, even the drama of civilization must have an end."

Buffalo Bill himself acknowledged that the West was playing out. In a June 1894 article for *Cosmopolitan* magazine, he conceded that "there is no longer any frontier. People live everywhere, all over the Rocky mountain region."

Cody could even feel it under his feet. He remembered that the open range's topsoil had been dry and loose: "It was possible to walk anywhere in that country, in the grass or out of it, at any time of the day or night, without wetting one's moccasins.... You slept out in your blanket at any season of the year, and when you awoke in the morning it was as dry as when you lay down." Now, he wrote, "heavy dews" fell, and those he blamed on progress. "I have a theory of my own to account for this phenomenon. The erection of wire-fences, which has unquestionably greatly increased the downfall of rain, has in the same way, by the attraction of electrical currents, brought about the dew."

Both Sherman and Cody understood what they had lost. So did many others. For years the nation's newspapers and magazines could sense the old life fading, and they chronicled its demise. Old-timers recalled their last buffalo hunt, their last wagon train, their last attack by outlaws or Indian raiders. In 1913, a motion picture crew set up at Pine Ridge Reservation with a cast of Oglala Lakota actors to film the massacre at Wounded Knee. Thus was born the cowboy movie, and it was fiction.

The *Weekly Capital-Commonwealth* in Topeka, Kansas, in 1889 headlined the obvious:

A Fading Race
A Frontier Feature Which Will Soon Be Seen No More

One of the most picturesque characters to be found in the story of American frontier life, the cowboy, will soon be seen no more. There will be great firms devoted to stock raising for many years to come, but the cowboy of the unfenced range has lost his occupation. The range has been covered first on one side and then on another by the flood tide of homesteaders, until there is no place left....

The Frenchman Paul de Rousiers, traveling the country to study American life, wrote, "This time we definitely say good-bye to the West.... We shall no longer consider the part it plays in the productive activity of the United States." Throughout the Midwest the talk was equally harsh. The *Kansas City Times* observed flatly, "The cowboy is not now what he used to be, and in 20 years the old-time rider will be a thing of the past."

The Great Cowboy Race of 1893 caught the country's imagination because it sought to dispel the notion of the vanishing frontiersman. Shortly before the riders galloped off, the *Chicago Daily Tribune* made note of what the cowboys were racing against: "Western Nebraska is not as it was a few years ago. The howl of the coyote has long given place to the whistle of the locomotive, and the prairie is no longer used for cattle grazing. Farmers have taken the place of cowboys, and only old-time cowboys remain." But the paper reported that the defiant cowboy participants would race regardless. Doc Middleton would saddle up. Emmett Albright declared, "By thunder, I'll be there on old Red Jacket, ready to show the boys where to stake out their horses as they come in."

In 1890, the U.S. Census Bureau announced the closing of the American frontier. The bureau's superintendent was Robert P. Porter, a journalist born in England who had come to America in his youth. He wrote for a newspaper in Chicago, engaged in Republican politics, and won entrée to President Benjamin Harrison. That brought Porter's nomination to oversee the country's eleventh census. The bureau then was a temporary assignment, with workers brought in every ten years to count heads.

"When I was appointed," Porter later told Congress, "I had nothing but one clerk and a messenger, and a desk with some white paper on it." He slowly built a staff, recruiting former agents from the last census, and in all he hired more than 2,500 employees. He sent them out into the cities and the towns and dispatched them to far corners of the vast and changing Western states.

They learned that fewer than two people per square mile lived in many sections of the West and that the number of American Indians had dropped by 150,000, or more than a third, over the past forty years. Porter and his team also determined that the frontier had been breached and the Pacific reached, and they decided that the Census Bureau would no longer track Western migration. By 1890, the bureau declared, "the unsettled area has been so broken by isolated bodies of settlements that there can hardly be said to be a frontier line." Western movement, the march across a continent, could no longer be measured. The frontier line no longer existed.

Those findings prompted historian Frederick Jackson Turner, in Chicago the summer of the cowboy race and the world's fair, to mourn the frontier as well. "The frontier has gone," he stated. "And with its going has closed the first period of American history." What Turner saw as the significance of the frontier movement was what the immigrants themselves had realized. "They were part of the growing American consciousness of itself," Turner said. The dream of the West had been lived.

Another historian, Emerson Hough, looked back twenty-five years after that summer of 1893 and the Great Cowboy Race. "The West has changed," he wrote. "The curtain has dropped between us and its wild and stirring scenes. The old days are gone. The house dog sits on the hill where yesterday the coyote sang." A lawyer and student of philosophy, writing in an age of airplanes and big cities and world war, Hough recognized that the pioneers' struggles were over, the cowboy roundups ridden. "We had a frontier once," he wrote. "It was our most priceless possession." It showed "our fighting edge, our unconquerable resolution, our undying faith. There, for a time at least, we were Americans."

The journalist Ray Stannard Baker would recall, in his *American Chronicle* autobiography, what he and his father, a bankrupt Michigan merchant, discovered after immigrating west. "He did not know, and neither did I as a boy, that we were living on the 'last frontier,'" Baker wrote. "There was no longer anywhere in America, or indeed in the world, for the ambitious or the discontented to go for free land, free forests, free rivers, for free opportunity."

Many of the "children of the West" knew this, too. They had pushed on and settled far away, seeking new adventures; when the Old West ended, much of the thrill went with it. "I sometimes wish I had stayed in Wyoming," wrote Doris Bowker Bennett, an old woman in 1976, in a memoir of her youth. "I was born and grew up in Wyoming on the edge of the Old West's last frontier, 'the West of the authentic Cowboy.'" A niece of one of the riders in the Great Cowboy Race, she remembered that "in spite of the rigorous climate and absence of many conveniences, we had what most of the world has lost and some of the country had lost then—a simple world of space, clean air and water, relatively untouched nature, and a sense of community that gave us children security. Although I chose to satisfy my curiosity about the outside world, I am glad that I was born where I was at the time I was. I had a rich childhood."

The old heroes had moved on, too; many, like Bennett, had left the West altogether. In 1887, Doc Holliday, a dentist turned gunslinger, was put to bed in Glenwood Springs, Colorado, suffering from tuberculosis. He was only thirty-six, and tickled to be dying with his boots off. General Philip "Little Phil" Sheridan, who had led many of the Indian campaigns and helped establish Yellowstone National Park, moved to Washington, D.C., and then to a summer cottage in Massachusetts, a world away from the Old West. There, in 1888, a life of heavy food and hard drinking caught up with him. Overweight and suffering a series of heart attacks, he was gone at fifty-seven. John Charles Frémont, the "Pathfinder" who had blazed the way west for the multitudes who followed, died in 1890 at his home on West Twenty-Fifth Street in New York. He was seventy-seven and had abandoned the frontier years ago. Even when appointed governor of the Arizona Territory, he chose not to move there and was forced to resign.

But some of the old heroes hung with it. As late as September 1907, a journalist for the *Columbus Evening Dispatch* in Ohio interviewed a famous visitor, a tall, silver-haired gentleman with a pale mustache and deep, searching eyes. He had brought with him his spectacular Wild West troupe of cowboys and Indians in full-dress ensembles, braves who faked the warpath and outlaws pretending to chase a Deadwood stagecoach.

"In all of my journeys," Buffalo Bill Cody told her, "I have always found that the West is an undiscovered country, and very few have the slightest conception as to what our West really is." At sixty-one, Buffalo Bill was not yet ready to give up the ghost of the Old West. He aimed to keep it alive, if only in his long-running Wild West show ring. There would always be one more curtain call, he hoped, one more gallop around the arena, one more time to aim and fire at clay pigeons.

"Busy? I'm always busy, but not so much that I cannot stop and talk to a newspaper woman," he told the reporter. "I could tell you so much of my beloved West that your hair would curl without the aid of a curling iron. Yes, I killed Yellow Hand in single combat. Sorry I did it? Not for the moment. He was one of the most desperate of fighting Indians, the man who supplied buffalo meat to the laborers building the railroad across the continent. But he went with the rest of them on the warpath."

The reporter thought Cody "particularly handsome." He knew what he was talking about, she wrote; he spoke in "an emphatic manner." And Buffalo Bill's eyes blazed when he praised the glory that had been the Wild West. "Indians! Don't say Indians to me," he thundered. "No one knows them better than I. Their friendships, their treachery, their habits of living. There are good and bad ones, and I know the lot of them. Living with them or near them since boyhood leaves little to the imagination."

Buffalo Bill leaned in toward the reporter. Like any clever promoter, he could be quite a salesman. "You are going to see the show? Yes? Well, let me tell you, it's a true picture of the West...."

Buffalo Bill Goes to the Fair | 4

William Frederick Cody became "Buffalo Bill," who became America's first international celebrity. Born in Iowa, first set on a horse in Kansas, and let loose in Nebraska and the vast regions of the wide-open frontier, he embodied the young country's drive for greatness. His was a life of hunting buffalo, battling Indians, and, as a show-man, reincarnating the epic Western adventure. In slaying the young warrior Yellow Hand, also known as Yellow Hair or, to the Cheyenne, Heova'ehe, Cody claimed the first scalp for Custer after the Battle of the Little Bighorn. In his last days in bed in his sister's home in Denver, his kidneys shutting down, he still dreamed of one more comeback in his Wild West career. The weary scout died reimagining the glory of his vanishing age.

A colossal figure in buckskin, on horseback or onstage, scoring record buffalo kills on the hunt or blasting clay pigeons in his show arena, Cody helped open the immigrant West and lived well past its closing. Touring Europe and its crowned heads in 1887, he stared in wonder as the British monarch Queen Victoria rose from her place of honor and saluted the U.S. flag streaming past her in his Wild West show. In the Chicago summer of 1893, he saw his show shatter all attendance expectations, often challenging the world's fair next door, his gate receipts piling up with the thrill of cowboys racing a thousand miles toward his front steps.

Ninety years earlier, Thomas Jefferson had sent Lewis and Clark on their journey of exploration, predicting that it would take a hundred generations to tame and populate the West. Americans conquered it in fewer than five. And during that time Cody championed nearly every turn of the sweeping Western saga.

With his silver mane and far-seeing stare, Buffalo Bill Cody helped to win the West and preserve it as the old frontier life was dying out. (Nebraska State Historical Society)

At twenty-one, he adopted the name "Buffalo Bill" while providing meat for Kansas railroad laborers and claiming 4,280 buffalo kills during an eighteen-month contract. He debuted on the stage in 1873, a year before the first gold nuggets were chipped out of the Black Hills. A decade later, he staged an "Old Glory Blowout" to fete the Fourth of July; the event was so successful it morphed into dress rehearsals for his Wild West shows. And in 1887, Cody marched triumphant into Europe with his marquee Wild West show, while back home the last of the native tribes had been shoved onto the reservation and the West itself was disappearing.

His Wild West was a corporation, his life the Western panorama. Dime novels heralded his exploits, though most of them were mere pulp fiction: Cody fighting a border duel, Cody tracking outlaws in the desert, Cody having it out at the Last Chance mining camp near Flagstaff, Arizona. "Every eye watched Buffalo Bill as he pulled the trigger," hyped one installment published in the summer of 1893. "All knew that he was a dead shot—a man who never missed a foe or game he fired upon."

His promoters shrewdly fixed his high brow and his lantern jaw in the fawning spotlight, papering billboards in advance of his traveling show and seizing upon free publicity such as the Great Cowboy Race to pad his box office. They prepared themselves for any turn in the world of show business, even restocking his corrals if the unexpected suddenly tripped them up. When his caravan collided with a freight train in rural North Carolina at four in the morning, upending rail cars and killing 110 horses, Cody's front men helped lift the show and its entourage back on track.

Boys thrilled to the click of his horses' hooves, and old men charmed by his theatrics relived their own dusty memories. Women's hearts raced when his deep-set eyes lit up like flaming arrows. Known publicly as a family man, Cody nevertheless pursued his opportunities for recreation, including one very public liaison with the daughter-in-law of railroad baron Jay Gould, the one-time "wealthiest man in the world." Cody's attempts to leave his wife spilled nastily into the courts; they ended up costing much money and more heartbreak for both him and his long-suffering Louisa, "Lulu," the mother of his four children. During the summer of 1893 in Chicago, Lulu made an unscheduled visit to see Bill, but she abruptly left town when told his hotel room already was occupied as "Mr. and Mrs. Cody's suite." For that indiscretion, Cody returned sheepishly to Nebraska at the end of the 1893 engagement and enthroned his unamused wife in the grandest mansion in North Platte, once owned by a silk merchant and featuring inlaid parquet floors and a sweeping staircase. The palace was dubbed the "Welcome Wigwam."

Sometimes Buffalo Bill could be well ahead of his time. "What we want to do is give our women even more liberty than they have," he said at the close of the first American century, endorsing an early cry for women's equality. "Let them do any kind of work that they see fit, and if they do it as well as men, give them the same pay." Other times he appeared well past his prime. "I have no future to look forward to," he wrote his sister Julia, lamenting his failing marriage. "No happiness or even contentment."

When not at his Scout's Rest Ranch outside North Platte, appeasing his wife, making a payroll, or entertaining guests in hotel rooms, Cody would turn out in his show ring, galloping about the arena, facing down shrieking Indians on the warpath, and reveling in the drum roll of applauding grandstands. To Cody's ears, the cheers soared like a frontier aria. If the real West was dead or dying, his Western circus was alive, with hands clapping, crowds hurrahing, feet stomping. A year after his record 1893 run in Chicago, he even stopped at Thomas Edison's studio in New Jersey, and some of his Indian actors were filmed nearly naked and whooping it up as in the good old days. In one twenty-one-second flicker, they reenacted the famed Lakota Ghost Dance.

Easterners first started marveling at Cody in 1872 as a daring scout and fearless hunter, not as an actor or showman. That year, someone else played him at New York's Bowery Theatre in a four-week production of *Buffalo Bill, the King of the Border Men*. Cody caught the show as a guest in a private box and was thunderstruck. Before the curtain fell he was introduced, and the audience roared. Nervous and tongue-tied, he managed but a few words, waving in his buckskin suit to the well-dressed theatergoers below. That was all it took. Buffalo Bill was hooked on the euphoria of acclaim. As Cody put it, "I was shown the elephant."

He was timid at first, and his knees knocked. For all his confidence in the saddle, Buffalo Bill was never a natural on the boards. In his initial struggles in stage acting on the East Coast, he often flubbed his lines. In one of his first premieres, before General Sheridan, a phalanx of Army officers, and a house of three thousand, he later recalled, his stage fright "broke me all up and I could not remember a word."

Yet in the open-air arena, Cody and his traveling troupe succeeded because they reincarnated what he and so many others had known on the rolling Western frontier. So it fell upon his broad shoulders to preserve America's great Western adventure, to make it breathe again, to present it to a modern world. "All the people back East want to find out just what the West looks like," he once told Lulu. "And you can't tell them on a stage. There ain't no room. So why not take the West right to them?"

The Western archaeologist Warren K. Moorehead would recall the day in the early 1880s when he was just a boy and the Wild West show came to his hometown, Newark, Ohio. "I shall ever remember my sensations when witnessing the grand buffalo hunt," he said. "Three or

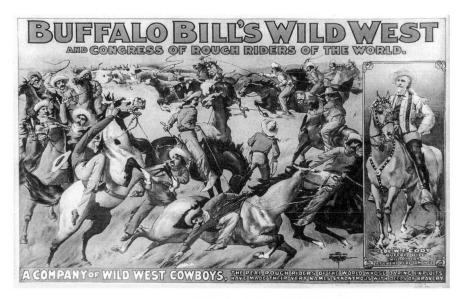

Buffalo Bill's enormously popular Wild West show made him wealthy, thrilled millions in the United States and abroad, and enshrined the daring, adventurousness, and endurance of America's cowboys. (Library of Congress)

four poor, old, scarred bison were driven into the fair-ground enclosure by some whooping cow-punchers. Buffalo Bill himself dashed up alongside the lumbering animals and from a Winchester repeater discharged numerous 'blanks' into the already powder-burned sides of the helpless creatures. The crowd roared with appreciation."

Cody scouted the reservations for native actors, including Sitting Bull for a time. He toured the old cow towns and enlisted cowboys and daredevils. He bought horses and stocked up on wagons, cattle and coaches, Gatling guns and grandstands, and eighteen-car trains to haul it all around. In an average week, his cast and crew could devour more than five thousand pounds of beef, four hundred pounds of ham, and eight hundred pounds of chicken. Two thousand loaves of bread were sliced and buttered. Six gallons of mustard were poured on, one barrel of pig's feet pried open, and five hundred pies served fresh from his coal-fired ovens.

Everything came in quantities as enormous as Cody's habits, particularly his affection for an uncorked bottle and a double shot glass. Repeatedly he was forced to promise he would lay off the spirits during the lengthy show seasons, which often ran for months at a time.

"I solemnly promise you that after this you will never see me under the influence of liquor," he once wrote to show promoter Nate Salsbury, his general manager. Then Cody thought better of what he had just pledged. "I may have to take two or three drinks today to brace up on," he admitted. And he corrected himself again. "This drinking surely ends today and your pard will be himself and on deck all the time." Salsbury warned Cody that he had better restrict himself to a single drink a day, and Cody promptly agreed. He poured a bottle of whiskey into a large schooner and carried it around with him—his one drink a day. Later he swore to Salsbury that when the shows were over, when he finally put down the rifle and took up retirement, he was going on a "drunk that is a drunk."

Drinking, for Buffalo Bill, came with the territory. It also helped boost his saddle-and-sirloin reputation as America's leading frontier hero. To him a drinking bender was "a hell of a toot" and an especially raucous night a "hoof-her-up." A year before he and his Wild West crew first headed out on the road, fifteen cowboys riding herd through Nebraska chanced upon Cody's ranch in North Platte. "Cody was at home and sitting on the veranda," recalled Frank C. Huss. "After hand-shaking and introductions, we were asked what we would have to drink. Each called for his favorite and each was supplied. There must have been a big supply on hand!"

Twice a day in his traveling extravaganzas, in large downtown venues or small fairgrounds, in the United States or in Europe, Buffalo Bill Cody reclaimed the daring and splendor of the old Wild West. In afternoon and evening performances, the acts featured trick ropers, broncho riders, and sharpshooters. The cast included Arab acrobats, Russian Cossacks, and Filipino horsemen. Annie Oakley would fire off spectacular hip shots at swirling targets. When outlaws robbed the Deadwood stagecoach, Cody's cowboys saved the day.

A typical opening act silenced the crowd with a bugle call, followed by a quarter-mile horse race featuring a cowboy, an Indian, and a Mexican *vaquero*. Pony Express riders relayed the mail, and Indian braves raced each other on foot and on horseback. "Cowboy fun time" spotlighted trick mules, bucking bronchos, and horsemen swooping small items off the ground. Ambushing Indians would attack a settler's cabin until a posse rode to the rescue "with enough firing of pistols to make a small boy howl with delight."

Cody, billed as the "Champion All-Round Shot of the World," would storm into the arena astride a favorite horse, armed with a shotgun, Winchester rifle, and pistol, while his Thoroughbred kicked up the dirt and sawdust floor. He would shoot at clay pigeons or composition balls, sending them spinning or shattering as he whirled in every direction. He would fire English style, the butt of the gun below his armpit. Then he would fire American style, the butt of the gun below his elbow. He could hit a ball in the air as he galloped past it, knocking down twenty clay pigeons in ninety seconds.

In Chicago in 1893, Buffalo Bill scored his high-water mark. When he set up camp that spring next to the World's Columbian Exposition—popularly known as the Chicago World's Fair—it marked Cody's most successful season ever; profits topped $1 million. It quickly became a must-see event, what one grizzled Chicago newspaper editor (who in his career had "seen just about everything worth seeing once") called "the greatest show" he had ever seen in his life.

In early 1892, Cody had returned to the United States after several seasons touring Europe. He sailed home on the luxury liner RMS *Umbria* to New York and concentrated on how to attach his hugely popular Wild West extravaganza to the Chicago World's Fair. It would be, Cody said, "the supreme effort" of his life.

But the Chicago fair promoters, who were raking in generous donations to build their promenades, house their exhibits, and electrify the White City, decided to lock him out. Cody's act, they said, "had a prime object ... to make money by a display of the savage and repulsive features of Indian life." The fair, they said, would in part honor Native Americans and highlight their efforts to adapt to the white world, but without all the savagery and banditry whooped up in Cody's show. And fair leaders scoffed at rumors that if denied a role inside the exposition, Cody would lease a spot next door. Too expensive, they said; "a fabulous price."

Cody remained determined. In Pittsburgh, he announced his plans to join the next year's fair. He spent a week in Lincoln and other parts of Nebraska and calmly went hunting, shooting two swans. He would tour England one more time, he said, before the fair opened in Chicago.

He staged his 1892 season at Earls Court in London. At a luncheon to celebrate the opening, he was feted by the U.S. minister (ambassador) and consul general, an English count, and the bishop of London. Spanish, French, Turkish, and Russian dignitaries partook as well. For the debut performance, twenty thousand people crowded into the court arena. Cody had brought with him a cast and accompaniment of four hundred, plus forty Sioux "braves and squaws." To kick off the first day, he purchased $370 worth of "Wild West" souvenir spoons for his lucky chosen friends and fans.

At Windsor, Queen Victoria presented Cody with a large gold seal embossed with her personal monogram and etched with the British Order of the Garter: "Honi soit qui mal y pense" (Shame be to him who thinks evil of it), words associated with Sir Gawain and the Knights of the Round Table.

As the Wild West drew enthusiastic London crowds, Cody continued to dream of Chicago and next year's world's fair. He sent scouts hunting for horses and riders from many countries, including Argentine gauchos, and planned to ship them to America for the Chicago engagement. "I am getting together the wildest, most novel, the largest show ever conceived for the World's Fair," he proudly announced in a June 1892 letter to the *Omaha Daily Bee*. He pledged that in Chicago he would be "repeating my success here in the metropolis of the world."

In England, Cody also was drawn to the increasingly popular sport of long-distance horse racing. To reporters in London, he spoke often about a recent Vienna–Berlin ride that left many horses ridden to death. "I'm not at all surprised that many of them came to grief," he said. "Blood is a good enough thing in its way, but in a long-distance ride of this kind it cannot, as a rule, hold its own against wiry bone and muscle."

To Cody, the European Thoroughbreds were no match for the heartier American Western-bred bronchos, and European riders no rivals to American cowboys. "The strain on the horses in such a ride is tremendous," Cody said. "But the strain on the rider is still greater." He did not think the sprint between Vienna and Berlin a "fair test of endurance either in men or horses." He rattled off Civil War campaigns and hard riding on the Plains that he said were "superior" to two hundred princes and high military officers racing just under four hundred miles between the capital of Austria and the capital of Germany in seventy-one hours.

Cody boasted to the European press that he could wallop any European rider in a true contest of long days and open terrain, and on a short track as well. "On the race course at Manchester several years ago I laid a bet that I would ride ten miles on 20 of my ponies faster than any other man on the same number of English Thoroughbreds," he said. "The English rider ... I beat him by 64 yards, and I guess that was about the hardest 20 minutes' work I ever did." He spoke of the great bursts of Pony Express mail riders "before the days of steam and telegraphs.... When Lincoln was standing for the presidency, the election returns had to be conveyed from Sacramento to St. Joseph"—from the capital of California to Pony Express headquarters in Missouri. "And mind you the track was nothing like so good as the road between Vienna and Berlin. Well, in the carrying of those mails the average rate of riding was 17 miles an hour. On one occasion I covered as much as 322 miles in one continuous ride, though not, of course, on the same horse, at an average speed of 15 miles an hour, and mind you, this was through hostile Indian territory too."

A reporter asked, "Was this your only feat of the kind?" Three times in the winter of 1869, Cody replied, he had dashed back and forth between Fort McPherson and Fort Kearney, ninety-five miles at a stretch. He recalled one forced ride of sixty hours when his horse weakened and they walked much of the way, only to see the horse bolt and kick when Cody tried to water it. The horse took off, and Cody chased it on foot some thirty-five miles, "within a half a mile of my destination." Then he knew the horse's days were done. "I gave it a bullet from my Winchester," he said, "and there an end."

Cody loved racing. He had grown up around horses, in the corral and on horseback. General Philip Sheridan's memoirs recalled a young Bill Cody ferrying military dispatches across the Kansas frontier in 1868, including one sixty-five-mile stretch "infected with Indians." Sheridan wrote that "Cody rode about 350 miles in less than 60 hours, and such an exhibition of endurance and courage" convinced the general to hire him as a lead scout.

In England in 1892, Cody was thinking of long-distance horse racing in America. He had his own ideas, and he told the press that his show promoter Nate Salsbury had offered to back fifty cowboys armed with revolvers against any "100 of the best of European cavalry." But Cody did not race against English riders, and his American bronchos did not take on Europe's uniformed cavalry. Instead he set sail a few weeks after the Vienna–Berlin disaster, bound back to New York. Much of his Wild West show baggage continued on to Chicago and was offloaded at the rail yards there. Buffalo Bill still was determined to star at the world's fair.

And he was restless. He hosted a company of English and Bavarian aristocrats on a hunting trip through the Rockies. Traveling across Arizona, Utah, and Colorado, he suggested a national game preserve in the Rocky Mountains. "The fate of the buffalo, which a few years ago roamed the plains in herds of tens of thousands, is to be the fate of all other game," he warned, "unless something is done to check the wholesale destruction of wild animals."

In January 1893, Cody traveled to Washington. Over dinner and cigars with friends not far from the White House, he discussed his game park idea and his Chicago plans. But the Interior Department rejected both proposals: no preserve and no official place for Buffalo Bill at the World's Columbian Exposition.

He tried again to change the minds of the fair promoters, but they insisted that the exposition was designed as a tribute to the modern world and the coming new century, and not as a look back at the legacy of the fading West. The fair's Committee on Ways and Means saw too much "incongruity" between the future world the fair would highlight and Cody and his cowboy past. The answer remained no.

Cody returned to Omaha, disappointed but unbowed. On March 21, he announced new plans to purchase "saddles and other goods and to fix upon rates with the Union Pacific railway company for the transportation, on April 1, of 300 horses from North Platte to the World's Fair."

"I leave for North Platte tonight," Cody declared. "We open up our Wild West show in Chicago one week before the beginning of the fair." He said Salsbury had leased a large lot between Sixty-Second and Sixty-Third streets, right next to the fair. The cost would be $180,000 for those fourteen acres of ground directly opposite and across the street from the fair's main entrance, no small sum. "Great Scott!" Cody had complained. "These Chicago real estate men simply want the earth."

"We shall have in our employ 400 people, 325 of whom will be performers," Cody reported. He promised Cossack, Arabian, Amazon, Chilean, Sioux, and cowboy riders; Mexican lasso champions; and English, German, French, and American soldiers. "You see," he boasted, "it is quite an undertaking. We have no syndicate back of us. Mr. Salsbury and myself are doing it all. To start our Chicago show will cost $275,000. We shall perform for about six months and two weeks and shall have seating capacity at each performance for 20,000."

Within three weeks, the first of Cody's horses and show luggage were unloaded from railcars at his new Chicago show grounds, the wooden rafters and grandstands rising next to the fair's glittering White City promenades. Crew members exercised the horses in the stall yards, while the clop of hammers constructing wooden seats accompanied the sound of water graciously spraying in the fair fountains. A giant landscape of Western landmarks, showcasing Pulpit Rock and Devil's Slide, was hoisted up as stage scenery for the Wild West, not far from the Ferris wheel soon to be swirling above Lake Michigan.

On the fairgrounds, promoters and the big moneymen in morning coats, hats, and canes inspected the exposition's finishing touches. At the Wild West arena, Cody printed fresh letterhead with a picture of Christopher Columbus—"Pilot of the Ocean, the first Pioneer"— opposite a picture of Cody—"Pilot of the Prairie, the last Pioneer."

In his show ads, Cody took direct aim at the fair and promised to outdazzle the White City. He would be "second to none." "The biggest outdoor animated amusement exploit extant or known, either ancient or modern," the ads boasted. "Action, skill, daring, danger defied; one thousand animated pictures in two hours given by flesh and blood; creation's greatest handiwork, nature's noblest mechanism, too natural and colossal for canvas or building. The grassy sward our carpet, heaven's blue canopy our covering. . . ." And when the city's poor children were denied free admission to the fair, Cody would promptly throw his gates wide open and place in their small hands free tickets to sit starstruck before his Wild West cowboys and Indians.

Cody's promotional campaign was a master stroke. "I am doing the business of my life," he wrote to his sister in August. With the Chicago season half over, he was well on his way to pocketing a fortune. "Am well, but hard worked."

Every rail line, trolley car, horse car, wagon, and bus leading to the fair stopped first at the front gate to the Wild West show. Even before either the fair or the show had opened, Chicago residents were flocking to the site to take a look around and size up the contests. Many were entranced by such sights as the arrival of the old Deadwood stagecoach, twenty-five head of buffalo, and the colored blankets and yellow feathers of the Arapahos, Sioux, Brulés, and Oglalas.

Seventy-six Sioux from the Pine Ridge Reservation had pulled into Chicago's Northwestern Depot, among them Jack Red Cloud and Chief Standing Bear. In a late-season snow dusting, they sparkled in eagle feathers, bear claws, and elk teeth, in blue trousers and buckskin jackets. Some stepped onto the train platform already face-painted, some adorned in yellow bonnets. At the show grounds, carpenters, reporters, and spectators crowded around. Some of the Sioux whooped and yelled on cue; others grimaced in their smeared paint.

"This," said Cody, introducing the members of his new cast, "is Rocky Bear, being a very honest Indian. He stands well with his tribe as well as the whites.... This is No Neck, who became famous as a scout while General Crook was conducting the Sioux campaign of 1876."

Rain-in-the-Face, a Lakota war chief who had helped surround and slay Custer, hobbled forward on crutches. Nearly sixty, he startled easily at the blast of trolley horns. For a while he crouched on the ground in the back, away from the city noises. He would headline the Wild West show, and he would visit the fair. But not, he said, rolling a cigarette to calm his nerves, "until my eyes are rested and I do not see so big."

Cody (or Pahaska, for "Long Hair," as the Lakotas called him) turned many of the Sioux loose upon the Chicago streets to promote ticket sales once the Wild West extravaganza was under way. They snacked on buttered popcorn and Cracker Jack, sipped soda water, and chewed gum. In uncomfortable suits and ties, some twirled walking canes and adorned their buttonholes with fresh flowers.

Chief Standing Bear rode to the top of the Ferris wheel, his two hundred eagle feathers floating in the high breeze. Others strolled along the beach at Lake Michigan, marveling at the vast body of water and the endless tide, paddling boats, and climbing atop the rainbow-colored ponies on the carnival merry-go-round. Around and around they whirled, the steam organ grinding out the Irish waltz "Maggie Murphy's Home," with its lyrics about "kisses on the sly." Chief No Neck held on tight, singing, "Yip, yip, yi, yi, yip!" Downtown, some rode office elevators, at first wide-eyed and frightened, hugging the sides.

The fair was set to open on May 1; Cody would beat it by a week. His glossy color programs already were printed, along with a sixty-four-page booklet filled with lithographs and articles touting Cody as the savior of the frontier. The booklet noted that the Old West was "a class that is rapidly disappearing from our country." Now this new 1893 season in Chicago would enshrine that past, the booklets pledged, and simplify "the work of the historian, the romancer, the painter, and the student of the future." And more: "America is making history faster than any other country in the world. Her pioneers are fast passing away. A few years more and the great struggle for possession will be ended, and generations will settle down to enjoy the homes their fathers located and fenced in for them."

Cody's green wooden gates swung open on April 26, 1893. From that first two-hour performance, the Wild West would run for six months, with two shows a day, a matinee and an evening gala. It would pull in upward of six million fans. Profits peaked from $700,000 to $1 million. By the time it ended in late October, it had forever transformed Cody from a one-time Army scout in a dwindling American West into the greatest showman of a modern world.

That first performance was staged at three in the afternoon. Guest invitations pictured Cody leaning on his rifle and decked out in his fat sombrero, high black boots, tan frayed coat, and yellow scarf. The show boasted a new name, too, long and wordy but full of Western self-righteousness: "Buffalo Bill's Wild West and Congress of Rough Riders of the World." Admission was fifty cents, a quarter for children under ten.

First came an overture and a grand procession of cowboys. The announcer would indulge the crowd. "In the East," he would say, "the few who excel are known to all. In the far West, the names we offer to you are the synonyms of skill, courage, and individual excellence."

A crew of cowboy rough riders relaxes between twice-a-day performances during Buffalo Bill's signature season next to the 1893 World's Columbian Exposition in Chicago. (Nebraska State Historical Society)

Fans would thrill, said the ads, to "450 People in the Saddle: Indians, Cowboys, Mexican Rurales, Spanish Gauchos, Vaqueros, Detachments of Cavalry, Soldiers of All Nations in International Drill. A Monster Musical." Herds of buffalo, wild steers, and bucking bronchos would roam the show floor in what everyone voted "a world beater."

"More than historic," proclaimed the Wild West posters plastered about Chicago and full of drawings of Cody leading a charge against Indian warriors, Cody heading up lines of military dragoons, Cody lowering his hat to the roar of applause. "It is history itself in living lessons, not the imitations of fancy, but the stupendous realism of facts. If any seek to imitate it, they defraud it. If any claim to rival it, they falsify it. If any copy its announcements, it is forgery."

Cody would proclaim, "Wild West, are you ready?" and the great show would launch to thunderous applause. Rain or shine, it did not matter; the new grandstands were full, breathless, and covered.

And it did rain. On the first day, the skies opened and torrents poured down on Cody and his show. Lightning flashed over the lakefront. The floor grimed to puddles and then to muck. Through a side door, the performers marched anyway; nothing could stop Cody now.

From the first the show sparked a series of rave reviews. "A sturdy young man clad in the uniform of the United States army stepped from one of the entrances," reported the *Chicago Record*. "In his hand was a bugle. He raised the instrument to his lips and sent the stirring notes of assembly around and through the camp."

Miss Annie Oakley, America's "Little Miss Sure Shot," a single star pinned on her upturned hat, blasted glass balls out of the air and sent them splattering into mud holes. Cody fired at clay pigeons, splintering them into clay chips. "A howling success," concluded the *Chicago Times*.

Riders chased each other around the ring, every man for himself, every race for blood. "Full of stirring action," noted the *Chicago Inter Ocean*.

Buffalo were lassoed, the stage was robbed, a settler's cabin was ambushed. "The merry crack of the rifle," exulted the *Chicago Post*. "The yell of the cowboy."

Sioux braves beat on drums, shook spears, shrieked, and lunged. "Everything was wild," enthused the *Chicago Dispatch*. "There was nothing tame about it."

The highest drama was reserved for Cody himself. Astride a powerful chestnut horse, he bolted across the mud-floor arena, wearing a long Astrakhan fur–trimmed overcoat and a big slouch hat. The rain by now was a deluge, but Cody galloped into the teeth of the storm. He reined up close to the grandstand rail. He doffed his big sombrero. He shook back his dripping gray locks, lifted his face, and shouted up to the wet heavens.

Whatever he said, it was lost to the slap of rain and the clap of thunder. Scarcely a word was heard. But those thousands in the stands and the hundreds more left stranded outside without a show ticket, men and boys leaning their ears between the board pickets, their eyes peering through the knot holes—all of them understood. They could not hear, but they got the message. The Old West was alive again. They cheered madly.

A Cowboy Race | 5

Reporter Amy Leslie found Buffalo Bill sitting in the shade. All season long, the *Chicago Daily News* correspondent had been touring the World's Columbian Exposition and writing of its elegance and grace, its brilliant Midway Plaisance, and its overwhelming exhibits. This warm afternoon in June 1893, she turned her pen to William Cody.

Following a brick walk lined with garden flowers, she approached his ivy-thatched cottage "in the shadiest corner" of his Wild West campground. Ducking through a door flap, she stepped across a woven Indian rug. The walls were covered with what she described as "rude pictures" of Western scenes. Cody, relaxing between shows, spoke to her not as much about his Wild West cast or his European conquests as he did about a cowboy race.

It was some years ago, he said, when he had raced in what was called a "Nebraska derby." A Mexican *caballero* pitted his steed against what Cody boasted was "the fastest horse on my ranch." Cody knew he could beat the Mexican. He had been eyeing his rival's horse for a day or two, tethered to a cluster of old adobe ruins and grazing listlessly.

"But the race day," Leslie wrote in her story, "the horse appeared in pattern trim, surmounted with a dapper little jockey the like of which North Platte had never seen. Cody had all his money on his own horse and a glimpse of the opponent showed him that he had been watching the wrong horse."

Cody believed he could win anyway, and he saddled up. The competitors steered their horses together and at the drop of a flag sped off. After about half the distance, Cody fell well behind and squinted at the jockey's chipper colors in the lead. The jockey glanced back at Cody. "How much of this do you want?" he taunted. Buffalo Bill pulled on his reins. "I guess this is far enough," he said.

About a thousand miles west of Chicago and Cody's cottage, the small community of Chadron, Nebraska, was not even ten years old that summer of 1893. But its founders and its town leaders were big-idea people, and they nurtured high hopes out on the Nebraska Panhandle, tucked in next to the badlands, Pine Ridge, and Wounded Knee. Their aim that year was to create their own showpiece in the West and thereby boost their former fur-trading post. They hoped to see the town rise up over the silent prairie and attract more home-steaders, draw in more banks and investments, and expand their business district along Second Street. One day, maybe, they could even challenge a thriving metropolis such as Chicago itself.

Their plan to accomplish all this was built on a cowboy race.

The settlement began as a creek-side trading post and within a decade had expanded into a frontier boom town. "These people," remembered H. D. Mead, an area rancher and town engineer, "endowed with the indomitable pluck and energy which never fail to succeed, suffered hardships and adversities, but always overcame them. There was scarcely a day in the years gone by but which presented difficulties before which a weaker people would have turned in despair. But over and through it all, they pressed onward."

Nebraska's Panhandle faded brown in winter, dripped wet in spring, and turned lush and green each summer. Red Cloud and his tribal Sioux once hunted its endless flatlands, the high buttes and snaky-tail canyons. The spectral Black Hills peaked just to the north. But after white families began arriving in covered wagons and by rail, horseback, and buckboard, all that changed. The old Pete Nelson ranch house on Bordeaux Creek was one of the first signposts for wagon trains and settlers looping into the White River Valley in the early 1880s. Next were the white tops of a tent city for the newest arrivals, then Chadron itself. In ten years' time, the town of Chadron was growing rapidly, and the Dawes County countryside had thick-ened with wheat, oats, corn, and sugar beets. W. W. Wilson farmed 640 acres, "all nicely fenced," he said. By 1892, after just six years on his tract, he estimated "the place was worth five times what it cost me."

The Dawes County Courthouse was dedicated in 1889. Thirty thousand dollars in lumber, brick, and labor were poured into it, and the building anchored Chadron as a place of reckoning on the once lawless High Plains. The courthouse was, reported the *Bee* newspaper in Omaha, "large and well built, and far superior to that of many of the more wealthy counties of the state." At the opening ceremony lawyers, judges, and local dignitaries lifted champagne bottles and clinked glasses, relieved that hired guns and cowboy vigilantes at last had been ridden out of their small patch of the prairie. No longer would they tolerate renegades storming through Chadron shooting chickens.

One of the courthouse's first customers was Orlan Carty, sentenced to two and a half years of hard labor at the state penitentiary for assault with intent to murder. "I hope that the sentence of this court will bring about a complete reformation," admonished Judge Moses P. Kinkaid, later a ten-term congressman in Washington whose signature measure expanded the Homestead Act. "You are a young man; you have been tried here by a jury of Dawes County. You had a fair trial. You have been well and ably defended. Nothing more could be done that was possible to do, and there is nothing left for the court but to pass sentence."

"Oh," responded Carty, breaking into tears. "How I pity my poor mother."

There still lingered a few flinty vestiges of the rugged past swirling about the dust and mud of the town's streets. Chadron's first saloon, Angel's Place, was known to be commandeered by as many as a hundred cowboys, most from the Three Crow Ranch, on rowdy weekends. "Not a bottle or glass was left unbroken," recalled one western Nebraska history. "Every article of furniture was shot to pieces, the stove was perforated, windows broken and the walls and ceilings riddled with bullets." Finally Angel pinned a star on an armed guard, "a hired man with whiskers that was some gun man himself." One day one of the cowboys, by the name of Bill Malone, strutted into Angel's Place and sized up the new guard, peering closely at his long red beard. Malone pulled on the beard. Then he lit up the bar with a few pistol shots right through the guard's whiskers, sending him fleeing for the next train to Omaha.

Chadron was filled with outsized characters. In the gambling halls, none was more notorious than "Opportunity Hank." An old frontiersman, he would fix a wild stare on any tinhorn who ventured to shuffle a deck of cards. "I'm a fighting man," Hank would growl. "Red Jacket," a gorgeous woman in her early days, survived three husbands (some said she killed them) and finally lived alone, cloistered, cranky, and ill-tempered, in a small shack outside of town, her last companion her Winchester rifle. The sheriff jailed her for shooting a man who trespassed on her claim but let her out when she set her cell on fire. She died in poverty, according to the state history, as "a dope fiend."

By the time of the Great Cowboy Race, the rutted cattle and trail days were folding up like a worn-out bedroll, and the old cow herders seemed to be relics of a bygone time. That year in Chadron, members of a state convention of physicians were surprised to spot a few "cowboys, horse thieves and bad men" still jangling their spurs and tumbling in and out of bars, including Angel's Place and the Red Front Saloon, reported the *Omaha Daily Bee*. The doctors were so charmed they took "Kodak snaps" of outlaw Doc Middleton and a younger fellow nicknamed "Rattlesnake Pete," though they did not realize he was merely a farmhand from central Kansas. Both would soon race to Chicago.

Meanwhile Chadron had continued to grow. The First National Bank, a wooden structure, was outfitted with fireproof safes and vaults. Pioneer woman Mary E. Smith Hayward ran the M. E. Smith and Company women's clothing store, "the finest of its kind in northwest Nebraska." The brick-and-stone $20,000 Nelson Opera House seated 650 and featured weekly entertainments. The Pace Theater doubled as a roller-skating rink. The two-story Union Block building traded in new furniture on the first floor, with a bordello up above.

What most impressed Chadron residents was the Blaine Hotel, framed out in 1888 but not furnished or opened for two more years. The delay was caused by overdue construction loans; some of the money was supplied by the Fremont, Elkhorn, and Missouri Valley Railroad to board its business passengers seeking new sales territory out west. By all accounts, the hotel was a modern-day dandy. Running water and indoor bathrooms were showcased on each of the three floors. Night lamps powered by coal-fired generators lit the hallways, with coal bins lined up on Second Street. Maids bending over "vacuum pumps" spruced up the thirty-eight guest rooms. The Blaine offered a grand banquet hall and ballroom, a billiard parlor, an elegant bar, a barbershop, its own laundry room, and a live-in apartment for the hotel manager. Above the front doorway stretched a second-floor rail balcony; from up there, the pistol shot would be fired to start the cowboy race.

By the time of the race, area newspapers were touting Chadron and Dawes County as a growing center for the coming century, a pioneer settlement that in a few short years had blossomed into a jewel of the New West. Dawes County, according to the *Daily Bee*, was "one of the best counties in the great commonwealth." Here for the march of immigrant wagon trains were "water-courses and bluffs, which make the finest of pasture and grazing." Here was "a large belt of [as] fine wheat land as can be found anywhere."

The county agricultural society had converted eighty acres outside of Chadron and "nicely fitted it up with fences, buildings, sheds and a first-class half-mile race track." Farms were selling for as much as $20 an acre as the railroad steamed through the center of the county, bringing cheaper goods, modern farm equipment, and always more settlers.

Indeed, "a wide-awake city is Chadron," concluded the *Daily Bee*. The population had soared to 3,500 by June 1893, and the community was "regarded as the best town in northwestern Nebraska." Plans were under way to build a new college campus, the old one having burned in a fire a few months back.

Before there was a race, before there was even a Chadron, there lived a small, stout widow named Fannie O'Linn. She almost always dressed in drab, dark clothing. Her thick gray hair was wound in a knot and plumped atop her head. She clomped around in flat shoes or low heels, wore wire-rimmed glasses, and sometimes placed a black hat on top of that thick hair. In winter—and the winters were fierce out on the Panhandle—she bundled up in a raglan coat.

Her full name was Frances Maria Brainard O'Linn. Her father had practiced law and presided as a county judge in Iowa. She had married a doctor and borne two boys and a girl before heading west in 1872. The family stopped first in Blair, Nebraska, on the Iowa line. Her husband died in 1880, and four years later Fannie and her children pressed on to Valentine, Nebraska, at that time the end of the railway tracks marching toward the Rockies. From there the family hired a freight schooner and pushed even farther, landing near a creek named after a long-gone French fur trapper.

The trading post had been built forty years earlier; it was run by Louis B. Chartran. He had lost his wife and three children to a series of misfortunes in the 1830s, and in his grief he had moved alone to the frontier. He made friends with the still unpredictable Sioux, swapping liquor, blankets, guns, and ammunition for their tanned buffalo robes. Some early maps placed the negotiating site on "Chartran's Creek" in honor of that first French trader. Settlers from Missouri took to calling it "Shattron." The Irish, German, and Norwegian immigrants who followed, struggling with the English language, called it simply "Chadron."

The O'Linns scooped a small shack out of the sod and hillside near the old trading junction and the White River. The walls were shorn up with log rafters, brush, and caked dirt. There they stayed until Fannie could "prove up" her claim, and there her son Egbert was killed when a gun misfired as he was scaring range cattle away from the family's haystacks.

The small O'Linn settlement gradually mushroomed: a post office run by Fannie, a few stores selling dry goods and air-tight canned goods, a stock pen, a saloon or two, a compact jail, and a small courtroom for a circuit-riding judge appeared. Then came the railroad. But the tracks swung wide of O'Linn's little spot, and the railway announced plans for a new depot out in the country. So Fannie and her few neighbors picked up and moved to the new train station. Pioneers remembered the sight of people tearing down their homes and loading buckboards and wagons, with horses and mules carting everything they owned—chairs, dishes, blankets, bathtubs—to create what became Chadron around that new depot.

"The road over the prairie and hill was a continuous procession of houses, stocks of merchandise, household goods and people," recalled E. E. Egan, who launched the settlement's first newspaper. "Many merchants left their goods on the shelves, moving the store complete. Ben Lowenthal completed the picture by keeping his store open for business while it was being trundled over the prairie." The evening before they all up and moved, some of the settlers gathered on the crest of a nearby hill for one long last look at the sod they had broken, the homes they had built, the lives they had planned. At sunset, remembered Egan, they raised a toast. "We bade her an affectionate farewell and then turned our faces to the future."

Less than a month earlier, the only occupant of the new Chadron town site had been a coyote. But within another month, Chadron covered almost six blocks. Mechanics, brick masons, and carpenters streamed in. Blacksmith shops, brick kilns, and wooden structures went up, some of the timber being hauled in from the Black Hills and beyond. That first year in Chadron, eight saloons swung open their doors. Another newspaper cranked up a printing press, and then another.

Fannie O'Linn reigned as the town's queen mother. Reading law books eventually won her a legal license and entrée into the bar of the U.S. Supreme Court, her sponsor being the Nebraska populist William Jennings Bryan. She not only hung out her law shingle; she also verified legal documents as a notary public, sold insurance and real estate, filed abstracts, and wrote loans. She attended births, consecrated marriages, and prayed at funerals. And she dealt with her own adversity. A second son, Hugh, was killed when he toppled off a train chugging east of St. Louis. Her son-in-law, Clarence Smith, was struck by a passing train.

While Fannie covered Chadron in her flat shoes and low heels, the cowboy known as "Billy the Bear" turned up in town with no feet at all. And yet his tough times, hard luck, and the snowdrifts that had buried him in the cold failed to keep him down. Billy would always lift himself up again.

Born Louis John Frederick Iaeger in Philadelphia, he was, he told friends, connected to royalty. His great-grandfather had served as the spiritual advisor to King Frederick the Great, the patron of the Prussian Enlightenment, or so maintained Iaeger family history. His father had built horse carriages in Hamburg, Pennsylvania, and after his parents died of injuries from an accident, young Billy was sent to an uncle in Arizona. But Billy longed for the open sea, and at eighteen he shipped off as a navigator aboard a grain tanker called the *St. John*, sailing the lanes between San Francisco and Liverpool, England, a borrowed copy of Mark Twain's *Innocents Abroad* tucked under his arm.

In Europe, he tramped around Paris and Milan but missed his homeland. So he sailed one last time, returning to the United States, and in San Francisco he worked as a proofreader for a series of volumes on Western America. He also interviewed pioneers and immigrants about their hardships in planting a new life on the frontier. In 1877, he joined an acting troupe. There he met his destiny.

"In the San Francisco grand opera house," he recalled, "I was cast in a fairy play called 'Snowflake.' I was a wicked bear and was supposed to drop dead at the touch of Cupid's wand. I fell directly under the heavy steel drop which started to descend on me. Simulating the dying spasms of a bear, as I imagined them, I worked myself to safety just in time to escape. My death quivers and agonies, combined with the situation, brought down the house."

It also brought Buffalo Bill Cody to his feet. He happened to be in the audience that evening, and when a shout rose up asking who in the world was playing the overly dramatic animal, Cody exclaimed, "Why, that's Billy the Bear!"

The name stuck, and so did their friendship. Billy moved out to North Platte, Nebraska, as Cody's private secretary at Scout's Rest. During an 1879 Cheyenne uprising on the Snake River, when ranches were burned and cattlemen scalped, he helped lead the settlers' resistance. In the early 1880s, he watered cattle along the Niobrara River. He bought the Sugar Creek Ranch in the Sand Hills. He took title to 1,500 horses in Texas and sold them in Kansas. He sunk thousands of dollars into an Idaho silver mine that dug up empty. He managed a ranch near Rock Creek, Wyoming, for investors planning to ship beef on the hoof back east. Then he met his destiny again.

Rushing on horseback to catch a train for Omaha, Billy became stranded in a sudden winter storm on January 31, 1883. For the next four days, the blizzard bore down on him. He abandoned his horse but could not find his own way out. To keep warm, he set fire to some fence logs, but they burned through. He huddled in the drifts as the wind howled, the snow mounted, and the white ice crinkled. Certain he would freeze to death, on the third day he wrapped his frost-bitten fingers around a lump of charcoal and in agony scratched out a farewell note to a friend. He expected it would be his epitaph.

"I got lost after I left the hills," Billy wrote. "It blew fearful. Oh, why did I go? I burned up Rufe's corral. Think this is Sheep creek. As soon as it clears up I am going to try again. Send my body to my sister, Mrs. J. J. Vandersloot, York county, Pennsylvania. Good-bye, old boy, and may God take my soul. Sell my horses to Henry."

Yet he did not quit. He plunged his frozen feet into snow piles well past his leather belt. On the fourth day, he spied a flickering lamp from a far-off cabin. Rising up out of the snow, he stretched his black and purple fingers around his six-shooter and managed a shot. The bullet shattered a window. Billy collapsed, but he was rescued.

Doctors amputated both of his legs below the knee. They took all of his fingers; the blizzard spared only his two thumbs. Released from a hospital, he was fitted with prosthetic limbs. He learned to crawl and then hobble, to stand erect and then balance himself. He practiced how to eat with a spoon and write with a pen. For a while he kept the books for Buffalo Bill once more, and Cody sometimes donated the funds for Billy's "artificials" from a manufacturer in St. Louis. Other times Billy took the train from "cow country" down to Omaha and rode back with a new pair of feet and two good hands.

But he never shed himself of the cold and the snow, never fully shook the chill, and in his diary notations he repeatedly reminded himself of what he had suffered through alone on the Wyoming tundra. "As anticipated last night the Storm is here in great Shape and 'King Blizzard' is at present in all his glory," he wrote in November 1886, almost three years after his own whiteout. "Like the old Soldier 'it reminds of me of old times.' Oh that I may never again see or feel those agonies I suffered when freezing on the Laramie Plains."

By then Billy had moved to Chadron, determined to reinvent himself once more. He started his diary on his first day in town in October 1885, plunging headlong into crowded saloons and bustling brothels. He recorded the tragedies of mothers dying in childbirth and children drowning in a creek bed, the occasional cowboy outbursts, and the dwindling Indian presence on the reservation badlands. What he particularly enjoyed writing about was the thrill of the impromptu horse races up and down the city streets as cowboys whipped and hollered and flashed past him like polished steel. Billy could no longer ride like that.

The future and the past: Billy "the Bear" Iaeger, a retired cowboy turned city slicker, and the deposed Oglala Lakota chief Red Cloud pose in the middle row of a group at Chadron, Nebraska, a new town displacing the old Sioux lands. (Dawes County Historical Museum)

Chadron residents were deep into racing, so much so that in 1886 they pushed horses around an oblong dirt track until the winner ran a hundred miles. Ten cowboys lurched off at sunrise, and before the race was half done, one horse slammed to a dead stop, dripping blood from its sides. Another somersaulted end over end. A third staggered, groaned, fell to its knees, and perished. Only three mangy mustangs limped on. First prize went to the mayor of Chadron, whose cow pony Old Baldy crossed the finish line "just able to walk in."

In five years, Billy closed out his diary. By then Chadron had been blessed with its new courthouse and the Blaine Hotel, a school building and an Episcopal church, a baseball diamond, electric lights, and a skating rink. Billy blossomed as well, rising to elder in the Elks lodge, staying active in the Fraternal Order of Eagles, and becoming treasurer of the Old Time Cowboys Association. He also served as a police judge and a justice of the peace. A "Democrat to the core," as he liked to boast, he repeatedly was elected city clerk, county court clerk, deputy federal court clerk, and a member of the Great Cowboy Race committee.

He won the endless devotion of the niece of one of those racing cowboys, the beautiful daughter of the prominent town physician. "Look at this three times a day regularly," his bride, Temperance, wrote on the back of her photograph when she presented it to him on their wedding day. "That should be sufficient." He did, and it was. For a long lifetime, they remained husband and wife, the parents of two fine-looking sons.

"As far back as I can remember," recalled one Chadron neighbor, Billy the Bear "had a two-wheeled cariole [wagon] that he could manipulate with his hands. It ran on the sidewalk and went quite fast. Later he was presented with a small electric carriage that putt-putted through the streets.... [He was] a wonderful little man, with a strong determination not to be a cripple.... He set himself above his infirmities."

Billy would glide about on his morning rounds on his cart wearing a bowler hat, a scarf or bow tie tight against his neck, a natty mustache, and sometimes a small cane under his arm. When he felt stronger, he walked upright on his two metal feet, slow but moving, the clank, clank, clank of his artificials proclaiming his steps. Later he learned to roller skate.

Billy stayed put in tiny Chadron for forty-five years. When he died there in 1930 after a series of strokes at age seventy-four, the downtown stores closed their doors for two hours on a busy Monday afternoon. At his funeral, the preacher opened his Bible to find that Billy had penciled in the exact passages he wanted read. "Read first 13 verses 51st Psalm," Billy had instructed. Verse 7 struck home: "Purge me with hyssop, and I shall be clean, / Wash me, and I shall be whiter than snow."

So much had changed since Billy the Bear had first hit town so long ago. "Chadron Neb Oct 14th 1885," began his first diary entry. "Arrived here and found every thing in a whirl ... excitement ... plenty of Cow-Boys in town and lots of gambling going.... John Keys, Allen, Harvey ... are running the gambling in the Gold Bar Saloon which has just opened up and Shows Signs of doing a big business."

"Oct 18th. Billy Carter and Tom Christan gave me the Hazzard Table in Carters Saloon, and I drew a good play from the Start."

He wrote about shady characters and the lure of alcohol and drugs: "J. W. O'Brien, O. S. Sloggy, Geo Minnick, headed by Geo Spaulding are again on a drunk in Carters.... After Supper, Mrs McNutt came around and as usual Succeeded in Stirring up a fuss.... Fannie Powers is all broke up about her dear Baby Jack being in jail and amuses herself by carrying ice cream, whiskey, opium and morphine to him."

Billy reported on the gunfire and sputtering exploits of the last wild cowboys, lit with enough liquor to bust up the new town. "Broken nosed Curley came back to Chadron from Douglas & the West, also little smitty and Vince. Nearly all the old Gang are back and things are commencing to loom up natural again."

His heart sped with the sudden cowboy races that erupted around town: "Just then a horse race sprung up and I let everything rest and attended to that, which took up the rema[i]nder of the day, and made Suckers out of all the Gang."

In one of his last entries, he described how far his adopted hometown had come since the West was wild, and how gentle the new life could be: "Sept. 1. Nice clear day in the morning but towards noon it commenced to blow and get dusty." That late summer afternoon he trotted a pony out to a friend's house for dinner; he visited other acquaintances as well. "We had 2 bottles of soda water. I spent a very pleasant day with Mr Sayrs and had a long and interesting chat with Mr De Lambert about the early days of Cow Punching and about how I got froze on the Laramie Plains."

In his very last diary entry, on January 21, 1890, he left just three words, ominous and forewarning, but hinting in their simplicity that he no longer feared the worst, for he had already endured it. "Stormy and snowing," he wrote.

◆──≍◆≍──◆

John Maher followed a different trail. A former schoolteacher, in Chadron he served as a town leader and government land office director, as a court reporter and stenographer. He also moonlighted as a Western correspondent and flourished as a freelance stringer for James Gordon Bennett Jr.'s *New York Herald*. It was through that connection, as one of the first reporters to reach Wounded Knee, that he first witnessed the might of the U.S. Army.

"It was a war of extermination," he reported. "It was difficult to restrain the troops. Tactics were almost abandoned. About the only tactic was to kill while it could be done, wherever an Indian could

Left to right: Billy "the Bear" Iaeger, Chief Red Cloud, and John Maher. (Dawes County Historical Museum)

be seen. Down into the creek and up over the bare hills they were followed by artillery and musketry fire, and for several minutes the engagement went on until not a live Indian was in sight."

Like Fannie O'Linn, Maher eventually earned a law degree. Unlike Billy the Bear, he left Chadron to explore other places. In Army uniform, he served during hostilities on the U.S.–Mexico border and in France during the First World War. Promoted to lieutenant colonel and chief disbursing officer, he oversaw finances for the Allied Expeditionary Force. From his Élysée Palace office in Paris, he handled the payout of some $500 million in war expenses.

He founded and served as first president of the Old Line Insurance Company, helped organize the American Legion, and headed up the Nebraska Progressive League. The son of a homesteader in Platte County, Nebraska, and a product of pioneer schools, Maher lived his last years abroad, touring the capitals of the world. He died an old man in Rome, stricken with heart failure, and he was buried in Arlington Cemetery, just across the river from Washington.

But little of that is why John Gillespie Maher is best remembered today.

Tall and ramrod straight, with a thick mustache and thinning hair, he often displayed a sardonic sneer. In his early years in Chadron, he was above all a hoaxer, a prankster, a teller of tall tales. The Eastern press thirsted for stories of the Indian warrior lurking over the next ridge, the daring cowboy riding the Plains, the rattlesnake coiled under a rock. Maher delivered. But many of the "news" items he sent zapping across the telegraph wires popped out of his own vivid imagination. In Chadron and around the Panhandle region, he was known to all as "the Paralyzer of the Truth."

"The Eastern newspapers were simply crying for Wild West news," Maher recalled many years later. "No tale was too preposterous, no supposition too ridiculous to be included in the columns of a New York newspaper provided the article carried a Western headline. At that time Chadron was a truly frontier town, made up of tent houses, gambling shacks and saloons. Nothing of national interest ever happened there. In fact, nothing ever happened, only a few cowboy fights. Nevertheless the East, enraptured with Buffalo Bill and his escapades and amazed at the discoveries of mammoth fossils in the Badlands, wanted news—and I needed money. So I sent them what they wanted."

After the Great Cowboy Race, Maher traveled to Chicago to cover the World's Columbian Exposition. In a column for the *Chadron Signal* titled "Farmer John at the Fair," he wrote that he had confessed to the Ferris wheel manager, "Occasionally I lied for the newspapers."

With his newspaper credentials, Maher and his hoaxes almost always were believed, at least initially. He wrote about a petrified man, complete with one foot sticking out of the dirt, discovered by fossil diggers in 1892 in the badlands north of Chadron. The mummified remains were paraded around the Midwest and for a while stored in a vault in Champaign, Illinois. Plans were drawn up to display them at the World's Columbian Exposition. The *Dawes County Journal* proclaimed the ancient cadaver a puzzle of anthropology: "The face resembles that of a Negro. But his shapely heels indicate Caucasian blood.... The medical fraternity and all others who have seen the specimen laugh at the idea that it is not genuine. It is undoubtedly the most perfect specimen of the kind ever discovered and is worth many thousands of dollars." Another newspaper testified that "even the toenails, teeth, eyebrows and pores of the skin are as natural as life."

In truth, Maher and friends had fashioned a sand-and-dirt cast from a soldier at nearby Fort Robinson and passed it off as a precious relic. Nevertheless, Maher said later, admitting the ruse with a chuckle, "that story provided me with columns for weeks."

When Chadron residents started heading to South Dakota and Wyoming in search of mineral wells and healthier water, Maher announced a new "soda springs" at the bottom of a Chadron well. He prepared news releases and reported that some invalids, after just one sip and a shout of hallelujah, "threw away their crutches." In truth, Maher had simply sunk some sacks of soda water into that old well bottom. There was no miracle cure.

One season he and his chums inflamed fears by reporting that British reprisals were being planned against Irish settlers in Nebraska's Niobrara River region. Towns such as Valentine and O'Neill were likely to be attacked, they warned, probably by British regiments marching south from Canada. He even mailed a crate labeled "rifles" to Irish immigrants in Valentine, available for self-defense. Cracked open, the box contained no firearms at all but rather, according to state historian Mari Sandoz, "a lot of Irish clubs cut, I hear, along the brush of Bordeaux creek in Northwestern Nebraska."

Another time, Maher claimed he had discovered the body of a Spanish prisoner during a visit to Louisiana and announced it was none other than the saboteur who sank the USS *Maine*. Actually, Maher had acquired a cadaver, placed it in a ruined fort, and set it afire. Voilà!—the missing "man who blew up the *Maine*."

He wrote of a sea monster lurking at the bottom of Nebraska's Alkali (now Walgren) Lake, and his accounts compared its head to an "oil barrel shiny black in the moonlight." The eyes glowed green and "spit fire." The mouth roared, and the teeth gnashed like rips of thunder. The creature would sneak ashore at night and devour a dozen calves at a time, flattening cornfields.

Many years later, Sandoz visited Maher in his office in Lincoln, hoping to clear up his history of hoaxes. He quickly brushed her aside and started in on another "fantastic version" about an old pioneer, a rattlesnake, and a horrible bite. The pioneer grabbed his .30-30 Winchester rifle, Maher told her, aimed at the snake, and in misfiring shot off his own hand.

John Maher long after he had abandoned Chadron, where he was notorious for his hoaxes, including one doozy about a thousand-mile horse race. (Nebraska State Historical Society)

Sandoz stopped him right there. She told him that the old pioneer in his "story" was her father, and she accused Maher of spooling out another "fantastic fabrication."

Maher turned pink. "You're the girl, the daughter who was with him when he was bitten?" he stammered. Yes, she was. "Well," he replied, "it was a damn good story the way I was telling it, wasn't it?"

Sometime in late 1892, a story began quietly circulating about a proposed cowboy race. Not an ordinary cowboy race down a dusty rural road or around a swirling oval track. This one, according to John Maher's reports to the Eastern newspapers, was going to be a big race, with real cowboys and Western-bred bronchos. It was going to capitalize on the long-distance horse-racing craze that was sweeping Europe. It was going to start from northwestern Nebraska and the Panhandle plains and lead straight to the steel-and-iron skyscrapers towering above Chicago, just in time for the next summer's world's fair. This one was going to be a thousand miles.

On November 9, 1892, the small-town *True Northerner* newspaper in Paw Paw, Michigan, picked up on the report and ran a brief, one-paragraph item in the middle of page 2—what appears to be one of the first published notices to surface about a cowboy race. "Will Ride to the Fair," announced the headline. The story fudged, noodled, and embellished some of the facts, but the idea was there. "The old-time cowboys of Northwestern Nebraska are going to the World's Fair," the story claimed. "It will be a pistol-shot mount and start, and the winner will get $1,000 and a gold medal. Side purses will be numerous. Over 300 old-time cowboys have agreed to enter the race, and have posted forfeits. A system of registry will be agreed upon to insure fair riding, and as many horses will be used as each rider may deem necessary."

Some of the big South Dakota ranchers and town leaders in Deadwood and Sturgis along the Black Hills, and in Chadron too, had been chewing over such a race for some time. But no cowboys had entered, and no gold medal had been struck. One weekend in Chadron, Emmett Albright, a cowhand from Texas, rode into town and over a beer at one of the saloons said an idea had been knocking around in his head about a long-distance "chase" to prove the Western broncho's durability and the cow man's endurance. He thought it a grand idea, especially if the cowboys could romp around Chicago and demonstrate their skills roping, riding, and "cutting" cattle. He thought they could draw a thousand or more fans for a show at the Union Stock Yards.

More news items began popping up, as though the race already were a done deal. Newspaper telegraph reports datelined Deadwood said $1,000 was being put up for a cowboy run from Chadron to the fair, to start next May 15. The *New York Sun* reported that the contest would prove the Western broncho could beat the time and endurance of the German and Austrian breeds in that fatal race of the summer before. "Westerners claim that their ponies can stand more hardship than any other four-legged thing on earth," according to the *Sun*.

Soon Chadron found itself over a barrel. Maher's latest prank had taken hold, and some in town worried that their city would be embarrassed for promising something it could never deliver. "The whole thing originated in the fertile brain of one of our local correspondents to the eastern press," complained the *Chadron Citizen*. "And well it might be to curb his imagination in the future."

In December 1892, an anxious rancher named McGinley, who owned the JA brand of horses in Sioux County, Nebraska, appeared on Chadron's streets, demanding, "Is there going to be a cowboy race, or not?" He proposed that some preliminary arrangements be laid down, and he called for a meeting to adopt a set of race rules, including a stipulation that horses not be ridden near to death the last fifty or hundred miles to the fair. He predicted that the cowboys would "jog" their horses about seventy-five miles a day to reach Chicago and suggested that "the best horses will be saddled and a grand rush will be made" in the final lap to the world's fair.

McGinley thought up to three hundred cowboys would enter. One of them, the notorious outlaw Doc Middleton, was among the first to raise a gloved hand. Emmett Albright, in his broad-brimmed Stetson and with a six-shooter strapped to his hip, hailed as "the finest rifle shot in these parts," announced that he was in, too. Winn Satterlee, the eleven-year-old son of the owner of the Blaine Hotel, begged to ride with them.

"Chadron is not as large a city as Chicago," noted the local *Dawes County Journal.* "But her people, like those of the city of the lakes, have some original ideas and purpose to cut something of a figure themselves at the big show. Hurrah for the Chadron–Chicago cowboy race!"

George Edward "Ed" Lemmon, the old-time cowhand from the Dakotas, cautioned that a trip of that many miles would not come easy in the saddle. "To ride 75 miles in one day is not out of the ordinary," he wrote in his log books.

Many men have done it. But to average that many miles for 13 days in a row would test men and horses to the limit.

The rider would not be mounting a fresh horse every relay and riding without regard for the horse, as he'd do if he knew he'd have a fresh mount at each stop. No, these men would have to save their horses' strength all they could.

Then, too, a rider with a fresh mount under him can stand a long ride much better than he can on a jaded horse. And if the road was rocky he'd have to let the horse pick his way, lest he sprain his leg or be lamed by a rock bruise. If the road led through hilly country with steep slopes he'd not dare ride at high speed either uphill or down, but would have to take advantage over every chance to make time when the temperature and the lay of the ground would let him.

But a real horseman understands his horse, and it is almost unbelievable how a good horse will respond to such a rider.

On Christmas Day 1892, the *Daily Bee* in Omaha thought Chadron could pull it off: "It is quite an undertaking for a city of this size to get up such a race, but there are some very energetic rustlers behind it and they say it will be carried out." The *Chadron Citizen* newspaper, in February 1893, boasted that its hometown was "getting a big lot of advertising all over the country." It was said that Nebraska alone might send three hundred riders, along with two hundred others from across the Western states. The purse money had fattened, and the finish line now would be the front door of the Nebraska state building at the Chicago Fair.

So on a Saturday night in March 1893, Billy the Bear, one of the race's biggest boosters, called a mass meeting to order inside Nelson's Opera House. E. D. Satterlee, owner of the Blaine Hotel, was elected chairman of the race committee. Harvey Weir was named committee secretary and Sheriff James Dahlman a committee member. In the back of the crowded hall, John Maher stood silent, a grin creasing his face.

They discussed raising more prize money, and how they hoped the race would come off as "a success with a big S." They adopted an initial set of rules:

—Cowboys could ride no more than two horses.
—Horses must be Western bred and raised.
—Saddles would be Western cowboy stock weighing not less than 35 pounds, and the combined weight of cowboy and saddle must be more than 150 pounds.
—Entries would close on June 1, with rider fees ranging from $10 to $25, depending on how soon the cash would be presented to the window teller at the Bank of Chadron.
—The cowboys would ride the morning of June 13 from the front of the Blaine Hotel, "this being the first day of the state's firemen's tournament."

No race route was laid out for the cowboys, but some committee officials began sketching the most direct path across the Nebraska Panhandle, over the Missouri River into Iowa, and over the Mississippi into Illinois, with a last dash for Chicago's Columbian Exposition. They would bill the race with that nicely rounded-out, precise number of one thousand miles, though some in Nebraska claimed it would be more like 1,040 miles with all the zigzagging and diverting around the Sand Hills and two big rivers. Computations today put the beeline distance at closer to nine hundred miles.

The panel completed one final task: they sent a wire to Buffalo Bill Cody and asked whether his show grounds next to the fair might not make the perfect finish line. Cody wired back to Sheriff Dahlman: "Am delighted to hear of the proposed thousand mile cowboy race from Chadron to Chicago (stop) Would appreciate having the race end at my Wild West Show in the Columbian Exposition (stop) Will donate five hundred dollars to be added to the purse of the winning ride (stop) Colonel (Buffalo Bill) Cody."

Not everyone was enthusiastic about pushing horses to the limit, though. To many there was a distinction between endurance and abuse. "It would be better for the 'boys' to choose some other amusement in coming to the great fair," the secretary of the Aurora, Illinois, Humane Society wrote in a letter to the *Chadron Citizen*. "Something that does not have about it the elements of cruelty."

George T. Angell, lawyer, philanthropist, and president of the Massachusetts Society for the Prevention of Cruelty to Animals, pictured "300 wild cowboys" driving their horses far too hard, "semibarbarians" on steeds at full gallop for days and nights "under whip and spur." He encouraged everyone along the route of the race to confront the cowboys "with hisses and cries of shame!" Angell believed that the Chadron race would be much worse than those in central Europe a year earlier. One of those horses, Angell said, was left "bleeding from her flanks, where she had been stabbed a hundred times with spurs, and from wales [weals] inflicted with the whip." Fifteen horses were disabled for life; "their sides are sunken in, their spines were twisted awry." At least eight of the Austrian horses died on the road.

What further agitated Angell was learning that the German Kaiser had hosted a postrace dinner to honor his riders. "If these gentlemen had undertaken this fine sport in Massachusetts," Angell warned, "instead of being dined they would quite likely have landed in a Massachusetts jail."

But interest in the West was building, drummed up by promotions such as one from the *Chicago Inter Ocean* that proclaimed the winner would gallop home "the Uncrowned King of the Cowboys."

Doc Middleton began laying down bets around Chadron, wagering up to $500 that he would arrive first in Chicago.

Clabe Young had for some years ridden bronchos for Buffalo Bill, and he would be sponsored by the state of Wyoming atop a big gray gelding that once ran wild and nearly attacked anyone who approached it. Young had won the horse in a poker game, named it Balmaceda, and broken it in. He had once been tried and acquitted of murder in Texas, and he had been wounded in a gunfight with Mexican smugglers. Now he was confident he could push his new horse a hundred miles or more a day to Chicago.

Jeptha Sweat, a Chadron youngster who had run off to Wyoming and worked a sheep ranch, trapped and hunted, shot a bear, and once raced for a $100 prize, said he would ride to Chicago. Narcisse Valleaux Jr., nicknamed "Young Nelse" of the Teton Range, announced he would slam his boots in the stirrups and race as well.

The committee announced more rules:

—The race would be open to the world.
—Each horse would be given a special commemorative
  brand.
—Riders would be required to register at designated stops.
—Anyone sneaking off for a train depot and "riding the rails"
  would be disqualified.
—Before the jump-off shot was fired, each rider would be
  handed an official map of the race route.

Originally from Minnesota, "Texas Ben" called himself a "titled cowboy" and said he was headed for Chadron and a spot in the line-up. From the Pine Ridge Reservation were expected a score of Oglala Lakota riders, including Big Bat, Yeast Powder Bill, and Yellow Bird. In Colorado, the people of San Miguel County rallied around a character called "Rattlesnake Bill," trusting in his "wonderful record" in the saddle. William Lessig and Joe Campbell, two other deeply tanned Colorado cowboys, rode in eight days to Chadron on one pony each, three hundred miles in all, just to show off their horses' strength. A young, feisty cowgirl named Emma Hutchinson was also trotting up from Denver, aiming to beat them all.

Sioux County, Nebraska, was backing "Rattlesnake Dick," a Yale graduate known for his predilection for snakeskins. Wiltz Earnest, the so-called Cowboy Giant at over seven feet tall, would ride. Huron, South Dakota, backed O. M. Bell, the local agent for the American Express company. He had recently picked out a new horse from a boxcar full of mounts.

Missouri and Iowa communities reported that they would put up several entrants, and as far away as Pennsylvania, local enthusiasts found someone to saddle up. Wyoming's list was growing, since many cowboys were idling and bored, or eager to escape fallout from the Powder River Range War in Johnson County. From the Bighorn Basin, Jack Flagg, who once had zigzagged his horse past a murdering posse of Wyoming cattlemen who had killed two of his friends, would compete. Kearney, Nebraska, promised to send a trio of cowboys: Tony Cornelius, Ed Finch, and Mike Sanders. When these three men "undertake a thing of this kind," promised the *Kearney Daily Hub*, "it means business."

Chadron itself would not be outdone. Along with Middleton and Albright, another hometown hero said he would ride. Jim Murray had traveled up from Texas in the 1870s as a boy, reached Omaha, and was bound for Montana when he decided that the Panhandle and Chadron were far enough. (He had stepped from the train with $1.50 in the pocket of his button-fly trousers; first off he bought some suspenders to help hold them up.)

Also bustling in and out of Chadron was John Berry, an area railway surveyor who had helped plat the city. He was mysteriously taking the morning express to Chadron and then departing on the night train home. All around town Berry kept his eyes trained and his ears alert. "When spoken to now-a-days on railroad matters," reported the *Chadron Citizen*, "he at once turns the subject to the cowboy race to Chicago, and the great advertisement the race is going to be for Chadron."

By the end of April 1893 the race seemed unstoppable, and Buffalo Bill had pledged his separate cash prize of $500, welcoming the haystack of free publicity. His adjutants Major John Burke and Nate Salsbury loved the idea, too. In their Chicago newspaper ads for their Wild West show, they began including updates on the race. In front of Cody's tent, they hammered up a wooden "Thousand Mile Tree" to mark the official finish line. The first cowboy in was to report to Buffalo Bill. He would shake his hand and declare him the winner.

To further sweeten the pot, the Colt Arms Company offered a specially manufactured "piece of side artillery"—a gold-plated revolver—as yet another prize. Colt called the pistol one of its cherished "cowboy companions." The .44-caliber revolver, with an ivory handle, blue-steel barrel, and gold-plated cylinder (page 205), was displayed in the front window of Hayes & Bargelt's jewelry store in downtown Chadron, its sparkle impossible to miss.

The Montgomery Ward dry-goods company in Chicago announced that it would toss in one of its finest leather saddles. The rancher H. D. Mead presented two locally known favorites, Doc Middleton and Charley Smith, with handcrafted leather bridles inscribed with silver plates: "World's Fair Cowboy Race, June 13, 1893." Separately, the Lowenthal Brothers' Second Street store chipped in a $25 saddle blanket and a $12 white Stetson hat for Middleton. The blanket was sewn with gold letters stitched in, reading, "Lowenthal Brothers, Chadron Nebraska Rider." The sweatband on Doc's new hat was printed in silver lettering: "Doc Middleton, Lowenthal Brothers' Rider to the World's Fair."

Criticism of the race heated up. At the state capital at Lincoln, a county judge grew disgusted with the idea. "Who does not pity as well as despise the man who shall sit for hours, for days and weeks astride some noble animal and see his quivering flanks, his distended nostrils and finally his faltering, failing limbs?" the judge asked. "Most of all to be despised is the man, or rather monster, who shall succeed in prolonging the torture."

From Barron, Wisconsin, a letter arrived on the Nebraska governor's desk from a group of bank executives, warning that the cowboy race would "see this country retrograding to the low place of the Romans in Nero's time." They complained that "the Spanish bull fighters" were equally brutal. In Philadelphia, the Women's Branch of the Pennsylvania Society for the Prevention of Cruelty to Animals met in their headquarters office on South Seventeenth Street and adopted a resolution condemning the race. Their president, Caroline Earle White, a pioneer in animal care who particularly championed horses, called for "prompt and efficient action" to put a halt to the cowboys and all the race mania. "Cruelty inevitably will be its result," she declared.

A few warnings escalated to threats: cowboys participating in the race might be handcuffed, arrested, and hauled off to jail. Many announced riders began changing their minds and dropping out. Soon the number fell to a couple dozen.

The critics kept up the pressure. At the annual session of the Illinois Humane Society on May 6 in their new meeting hall on Chicago's State Street, John G. Shortall, president of the national and Illinois societies, urged the state legislature to pass a bill against the animal cruelty involved in such a long-distance cowboy race. He called it comparable to other "brutal fights and a disgrace to the community." Another critic, the Reverend David Swing, took the Sunday pulpit at the Central Music Hall in Chicago, a towering theater structure with thundering acoustics and a giant American flag. The city's most popular preacher, Swing condemned the race as "both stupid and brutal" and said, "The scheme is too inhuman for our age and nation. It should be instantly abandoned.... To think that there are men here in this city and in the far West who could deliberately plan an amusement so perfectly infamous."

Protests spread to the state houses, and Nebraska Governor Lorenzo Crounse's desk spilled over with letters and telegrams of complaint. "Stop it if possible," demanded a group of Nebraska women, many from Chadron. "It is to be a blot on the name of America, civilization and Nebraska in particular." The Wisconsin Humane Society urged the governor to "think of the unutterable suffering and death of some of the poor helpless innocent horses at the mercy of those who think only of their reward." They suggested that "true mercy is nobility's true badge." The American Anti-Vivisection Society called the cowboy race no better than a "bull-fight or a pigeon-shooting tournament."

Members of the race's coordinating panel, now officially called the Chadron Citizens' Committee, ignored them. Instead they invited Governor Crounse to fire the pistol to start the cowboys to Chicago. Crounse declined, but he also declined to lift his hand to stop the race, his office arguing that the governor did not possess the legal authority to bar any cowboys from racing horses anywhere.

So the protesters turned again to Chicago. Shortall met with Cody and Salsbury and urged them to drop their sponsorship. He told them their pledge of additional prize money and their "being so well known in the West" was only encouraging trouble. Salsbury responded with an extraordinary May 19 letter to race committee secretary Harvey Weir, reminding him that many of the nation's newspapers, especially the Eastern press, were united with the humane society groups in wanting to shut down the race.

"It is quite impossible to make them understand that cruelty will not be practiced in the endeavor by individuals to win the race," Salsbury cautioned. The committee must convince the country that the cowboys would not abuse their horses. "You may be sure," he wrote Weir, "that unless you do this and do it with perfect candor and honesty, the race will never terminate in the city of Chicago." If those assurances were not made, he told Weir, Cody might pull out. "So far as our connection with the race is concerned, you know that our offer was made in perfect good faith. But at the same time we will not assume any part of any discredit that may be attached to it by the better class of the community, and unless convincing proof can be given that cruelty in no form will be practiced, we shall withdraw our offer."

Salsbury also told Weir that a skeptical public would rise up and "completely frustrate the success of your plans," something the Wild West show wanted no part of. He noted that "Colonel Cody is an officer in good standing" of the Humane Society and also serves as "an officer of the state of Nebraska." With that in mind, Salsbury recommended that the Chadron committee members "either abandon the race entirely or promote it on such lines as are unmistakably opposed to any form of cruelty." He enclosed a copy of the laws of Illinois "governing matters of this kind" and issued a final warning: "The Humane Society is making no idle threats but has power under the law to greatly interfere with your plans."

For Salsbury and Buffalo Bill, it was a brilliant public relations move to distance themselves from the troubled Chadron committee; forty letters a day were arriving in Cody's Wild West mail bag demanding he halt the cowboys or at least stop egging them on. But they could not personally block the cowboys. And Cody insisted that his role was nothing more than offering the additional $500 in prize money and declaring the first cowboy across his finish line the winner.

Weir answered Salsbury in vague terms, saying the horses would be well cared for and that the race now would begin June 13. He also stated that the gold Colt pistol would be shipped to Chicago for Buffalo Bill to present to the winner.

Soon another letter arrived in Chadron, this one from Paul Fontaine, secretary of the Minneapolis Humane Society, and it leveled the gravest threat of all. "Those who undertake to make that race will be arrested, tried and punished," Fontaine warned in the letter, made public on May 20. "This is not a matter of sentiment void of sense. The law-abiding people of Iowa, Wisconsin, Illinois, Nebraska and Minnesota will make their power felt.... Again we repeat, the law against this proposed cow boy race must be enforced at all hazard."

More cowboys pulled out; fewer than twenty riders now remained. Many felt insulted by Eastern demagogues telling Western frontiersmen how to conduct their affairs

In a third letter to Weir, less than three weeks before the race, Shortall "respectfully" asked Weir to read the letter out loud to all "those contemplating the long distance race between Chadron and Chicago." He cited Illinois laws and fines and threatened arrest warrants for anyone "overloading, overdriving, overworking, cruelly beating, torturing, tormenting, humiliating, or cruelly killing any animal." He believed it was "not possible to make a contest of endurance and speed between horses for 50 miles," no less all the way to Chicago. He warned that state fines could run as high as $200. "Such violation of the law being from hour to hour, arrest after arrest of the same individual can, and will, be made," he wrote.

The home stretch for the race would be the worst on the horses, and in DeKalb, Illinois, the last big town before Chicago, the local *Chronicle* noted that "right here is where the hard riding will begin. The race from this point to the city will be hot, and the way will be lined with officers of the Humane Society." The newspaper dismissed it as a "gigantic horse race" to be unleashed "in hot weather and over all sorts of roads, for a paltry prize, and that these poor, dumb beasts are to be maimed and killed to gratify a beastly love of excitement."

Governor John Peter Altgeld of Illinois warned that any cowboys crossing the Mississippi River into his state could be arrested before their saddles were dry. In Iowa, Governor Horace Boies prepared to grant local sheriffs special authority to collar any riders merely suspected of mistreating their horses. He cited state statutes against animal cruelty.

Many newspapers both in the East and the West continued editorializing against the race. "Everything demands its suppression," opined the *Intelligencer* in Wheeling, West Virginia, "and nothing commends it to popular approval or favor." The *Omaha Daily Bee* commented that "the poor bronchos will be hard pressed under whip and spur, night and day, through the terrible ordeal, in weather that may prove to be the hottest of the year." The *Philadelphia Press* concurred: "A cruel contest ... a barbarous trial of endurance and speed."

In Boston, George Angell and his Massachusetts animal protection society offered their own reward of $100 and a gold medal "to the man or woman who shall do most to prevent this terrible race which if accomplished will be, in the view of all the humane people of the world both Christian and heathen, a national disgrace."

Others fired back at humane society officials and warned them to back off. An anonymous letter writer identifying himself as "the last of the Dalton's," a reference to the Dalton Gang in frontier Kansas, told the humane leaders to "shut that fly trap of yours or I will shut it for you, that you will never open it again. It is none of your business what we do." He called for bloodshed, and he signed the letter, "Your Will Be Slayer."

In Chadron, more of the cowboys packed up for home. A few stuck around, exercising their horses twenty to thirty miles a day. Doc Middleton was putting one of his horses through its paces up and down Second Street. Barns and livery stables were watering, combing, and bedding down the horses. The brand-new leather saddle from Montgomery Ward was en route, and that heavy gold Colt revolver gleamed in the downtown jewelry store window, primed to fire the opening shot.

June came at last, and with it rumors that Chadron might back down. The first of the month found Doc Middleton in a packed Fourth Street saloon; at over six feet tall, he was easy to spot above the heads of his drinking pals. His scraggly brown beard hung near to his holsters. He wanted everyone to know that he was going to race even if he had to ride alone.

"The reports to the effect that the Great Cowboy Race has been declared to be off are not true," Doc insisted. "The humane societies have caused us some uneasiness, but we want them to cooperate with us. They will find that there will be no cruelty to animals. We know better what a broncho can stand than they do and will use judgment in handling our horses."

Middleton said that because two horses would be allowed each rider, one could be led while the other was ridden, giving the horses a relative break. "I expect it will take us at least eight days to reach Sioux City" at the Iowa line, he said. "I have no idea what number will finish. Some of the horses will get too leg weary to finish."

Chadron's Sheriff James Dahlman backed the old outlaw. He announced that he would ignore the reward money and gold medals posted by the humane societies to stop the race, and he would make no arrests.

Still the opponents pressed on. Humane society officers formed a special committee in Dubuque, Iowa, announcing that they were "determined to see that the riders do not enter Chicago." They hoped at least to stop them in Dubuque. In the churches there, ministers preached frequently against animal cruelty. Handbills were passed around, and posters were tacked up on trees, barns, and telegraph poles all along the suspected race route, calling for the arrest and conviction of any cowboys stampeding their horses.

Shortall fired off another letter to Governor Boies, repeating that the race would be a "violation of the law in Iowa." Boies responded by directing county sheriffs to make arrests the moment any cowboys from Nebraska crossed the Missouri River on an overworked horse. "To justify an arrest in this state," the governor told the lawmen, "it will not be sufficient to prove simply that these men were engaged in a race. To this must be added the fact that while in your county they violated the statute by over-riding their animals."

Jack Hale, a prominent South Dakota stockman, came to Chadron and offered some of his horses for the race. Reports had cowboys Emmett Albright and Joe Gillespie working their ponies out in the rural sections of the county, near Crawford. Emma Hutchinson was also reported to be still on her way, though the papers said "nothing has been heard of her since leaving Denver."

The streets of Chadron hummed. A traveling circus stopped in town for a summer run, and a convention of medical surgeons was in full swing. The state firemen were arriving, too. Yet most eyes were trained on the cowboys, as some were galloping their ponies around the Blaine Hotel, just to show they were fearless.

John Maher introduced the cowboys to various out-of-town visitors. "A hundred Kodaks were sprung to take pictures of the group," reported the *Chadron Signal*. "And when it was announced that Doc Middleton's horse, which came from Dr. G. P. Waller's pasture, was the one that he rode from Crow Butte to Omaha pursued at every jump by howling Sioux Indians, several ladies insisted on hugging the horse while Doc looked on rather sheepishly."

The circus paraded down Second Street, and the ruckus emptied the saloons. James "Rattlesnake Pete" Stephens of Kansas, with a bellyful of "John Larkin's Poison-Weed Sagwa," rushed outside with other drunken cowboys. They leaped on their horses and chased after the circus, jabbing the elephants and circling the clowns, leaning down to pull their hair. Two policemen brandished batons, but the cowboys scampered away.

Back in Illinois, Shortall had not given up. He enlisted veterinarians to testify about the dangers of long-distance riding. He was collecting affidavits and taking depositions. In Iowa, rewards now offering up to $500 were printed in local newspapers for any evidence of "unjustifiable cruelty." The *Chicago Inter Ocean*, one of the most influential newspapers in Illinois, called upon Buffalo Bill to "exercise his influence to put a stop to the outrage," arguing that "he, more than any other man, can prevent the riders from leaving Chadron."

By then, though, Cody was all in. His publicity men were printing up newspaper advertisements heralding the cowboys racing to his Wild West arena next to the fair. His friend Henri Leon, widely known as long-haired "Broncho Harry," told humane society officials that the cowboys were going to ride "fully armed" with pistols and "would fight should anyone attempt to delay them." He also read an open letter to Shortall. "If there be any interference ...," he warned, "the perpetrators shall receive a full meal of genuine western feed—i.e. buckshot, small shot or anything at all, to hold our own." He said the cowboys would carry two guns and a knife apiece. "The men in the race are not in the habit of having people cross their paths without doing some shooting," he added.

Chicago preacher David Swing answered for Shortall on June 8, the race now less than a week away. "The average cowboy is heartless," Swing said. "They brand, spur, beat and ride without mercy. They expect to work their horses to death in three years; new ones are cheap."

For Chadron, the last-minute threats came too late; the town was all in, too. Dr. G. P. Waller would take the train and carry the $1,000 purse to Chicago. In a final town meeting, committee officials decided to hold the entries open until the day of the race. The start was now set for the coming Tuesday, June 13.

Bets were pasted around town, with Middleton in the thick of the action. Horses were groomed and rested, and they would be fed a "special" meal the morning of the race. The committee drew up a race slogan: "He who wears the spurs, must win them." Boasted the *Chadron Citizen*: "There are plenty of men in the West who have ridden to exceed 100 miles a day for two or three consecutive days.... Our eastern friends are giving too little credit to the cowboy and his steed, and if any of the Humane people wish to come out here, or if they are in Chicago when the race ends, they can see that they have judged the participants in the Great Cowboy Race by the wrong standard."

On June 11, two days before race time, Shortall tried once more to halt the proceedings. "Out on the Plains, horseflesh is cheap," he complained. "Not much attention is paid to the comfort or discomfort of animals." He had received hundreds of letters urging him to fight on. He had written governors, enlisted county sheriffs, and pleaded to the humanity of the fading Western cowboy. He had "begged" Chadron to change its mind. Now all he had left was to call upon "the strong arm of the law." He vowed one last time: "We can and shall have the riders arrested every hour or oftener." And as often as they make bail in county jails from Chadron to Chicago, Shortall cautioned, "they will be re-arrested."

But his words were like empty dust on the Nebraska Panhandle. Some three thousand spectators (some said five thousand) were streaming into Chadron, filling up the Blaine and the smaller hotels, renting back bedrooms in local homes, the straw and the haylofts in the horse barns, and any extra boot space along the foot rail in the town saloons. Farmers and ranchers and those still homesteading in sod houses hitched up wagon teams and drove into town. From the

Black Hills they came, and from over on the Wyoming flats and all along the Niobrara River Valley.

Banners were flying along Chadron's Second Street, its main road. The town band rehearsed outdoors, its cymbals and drums stirring up the warm summer air. Young boys reserved lampposts and tree branches for the best perches when the cowboys would thunder off beyond the low-slung skyline. On the evening of June 12, buggies and wagons were lining up along the eastern edges of town, poised to chase the cowboys and cheer them on to Chicago.

That evening, a pair of determined animal rights advocates, Paul Fontaine and the veterinarian W. W. Tatro, emissaries from the Minneapolis Humane Society, were aboard an overnight train to Chadron. The locomotive was chugging at fifty to sixty miles an hour across the darkened prairie and making a number of stops. According to the chalkboard at the Chadron depot, it was expected in by late morning. Barring any breakdowns, they were hoping to arrive with just a few hours left before the cowboys roared off. And if they made it, they were going to stop the race.

Race Day | 6

Everyone knew that the morning train was coming. And they knew that Minneapolis Humane Society officials would be aboard, determined to shut down the race. They knew arrests might be made and that more of the cowboys were opting out and starting back home. This knowledge prompted the race committee to scratch the planned early-morning start time on Tuesday, June 13, 1893, and instead launch the cowboys to Chicago at 5 p.m. That would give them time to hear the protesters out, and maybe reach a compromise and save what was left of the Great Cowboy Race.

It would also give them time to settle down some of the protesters at home. Many of the women of Chadron wanted the race stopped, too. The day before, they had papered the streets with posters and handbills announcing a June 12 evening meeting at the Congregational Church. The pews were soon filled with sixty people, and the gathering was also promoted by several ministers, a judge, and a professor.

The meeting was gaveled to order just before sundown, and they elected Mary E. Smith Hayward as chairwoman to speak on their behalf. An avid reader from Susquehanna County, Pennsylvania, she had moved West to see with her own eyes what she had learned from the pages of library books; her favorite was titled *Western Life*. She had hoped to reach the Pacific, but the railroad stretched only as far as Valentine, Nebraska. So she boarded the stagecoach and kept traveling, staying one night in a boarding room with five smelly dogs next to a rowdy saloon that she later learned belonged to Doc Middleton. She pushed on, finally making her home along Chadron Creek. She raised vegetables, filed a timber claim, married a future city mayor, and opened a popular women's clothing store at the corner of Second Street and Chadron Avenue. A horsewoman herself, she defended animal rights, planted trees on the courthouse square, and led the city's Woman's Suffrage Club.

That night in the Congregational Church, she silenced the anxious crowd. She urged compassion, reason, and true civic pride. After a "considerable discussion," she pushed through a three-point resolution opposing the cowboy race:

> RESOLVED: That we, citizens of Chadron, Neb., assembled in mass meeting this Monday evening, June 12, express our sentiment of opposition to the cruel treatment of animals under all circumstances, and our hearty appreciation of the widespread desire to prevent the infliction of cruelty upon the horses to be used in the cowboy race which starts from this city for Chicago tomorrow afternoon.
>
> RESOLVED: That we are in perfect accord with the officers of the Humane Society in the endeavor to prevent the infliction of any cruelty upon the horses, and will readily cooperate in punishing the offenders.
>
> RESOLVED: That owing to the base misrepresentations of our city and surrounding region by the eastern press, we emphatically protest against the characterization of those who live here as belonging to the brutal, lawless and desperado class.

Those jammed inside the church, many of them the wives of some of Chadron's city leaders, made it clear they were adamantly against cowboys beating their horses to win a thousand-mile thunder to Chicago. They strongly supported the Minneapolis Humane Society officials and were angry with the Eastern press for making Chadron a national laughingstock. The women returned home convinced they had taken a noble stand, and confident that the Chadron hucksters would come to their senses. Indeed, when dawn broke the next morning and the train neared the city, more of the cowboys began asking for refunds and saddling up their horses for home.

H. J. "Harry" Rutter was one who bailed out. He had ridden down in May from the N Bar N Ranch in eastern Montana and signed up for the race. Born in Indiana and raised in Texas, he had, over a fifty-year career extending well into the next century, supported his family in Montana's Milk River Valley as a cowpuncher, stockman, lawman, and civic leader. But cowboying was his strongest suit. He had started out at nineteen in Texas. At twenty-seven, he moved north to scout for fresh grass. At thirty-three, he served as a trail boss for a crew working 1,600 horses and 30,000 head of cattle, and in the wintertime he brought along twelve blankets for his bedding. E. C. "Teddy Blue" Abbott, a noted cowboy memoirist, recalled seeing Rutter and another cowboy water two thousand head of cattle at Skunk Springs, just the two of them. "It was the slickest piece of cow work I ever saw in my life," said Teddy Blue.

But Rutter was not all rugged cowboy and trail herder; he had his principles. For a while he bunked in Teddy Blue's cabin, where a pair of ruffled drawers once belonging to "Cowboy Annie" were hanging prominently on a forked stick in the wall. Rutter tore the drawers down and tossed them into the wood-burning stove. "Wasn't decent," he said.

Rutter recognized that cowboying was largely a young man's endeavor and that the sun was setting on the Old West. A couple of years after he skipped the Great Cowboy Race, he staked a claim on a Milk River homestead and pinned on an undersheriff's star. He chased horse and cattle thieves, wranglers, and outlaws and found time to pursue a bride, too. His target was Elsie Clough, the daughter of a construction engineer on the Great Northern Railway. One evening he rode over for a visit only to learn that Elsie had left for a dance forty miles away on the Montana–Canada border. Rutter climbed back on his horse. "That was the longest forty miles I've ever covered in the saddle," he later said. "But I got there before the dance was over."

He married Elsie in Glasgow, Montana. She was a schoolteacher and later superintendent of schools. He went on to serve as county commissioner, postmaster, church elder, and a bank director. He assumed all the trademarks of a city slicker—he trimmed his mustache, snapped on a natty bow tie, and sported a dark derby hat. By then the cowboy days were numbered and had been for some time. "The last of the big herds of buffalo had been killed off in this territory in 1881 and 1882," he later recalled. All that was left was range squatters picking through the buffalo bones.

With his daughters, granddaughters, and great-granddaughter, he shared stories about "Long Whiskers," the camp cook who had stirred a batter of pancakes and flopped them one at a time into a pan of sizzling bacon fat; about Dodge City, Kansas, and its junction of trail drives reeking with cow dung, choked with cattle dust, and roaring with six-guns; and about the mining camps around Deadwood, South Dakota, where gamblers and gunmen overran the streets and saloons.

In 1893, still a young man at thirty-four, Rutter realized that getting into trouble in Chadron with Humane Society representatives and a sheriff's posse in Iowa or Illinois while running a foolhardy horse race to Chicago was not going to do him any favors as a future lawman. "I was making plans for a home and I was anxious to be independent," he later remembered. He wanted someday to "concentrate with better peace of mind" on ridding the West of "the lawless class that was holding us from becoming civilized." Going to jail for a cowboy race would not get him there. So he pointed his horse north and cleared out of Chadron.

Heading toward Chadron, however, was Emma Hutchinson. Thirty-three years old, a cowhand, rancher, and Sunday school teacher, she had sent word a month earlier from her home in Denver that she would race to Chicago. No man or horse could beat her, she claimed, and she would aim to reach Chicago in twenty days or less. She vowed to ride home with that prize Colt revolver tucked safely in her saddle bags, if not cradled in her holster.

She had been born in a barn in Wisconsin, raised in the Montana mountains, and for a dozen years had worked the Western horse and cattle roundups. She was, newspaper accounts said, "the complete female vaquero." She "practically lived, ate and slept in the saddle." She had "endured all the privations and hardships of the frontier." Indeed, she had undertaken her share of long-distance rides already, including one 450-mile, seven-day slog with a single string of horses. The winds picked up, the rains fell, and many nights she "slept shelterless in a constant storm." But she rode on.

Hutchinson seemed the perfect cowgirl to outpace the cowboys. Down city streets she rode sidesaddle. Out on the prairie handling stock, she wore a divided skirt and handled a horse like a man. Indians reverently called her "Lightning Squaw." She was the only person her horse, Outlaw, ever allowed close enough to touch. They rarely parted.

She vowed to ride Outlaw into Chadron and show up all the big-headed, big-hatted cowboys. At eighty-two pounds, she weighed far less than any of her male challengers, even though some said Emma appeared "a little plump." "Do I expect to win the race?" she said to a journalist. "I most certainly do. . . . I am counting on seeing Colonel Cody in Chicago. . . . I will follow my usual plan. I will aim to eat only the simplest fare and, instead of any stimulants, will drink only milk. . . . The horse will be thoroughly rubbed down every night, and if I have a reason to fear that he will be 'salted' or in any way disabled by my contestants or anyone else I shall sleep in the stall with him. In riding I shall get out and on the road each morning as early as I can see and ride until 10 or 11 o'clock, when I will rest and refresh the horse for three or four hours, taking the road again and riding until dark. I do not like night riding, for it makes a horse nervous. . . . I expect to win by endurance."

So sure was Hutchinson that she sent a letter to Buffalo Bill Cody in Chicago. "Look out for me," she told him. Her words were no idle bluster. The newspapers reported that Emma was "one of the best offhand judges of horseflesh" on the range and "given a bunch of horses, [she] can usually pick the winner for a race."

She seemed a darling from the start, to many just the ticket to give the Great Cowboy Race an added boost and drum up even more money and interest in Chadron. She even had made her way into a poem by Cy Warman, a failed wheat broker turned Denver railroad man turned author and warbler and—eventually—"the Poet of the Rockies." Just a year earlier, Warman had proven his own stamina by riding from New York to Chicago in the cab of a steam locomotive called the *Exposition Flyer.* Warman knew a lot about long-distance feats of endurance, and after arriving in Chicago he submitted a story to *McClure's* magazine describing his railroad trip as "a thousand miles in a night." His lines about Hutchinson resemble a limerick:

Emma is her name,
Single is her station,
Her eyes are blue,
Her heart is true,
And she rides like thunderation.

Back on May 7, Hutchinson had formally notified Harvey Weir, secretary of the Chadron Citizens' Committee sponsoring the cowboy race, of her "purpose" in running the race. Weir quickly called another committee meeting. He told the group that she had secured a financial backer in Denver also willing to wager a few thousand extra dollars in side money that she could arrive first in Chicago. The committee agreed to let Emma race—in skirts or pants, whatever she fancied. So ten days later, Hutchinson wired from Denver that she would be leaving soon for Chadron with two horses, "riding by easy stages in order to acclimate the animals gradually." She said she would "exercise them daily," covering twenty-five to thirty miles a day "up to the time the start is made in the race."

She saddled up and trotted off, down the eastern slope of the Rockies and onto the thick spring grass of the High Plains. Riding with her was a growing public fascination with cowgirls and female equestrians who were challenging the notion of the West as an arena for male derring-do.

One of the most famous of American women, Elizabeth Custer, wife of the "martyr" of the Little Bighorn, had once "eclipsed all her nineteenth century sisters in horseback riding, for to her it was a necessity, not a luxury." Mrs. Custer believed women could "manage horses with more judgment than men," that a woman was lighter in the saddle and swayed gently with the bounce of the horse's trot, "in harmony."

Other American horsewomen also captured the popular imagination. Mrs. E. S. Beach, a New York riding instructor who had earned her spurs at the age of five, devoted ten hours a day to the stirrups. "My longest ride was the big tree district in California," she said. "I was in the saddle for several weeks steadily and rode over much rough country."

Elizabeth Jordan spent a month on horseback climbing up and over the Virginia and Tennessee hill countries. Her one regret was that the cliffs let in little sunlight. "The distance between towns was too great, and the darkness came over the paths too quickly," she said. Alice MacGowan rode through Tennessee and down to Texas, and once circled for days around the Blue Ridge Mountains of Tennessee and North Carolina. She carried a small bag of food and water and stopped at mountain cabins when her supplies ran low.

"Broncho Kate" Chapman was just seventeen in the year of the cowboy race but already had forged a name for herself as the "most fearless rider in the world." She had roped a particularly unruly wild mustang (considered the "worst horse" that ever lived), saddled it in a small corral, and climbed atop it. When she lifted the horse's blindfold, "the brute began a terrible battle in which the girl finally came out victor and rode the horse at will wherever she pleased." The daughter of a frontier cattleman, Kate had been riding since she was a toddler of three. Now a young woman, she was charming and fun, and, it was said, "there was not a man in the country but would walk if she would take his animal."

So Emma Hutchinson of Denver was in good company trotting out to the Nebraska Panhandle. But by June 5 she still had not arrived, and that caused deep concern. Some worried she might have taken ill or ended up lost. Or maybe had abandoned her long skirts and floppy straw hat for a sturdier suit of cowboy jacket and jeans.

Another week wore on, and by June 12, the day before the start of the race, she still had not tethered Outlaw to a hitch rail in Chadron. Race secretary Weir began making some discreet inquiries. Sheriff Dahlman was asked to hold the race until she galloped into town or was located or rescued on the Plains. But Dahlman turned down all suggestions of a delay or a postponement, and the committee agreed to hold her entry open until race day.

In those last hours she still did not show. In her place she sent a letter, explaining that her financial supporter had backed out. None too happy, she had been forced to turn her horse around and start home for Denver.

Harry Rutter had pulled out, Emma Hutchinson was a no-show, and when race day dawned in Chadron, other cowboys nervously elbowed around the railroad depot and along Second Street, struggling with their own last-minute jitters. Heads were counted, and only eight fidgeting cowboys still stood firm, insisting they would ride in the face of angry Humane Society protesters and armed sheriffs' posses.

Their horses—two each—were led over to Forbes's blacksmith shop and branded by Sheriff Dahlman with the hot-iron number 2 on the right side of the neck, a mark the racing committee would recognize along the route. That drew more of the curious out into the downtown streets, the stores closing, the crowds thickening.

Yet elsewhere in Nebraska and around the nation, the Great Cowboy Race continued to raise the tempers of both those who wanted it stopped and those anxious to hear that pistol shot sending the cowboys off to Chicago. "These human cranks who protest against the cruelty of the race do not know much about the broncho of the great West," wrote W. B. Lower in a letter to the nearby *O'Neill (NE) Frontier* newspaper. He complained that the "eastern people underestimate the humanity and morality of Westerners.... Eastern people are giving very little credit to the cowboy and his steed, and it will soon be manifested that they have been judging the cowboy of the Plains and the great west by a wrong standard." Let the cowboys ride, Lower proclaimed. Let the horses run. Should the outlaw Doc Middleton prevail, he and Buffalo Bill will be "the most popular things at the fair."

T. H. McPherson, a stockman from Dakota Junction, Nebraska, visited the Sioux City, Iowa, part of the race route and suggested that the sheriffs arrest the Humane Society officials instead and leave the cowboys untouched. "The kicking you notice comes from the East," he told a Sioux City newspaperman. "But the general opinion in the cattle country is that the Humane Society is interfering in what it knows nothing about. We know what a broncho will stand, while most of the eastern people who are objecting to the race never even saw one." McPherson said that the train heading into Chadron might as well turn around and start back east. The race committee managers were "not the kind of people to be scared out."

At the state capitol in Lincoln, another letter landed on Governor Crounse's desk on race day. This one hit with a thud, calling the race a "cruel and barbarous enterprise." It ran three pages, handwritten on stationery from the *Weekly Review* in Boston, a New England journal with a large circulation and a heavy hand in American politics, literature, science, and the arts. The writer was E. C. Walker, a free-love and free-thought firebrand from the East Coast, and he came straight to the point: "These cowboys and their abettors, including yourself, have a perfect right to run all the races to Chicago against time that may be wished," he told the governor. "But more have the right to compel horses to stand up if they can against the awful strain. No Vienna–Berlin savagery is needed in this country. Bull fights and gladiator shows would not be more cruel and demoralizing." Others, too, rallied around the Chadron women and the humane societies.

A writer identifying himself only as "the Rustler" dispatched an angry missive from Buffalo, Wyoming, demanding that the race be stopped, not for humane reasons and not to dodge arrests, but because the whole thing was rigged. His complaint ran in full in much of the Western press and was picked up back east, too. He belittled the race as nothing more than an "advertising scheme" for Chadron and local favorite Doc Middleton, and he said some of the cowboys who would run strong in the race were quietly being eased out to boost Doc's chances.

Army Captain E. L. Huggins, a Medal of Honor winner and Indian fighter on General Nelson A. Miles's staff, warned that too much whip and spur would forever tarnish the heroic reputation of the American frontiersman. He spoke from the perspective of a career horseman and commander of the Army's 2nd Cavalry. "The race will not reflect any great credit on the men who take part in it or the man who wins it," Huggins said. "It is really a question of endurance on the part of the ponies and not of the men. The weakest cowboy in the race can use up four or five ponies in riding from Chadron to Chicago, so that it is a test of the endurance of the animals."

Huggins admitted he did not know the riders and had not seen their horses, and he was unfamiliar with the route and the terrain. Nevertheless, he cautioned, "there is very little excuse for it." Each cowboy, he said, "must decide when to push his pony hard and when to rest him in order to preserve the animal's strength. But at best it will be hard on the animals."

In Chicago, the Reverend F. M. Bristol, pastor of Trinity Methodist Church, deplored cowboys' digging metal spurs into their horses' flanks as "a cruel thing ... simply unadulterated cruelty." He called on the American Humane Association to block the cowboys before they reached the Mississippi River and urged Illinois county sheriffs to arrest the cowboys and seize their horses. "They will receive a lesson which they need," Bristol said. "There is nothing to be gained by it, nothing to be learned from it." The law simply must be obeyed. "If they have not killed their horses before they get to Illinois, they should be put under arrest and the ponies taken from them. They should, every one, be prosecuted under the laws of this state."

John Shortall, who as president of both the Humane Society of Chicago and the American Humane Association had been arguing against the race from the start, mounted a final assault. And he laughed off the "implied threats" that the cowboys might shoot any humane workers who tried to interfere. "They will be quite able to take care of themselves," Shortall said of the animal protection agents.

He predicted that while the cowboys and their horses would likely thunder through Nebraska and probably squeak past Iowa, they would not be crossing the Mississippi. "I do not care to make public our plans just now," he demurred. He revealed only that eight of his agents had been dispatched to posts along the expected route, and mentioned also the two that would be stepping off the train at the Chadron train depot. The agents would, Shortall vowed, "deal properly and vigorously with this matter and enforce the law."

Asked a reporter, "Have you heard the 'bluff' about the cowboys being armed and ready to shoot?" "I heard of it," Shortall replied, "but I do not regard that as a 'bluff.' It was only the foolish talk of an irresponsible individual. But it makes no difference what the cowboys think or say they will do. They may carry all the guns they want to, but they will shoot nobody. Our men are courageous and active, and I have no doubt they will not be intimidated from doing their duty by the fact that a man guilty of cruelty to a dumb beast has a gun. This Humane Society takes 'bluffs' from nobody."

Meanwhile, Paul Fontaine and W. W. Tatro, the executives from the Minneapolis Humane Society, picked up their bags at the Chadron train station on the morning of the race. They had telegraphed ahead that they were being sent by a conglomerate of animal rights activists to hash out some kind of compromise or, as Shortall was vowing in Chicago, to shut down the race.

The duo was tired and hungry but determined to get to work. They met with some of the riders, shaking hands and sizing up one another. They toured the horse stalls, barns, and livery stables. Tatro, a veterinary doctor and breeder of fine horses, examined the animals' legs and backs and assessed their strength. Shortly before noon, Fontaine and Tatro pronounced the horses healthy and well-bred, "in good condition" at that time. Then everyone proceeded down Second Street to the Blaine Hotel. The time was 11 a.m., just six hours before the cowboys were scheduled to storm off for Chicago.

Fontaine and Tatro said they wanted to speak to all who were "interested" in the race. Inside the hotel they greeted committee members and town leaders, including Billy the Bear and John Maher. Fontaine said they had come to Chadron because "the race would be cruel" and "there was a strong feeling against it." He was very direct: he and Tatro were in Chadron to compromise or to close the race down.

So the Humane Society emissaries, the race committee members, the cowboys, various town leaders, and everyone else who had squeezed inside the hotel lobby now shoved into a larger meeting hall. Wooden chairs were lined up, the heavy windows raised to let in more air (and flies), and each side faced the other. Chadron Mayor Augustine A. Record presided. The room was stuffy and hot and heavy with doubt: Was there any wiggle room, any common ground?

Fontaine rose and faced the group, repeating what he had said while leaving the train station, greeting the cowboys, and inspecting their horses. "Our duty is an unpleasant one," he explained. He spoke for a half hour. "It seems like meddling, perhaps. But if the race started and there was any cruelty practiced, arrests would most certainly be made."

Tatro echoed Fontaine's concerns. Animal cruelty was illegal, he warned, and state laws must be enforced. No cowboy, no horse owner, no stock breeder, no town booster stood above the law.

Mayor Record invited the race managers and promoters to speak. First up was Jack Hale, the widely respected rancher and stockman from near Sturgis, South Dakota. He owned a horse named Poison that one of the cowboys planned to ride, and he spoke on his horse's behalf and for all the cowboys. He began by agreeing with Fontaine and Tatro that riders should be "arrested and punished" if they abused their horses. That, he said, would only be "right and proper."

But there was a difference here, Hale stressed. "If a man wanted to ride from here to Chicago, if he went about his business and used his horses right, he should be let alone. But if he abused his horses, it was time to arrest and punish him for it. If the man who an owner of a horse had employed to ride was guilty of such a thing, he ought to be arrested. And if the Humane Society put him in jail, I would not help him out."

The cowboys and race promoters squirmed in their seats. In the back and up against the walls, some turned away.

Cay: H.W TTENBACK   JACK HALL   TOM MIX   H R Forsyth
WEBER

Jack Hale (*center*), with cowboy film actor Tom Mix to his left. Hale was a rancher who brokered the compromise to establish Humane Society inspection stations along the race route. (Minnilusa Historical Association, Rapid City, South Dakota)

Hale spoke about those back east who for years had ridiculed the men who braved the frontier and tamed the West. To him, he said, the Eastern snobs were hypocrites. "I have seen Eastern gentlemen spur their horses on the race track until the blood ran to the ground. Why weren't they arrested?" he asked. "It looks to me the Humane people want to nab the cowboys and make some money out of it. If, as they imagine, the riders in this race are going through under whip and spur, then arrest them. But first wait and see whether they are guilty of such a thing."

Hale told the group that in the Black Hills region he had seen plenty of doctors, lawyers, and even ministers mistreat their horses. But "that class of men," he said to a roar of laughter, "were not looked upon as being worse than cowboys."

Sheriff Dahlman, a race committee member, took the floor. Let's instruct the riders to use good judgment; let's urge them to care for their horses, he said. Considerable expense and trouble had already been involved in getting many of the riders here, not to mention the several thousand country homesteaders and out-town-visitors bunching up outside the hotel entrance, eager to hear whether the race was on or not.

The race committee, the sheriff warned Fontaine and Tatro, "is not going to back down.... The race is going to start, and the money to pay the purse will be sent to Chicago. They will carry out their agreement, and the riders will be told that if they keep their horses in good shape they have a right to go through unmolested."

Dahlman spoke well, his words not threatening but forceful. He displayed the early signs of his subsequent long and distinguished political career: sheriff for three terms, mayor in Chadron, and, for many years more, the beloved mayor of the state's largest city, Omaha. He had known Buffalo Bill Cody back in the 1870s, a friendship Dahlman was always "proud to say still holds good." He would eventually round out his career as the U.S. Marshal for the state of Nebraska.

Like many of the older men meeting in the Blaine Hotel, Dahlman had started out as a young cattle herder and cowboy, working stock in western Nebraska and at the mouth of Antelope Creek on the Niobrara River, once a sacred crossroads of the old Sioux Nation. He had struggled through the snowstorms of Nebraska winters, some lasting three days or longer, and he had fired up cow dung and buffalo chips to warm his feet and hands. After a particularly harsh blizzard, he recalled, "we gathered up the saddle horses and made another start, and sent out scouting parties. We soon began to strike cattle perfectly contented in their new home amidst the splendid grass and water in the valleys, now the great hay meadows of the west."

James Dahlman loved Nebraska, he loved horses, and above all he admired courage and daring. So he was going to see this cowboy race through. He called the rewards of $500 or more offered to arrest the riders "nonsense." This was not going to be a breakneck kind of race. This was about pacing and timing. "These horses and these cowboys are hardened and in good condition," he said. "They can make a ride of sixteen or seventeen days at a moderate speed without hurting themselves."

Before sitting down, Sheriff Dahlman added a final word of defiance: "So far as the race being an injury to our city, we do not think it would have that effect."

Secretary Weir predicted that all the protests would blow over. He recalled complaints during the Indian Wars about how white settlers were decimating the native peoples, and how that hurt the country. "But Chadron is still here and doing business," Weir said, "and can conduct the cowboy race with credit to herself."

Hale rose again, this time to offer a compromise. Why not have Fontaine and Tatro follow the race by train along with Weir and other committee members, and set up inspection and checkpoint stations to examine the horses? Two other South Dakota ranchers liked the idea. So did much of the room. The five o'clock hour was looming, and the race would soon be on; almost everyone was growing anxious.

Tatro stood and bowed. "Our time is your time," he said, agreeing to the compromise. "We will gladly go to see that there is fair play."

A local newspaper editor agreed that it was "not right to pre-judge the race." See what happens first; see how the cowboys ride, how the bronchos hold up. "Then you'll have a better idea of the treatment of the horses," he said. A retired colonel complained that all the race talk had begun months ago as a lark with a short news-paper item, and for too long it "had been advertised a little too much." He said it was time to stop conflating and hyping the race with wild stories about Western outlaws and cowboys with fake names like "Rattlesnake Pete." In a jab at John Maher, he added, "We need to have the lying newspaper correspondents tell the truth."

Mayor Record said he would be just as happy to "shut off the correspondents who have a weakness for stretching the facts." He turned to Fontaine and Tatro and said, "I can't blame you for inter-fering" after all the tall tales Easterners had read about this fantastic cowboy race. "You've formed the wrong opinion," he told them.

Fontaine scanned the audience. He had been warned not to come to Chadron unarmed, he confessed, yet he felt secure with-out carrying any pistols: "They said I would not be safe among a lot of cowboys, so great was the fear of our Eastern friends. But instead of being insulted or threatened, you have treated us very kindly since coming here. You have almost converted me," Fontaine added, to the notion that the race could be run without abuse, without arrests, and without the slamming of jail cell doors.

Even Doc Middleton, the outlaw, horse thief, and rumored mur-derer, did not seem all that bad. "We found him a very nice fellow," Fontaine said. "And he found our people had heads and hearts and hands willing to do what was right. We had come here to establish a principle that dumb animals have a right to protection, and if the race must go, it should end without any cruelty."

But Fontaine had no kind words for John Maher. "This trouble could have all been avoided if your home correspondent had set the matter right," Fontaine said. "In justice to the riders, the town and the state, I shall endeavor so far as I can to set the matter right."

The speeches were done, the meeting was over, the room fell quiet. Filing out, the men shook hands and patted backs. Everyone knew where everyone else stood; everything seemed reasonable at last. The cowboys would race, Humane Society inspectors would follow by train, and the horses would be examined at a series of way stations along the course. Any cruelty, any harm, and a cowboy would be out. The local sheriff would decide where any abusive rider spent the rest of the race.

So ended the meeting in the Blaine Hotel, and so ended any last chance to stop the cowboys. In a few hours, the Colt revolver would be fired from the second-story hotel balcony. Secretary Weir plopped a floppy white Stetson over his head that nearly covered his ears. Tonight he would take the biggest prize in the race and board the first train headed east. He would follow the pace of the cowboys, too. And when he arrived in Chicago, Weir would hand the golden Colt revolver to the greatest showman on earth: Buffalo Bill, who would present it to the winner.

Post Time | 7

Late in the afternoon, a line of cowboys turned the corner onto Second Street and eased their horses in front of the Blaine Hotel. With all of the day's fits and starts, the starting time for the race had been moved to 6 p.m. So the cowboys, eight in all, settled in their saddles and steadied their horses. After six months of protests, angry defiance, and nagging indecision, post time at last had arrived for the Great Cowboy Race. In fifteen minutes, the competitors would rush off on a thousand-mile sprint across three states and two mighty American rivers, aiming for the Chicago World's Fair, its fabulous White City, and Buffalo Bill's front door.

Town dignitaries were assembling on the second-floor balcony over the hotel entryway. In a small spot of shade next to the train depot, Jester's Freak Band, a local cornet ensemble in fancy braided uniforms, stirred the crowds. Chadron's downtown merchants closed their shop doors but left their windows raised high. They craned their necks far out over the windowsills, their eyes and ears kept sharp. The more adventurous climbed up on rooftops, seeking the best seats and the better views. Trees made a good perch, too; so did gas lamp poles and hitching posts (for small boys who could stand still, stretch high, and keep from fidgeting).

The crush of people filled the cross streets and the wide wooden boardwalks and back alleys, in some places standing ten or more deep. On both sides of the road a half mile out of town, the anxious jousted their buggies, their buckboards, and their bicycles for the best spots. Others clambered up a small hill even farther east, hoping for a final glimpse of the cowboys when they roared off for Chicago.

Flags waved in the warm air, handkerchiefs too. Hats were doffed, cheers rose up, boys whistled, and girls shrieked. Fancy new Kodak cameras were swung into position. Some in the crowd scooped up late editions of the local newspapers, one proclaiming in a burst of civic pride: "Never before in the history of Chadron has there been an event in which the eyes of the world were directed toward our city."

All stood still, all hushed, all waited.

Then John Berry pulled up on a chestnut stallion named Poison, and he slipped into line with the cowboys. Never a man to talk much, he did not have to now. It was clear he meant to race. Many recognized him as the railroad man and surveyor who for years had swung through Nebraska, Wyoming, and the Rocky Mountains seeking new paths for railroad track lines, and they had heard that when the official race route was being planned for the Chicago fair, Berry had helped draw it. The official map was supposed to have been kept folded and hidden from the cowboys and not shared until moments before the trigger on that Colt revolver was squeezed on the hotel balcony. But Berry had known the secret route for a week or more now. If allowed to race, he would have a significant head start.

Worse yet, he was no cowboy.

Sitting there on Poison, Berry did not speak. Not until some started to grumble did he realize that he had better say something. So he leaned over his horse's mane and explained that he had not initially intended to enter the contest. But the cowboy who was supposed to ride Poison had unexpectedly fallen ill, and the horse's owner, Jack Hale (the same Jack Hale who had brokered the compromise with the Humane Society officials earlier in the day), had asked him to fill in at the last minute.

Few believed it.

Berry insisted it was true. He had expected a good bit of grousing if he tried to race along the same route that he had helped carve out and had committed to memory. He feared that someone in Chadron's crowded streets or during the race or especially near the finish line in Chicago might be furious enough to poison Poison.

Few cared to hear that either. The situation did not sit right, and once again the race was delayed. Committee members decided they had better huddle once more. Some suspected Berry was pulling a "cute trick" to sneak into the race with a wide advantage over the others. The committee members climbed down from the hotel balcony and reconvened inside the lobby.

Steely-eyed John Berry, whom many called the "Silent Man." A railroad surveyor and not a cowboy, he would race the thousand miles "under protest." (Courtesy of William McDowell)

In short order, they voted unanimously to bar Berry from the official competition. They could not keep him from riding, though. There was no legal way to stop a man on a horse from riding almost anywhere. The West might have been tamed, but much of it was still wide open, lawless in the sense that the law out in the open country was often a day and a night's ride away. Nevertheless, the committee declared that Berry would not qualify for any of the prize money or awards should he beat the eight cowboys to Buffalo Bill's Wild West show. Nine riders would race, but only one of them—and that one a true cowboy—could win.

Berry kept Poison in line. When he heard the committee's ruling, he did not budge or climb down. Even when some in the crowd started to jeer that he was trying to "poison" the race, Berry held steady and calm, prepared like the others to get started for Chicago. Nor would he mind that the *Chadron Citizen* newspaper disparaged him in its next edition, speculating that he wanted in the race not for personal glory but rather personal wealth. "It is said that big money, some $2,500, is offered for the winning horses," the paper alleged, "and John isn't going to Chicago for his health."

The committee paused to take a group portrait of their nine riders (see page 130). They had strapped saddlebags, bedrolls, blankets, chunks of bacon, and cans of beans on their horses and, for some, a pistol or two. Photographers from the local Foss and Eaton studio stepped up and arranged the shot. The bright flash from their big box cameras captured images that soon would brighten newspapers and magazines around the country. "A finer looking body of men and horses it would be hard to find," the *Omaha Daily Bee* gushed. "They stood grouped together for the benefit of an enterprising local photographer, decked out in the accouterments of the wild and woolly west and surrounded on every side by eager friends. They presented a most picturesque sight, one to be seen but once in a lifetime."

Berry now had the last word. He would race with the others, he said, "but under protest." If he won, the matter of the prize money, the new Montgomery Ward saddle, and the Colt revolver could be settled in Chicago. Buffalo Bill had been appointed to declare the winner and divide the spoils, not the crowd in Chadron and not the members of the race committee. They had long ago handed that responsibility over to Cody, who was waiting for the first of the nine horsemen to reach his doorstep, be he a cowboy or otherwise.

But John Berry was not a cowboy. He was a railroad man. Born in November 1854 in the seaport village of Lynn, Massachusetts, he had moved west and found work with the Fremont, Elkhorn, and Missouri Valley Railroad and other lines chugging through the Nebraska Panhandle and beyond. The tracks bypassed Fannie O'Linn's tar soddie and tiny settlement and plunked down a new depot that spawned the town of Chadron.

In helping plat the new city, Berry set up a large booth with a small roof for shade and started selling town lots. The bidding began on a Saturday, the first day of August 1885. He and others had designed Main Street to be the commercial center, but most of the merchants and businessmen chose Second Street instead. At first it had little more than a saloon and a brace of restaurants, and they kept the doors open all night. New settlers slept in tents or under the twinkling summer stars until the railroad built a headquarters, digging earth, hammering boards, and anchoring it near the depot. Bidding was brisk, and some of the choicest lots drew ten times their value. By nightfall on the first day, Berry had collected more than $52,000 in cash. No bank had yet opened in Chadron, so he kept the bundle, which he called a "piece of money," and slept over it for several nights.

Then he hopped a construction train east to Valentine, Nebraska, and found a bank for safekeeping.

Some recalled Berry as a "sphinx-like scout for the railroad." Back in 1882, he had helped lay the right-of-way for another Nebraska community that he proudly named Johnstown after himself. He named some of the new roads for his family and friends—Carpenter Street for Uncle Dan and Frame Street for Jake and Elias. Over the years, he scrambled up and down the line as a land agent, surveyor, and engineer. Earlier he had driven the mail by stage to Fort Niobrara during the hostilities with the Sioux. He punched farther west, too, past Denver, searching for new train routes up and over the Rockies. He knew the region so well he did not need a map to find the quickest trail in or out of the West. After he helped pick the route of the cowboy race, the *Omaha Daily Bee* declared, "Rest assured that it will be the best." Those who knew Berry's work called him "the Pathfinder."

He sported a small-brimmed hat and a walrus-thick, rust-red mustache. He seemed more town-like than any cowboy, according to the *Chicago Herald*, which described him halfway through the race: "Nor was he rigged out in buckskin, jingling spurs, broad hat and revolvers. He was a small, thin-waisted man with a bright eye, a red mustache, a home-sick hat and a gore in the back of his $3 trousers." Another paper observed that despite his small size, "he had all of the natural endowments for endurance."

He did not tolerate fools. When he was helping design a new saloon in Douglas, Wyoming, he grew weary of drunken cowboys taking target practice on his gas lamps. "There's no particular harm in shooting out the lights, boys," he told them. "But it strikes me you'd lose a heap of time between drinks. And no man gets a drink over this bar in the dark. He might get water by mistake, and then I'd be down to Laramie for homicide."

A niece, Doris Bowker Bennett, recalled in a memoir she titled *A Girl in Wyoming: 1905–1922* that Uncle John was twenty years older than his seventeen-year-old bride, Winifred Howell. They stood at the altar in 1890 in Newcastle, Wyoming, three years before the Great Cowboy Race. Winifred hailed from Halifax, Nova Scotia. She and her mother had moved to her father's log ranch house on Skull Creek on the eastern edge of Nebraska back when her father was digging for Wyoming gold. They rode out west to join him, first in a stagecoach, then in a mule-drawn wagon.

Bennett wrote that "during the Indian wars [Berry] carried mail by stage coach through Nebraska and South Dakota.... Later he became a pathfinder for the C.B.&Q. and laid out the routes for the rails" of the old Chicago, Burlington, and Quincy line.

John and Winifred's marriage license was the first issued in newly founded Weston County in the newly admitted state of Wyoming, and they were the first newlyweds to board the train at the new CB&Q station. "Mr. Berry is well known all over the West having been in the employ of the railroad for a number of years as a right-of-way man and inspector of the frontier country," noted the wedding announcement in the local *Republican* newspaper. "There is scarcely a ravine or hill in Wyoming or mountain that he has not visited and perhaps no man in the west is as well posted upon the actual resources of Wyoming as Mr. Berry." The announcement called the bride "a young and accomplished lady and among the fairest of the fair." It added, none too happily, "We don't know what our young men are about, to allow these railroad chaps to come out here and select and carry away the fairest of Wyoming's flowers."

Berry would have made an ideal catch in eastern Wyoming or almost anywhere else. "He was not a gambler, did not drink or smoke, and because of his quiet manner was known to friends as 'Silent John,'" his niece Bennett wrote. "He never was a heavy eater and paid little attention to food," all of which kept him small and lean in the saddle and a light burden for any horse, someone hard to beat on a thousand-mile run.

Others described him as "being about as close to the classic figure of the western good man opposed to the western bad man as was possible for a creature of flesh and blood. He was slight, soft spoken, modest, hard working, intelligent and kindly."

A nephew, David Howell in Wyoming, said his father had helped Berry in some of his railroad surveying. "They went all through the mountains in southern Wyoming trying to find different routes," he said. "And Aunt Winnie was a lovely lady, loved to laugh. A big, pretty, heavy-set gal. She giggled all over when she laughed." She and John reared two daughters, Beryl and Ruth.

Jack Hale had early on spotted talent in John Berry. The South Dakota cattleman and stock herder from near the Black Hills had also ranched under the shade of Devils Tower. He grew well acquainted with Berry's work for the railroad carrying families and jobs to the expanding West. When Hale had offered his compromise to the Minneapolis Humane Society officials, he knew he would have a horse in this race. And when he asked John Berry to step in for an ailing cowboy and race his horse Poison, he knew Berry would do it.

But Berry never spoke much about it. Even over the long march of years, when children begged to hear about the Great Cowboy Race, Berry had little to offer. He never told Winifred much, either. About all she ever got out of him was that somewhere in Iowa—or was it Illinois?—he happened upon a train platform and spotted a bucket of milk. Tired and thirsty, he dipped a ladle into the pail and drew out a big cup of milk.

An angry farmer complained. "Hey, fella, that milk cost me money." John was so sure he was going to win that he flipped the farmer a quarter. "Here," he said. "I'll have money to burn."

Some said he was racing to raise funds for a down payment on a new ranch in Wyoming, that he was short a thousand dollars or so. But he never spoke about that, either. He did offer one other story from the race, about when he finally came crashing into Chicago nearly dead and beaten and was put up in a hotel bed. He awoke hours later and his bleary eyes fixed on a sign someone had tacked over the doorway. "Silence!" it warned. "John Berry Sleeps Here!"

For a sad-faced, silent man, that made him smile.

Not so modest or soft-spoken was Doc Middleton. The former outlaw, horse thief, and rumored murderer had exercised his horse up and down the Chadron city streets for two days. Women snatched souvenir strands from his horse's tail. They might just have likely dreamed about a lock of Doc's beard; it fell nigh to his holsters. Or maybe they craved a more intimate look at his gold tooth.

When Doc pulled up on his lead horse, Geronimo, a mighty yell rose from the rooftops. With his piercing, dark gray eyes under a new wide-brimmed hat, he bent low to kiss his wife, Rene, and two of their young children. Then he turned, smiled, and waved his hat to his Chadron cheerleaders. The day seemed his.

Middleton was now forty-two years old. He once had run two criminal outfits, the Pony Boys and the Hoodoo Gang. He had been

A cowboy outlaw, horse thief, and leader of the Pony Boys and the Hoodoo Gang, Doc Middleton was the odds-on local favorite to beat them all to Chicago. (Nebraska State Historical Society)

in and out of jails and prisons throughout the West, and had been ambushed and captured by a posse hired by the Wyoming Stock Growers Association. It was said he had settled down some before moving to Chadron with his third wife and their family. She was only fifteen when they had eloped in Neligh, Nebraska; he was thirty-three.

He was sharp with cards but nothing to talk about as a cowhand. For ranchers, he was a horse thief who fenced his loot up north. For the Sioux, he was a menace who preyed on their herds. Wanted posters featuring his rugged good looks and offering from $100 to $1,000 wallpapered the Nebraska and Wyoming countryside. He most likely was born in Texas, though his death certificate said he first breathed air in Mississippi. From the South up to northern Wyoming, he was known by a string of aliases: Dick Milton, Texas Jack, Jack Lyons, Gold-Tooth Jack, and Gold-Tooth Charley. He sometimes said his name was David, sheepishly adding that he was merely a "dealer in stock."

Where the "Doc" came from, no tongue could tell. His birth name most likely was James Riley, but that had to change to fit the times. His confederates were lusty, dangerous, hard-bitten toughs, men such as Kid Wade, Lame Johnnie, Lengthy Johnson, Sixteen String Jack, and Curly Grimes. A name like James Riley just was not going to cut it out west. So he became Doc to fit his own special brand of prairie house calls. He ruled his gangs with an "iron nerve," and yet he claimed many of his ill-gotten proceeds went to helping the poor and the needy immigrants huddled in covered wagons crossing the Great Plains. Some went so far as to revere him as the "unwickedest outlaw" in the country. He considered himself a Robin Hood of the West, a Rob Roy of the Niobrara.

Once he came across a bored cowboy at a cattle ranch shooting at the feet of an old man, making the old man dance. The old man was tiring and begging to sit down. An angry Middleton turned his guns on the cowboy and made him dance.

Another time a greenhorn came riding past Doc in a hurry. Middleton slowed him down. "Where you bound?" he asked. "They say there's a damned old horse thief named Dick Milton who is scaring everybody," came the reply. "I sure wish I could get a look at him. He wouldn't scare me." Doc drew his pistol. "Young man, you're talking to Dick Milton." Then he took the greenhorn's guns and stole his horse.

On a Union Pacific train out of Denver, Doc elbowed into a twenty-five-cent-limit game of poker. Out the window, someone spotted a line of free-range cattle, and one of the gamblers, a Texan named J. S. Robb, swung around and took a long look. When he turned back to the game, Robb noticed he had drawn four kings.

"If the limit was off, I would bet $5 on this hand," Robb said. "If you did," said Middleton, "I would raise you $10."

They quarreled a bit and upped the wager to $15. Middleton then turned over four aces. Robb instantly realized he'd been had. He placed his six-shooter on the card table. "My friend," he told Middleton, "I guess I will have to trouble you to hand me back that money."

Doc had stolen his first horse at the age of fourteen. Word spread that he had shot and killed a soldier in a dance hall brawl, clubbed a man to death for threatening his grandmother, and fatally beat and whipped a cowhand during a squabble inside a Texas corral. At eighteen he murdered a schoolteacher for defiling his sister. In a Huntsville, Texas, prison for horse stealing, he broke out and fled the Lone Star State for good. Others said that when he was twenty he killed several men in Newton, Kansas, for murdering the town marshal, a man who had befriended the young Doc.

During a two-year spree in the late 1870s, Middleton and his Pony Boys and Hoodoo gangsters stole more than three thousand horses, mostly along the Niobrara River Valley. When it was forbidden to sell whiskey to the Indians, he shipped wagons full of chicken carcasses to the reservations, the chickens stuffed with half pints. When the railroads replaced the cattle drives, he stole from the cattle cars.

Stories circulated through Nebraska, Wyoming, and the territories that Doc and his gangs hid in dugouts along the Niobrara, well beyond the reach of the law. "A great many efforts have been made to capture Doc Middleton," the *Daily Leader* in Cheyenne, Wyoming, reported in April 1879. "But as yet he is still at large. He has had many escapes and adventures and is regarded as the luckiest outlaw who ever infested the western frontier."

Tall and handsome, elusive and ornery, for a while he led as many as a hundred bandits terrorizing the countryside. "He has no education but is a smooth talker, and was born to command," according to the *Cheyenne Daily Sun* in 1879. "He is loved by his men and yet they fear him.... He carries two trusty revolvers and is regarded a dead shot." Some called him the "Man with the Golden Tooth" after part of a tooth was chipped out and rebuilt with gold filling. Others mocked him as "the golden-toothed lover of other folks' cattle."

The railroad magnates and the stockmen at last did him in. He was run to ground in a canyon shootout that ended with two of his gangsters dead and a lawman seriously wounded. The authorities took Middleton into custody and sent him up for grand larceny and stealing horses. He pled guilty in a Cheyenne courtroom, and the judge gave him five years. They slapped handcuffs on his wrists and led him away in a horse-drawn bus to the railroad depot and from there to prison. Crowding into the bus with Middleton was a well-armed security detail—a deputy warden, a sheriff, a deputy sheriff, a police officer, and, carrying just his notepad and pencil, a Cheyenne newspaper reporter.

Doc did not much seem to care; little of it fazed him. Being escorted to prison seemed mostly an inconvenience. "It's pretty hard," he mused in the bus. "But I've made up my mind to take it philosophically. I expect that five years down there will seem as long as ten out here on the free prairie."

They were taking him to the fairly new Nebraska State Penitentiary in Lincoln because a fire had closed the Wyoming Territorial Prison near Laramie. What was left of those burned walls and charred cinder blocks did not seem likely to hold someone as mean and treacherous as Doc Middleton. Deputy Warden C. J. Nobels told him that many of the Wyoming prisoners liked the Lincoln facilities. Nice new quarters, they said; easy street. "Well," said Middleton, "I'm glad to hear it. I'm not used to being caged up that way. I don't think my punishment is just." To read the Nebraska papers, he complained, "you would think I'm the worst man in the world."

The reporter asked why his wife had not come to Cheyenne for one last kiss before he was hauled off to prison. The question stopped Middleton. For all his toughness and defiance, Doc let out a long, pitiful sigh. His voice trembled, and he began to cry. "Because she didn't intend to come," he barked back. "I did not expect her. There was no truth to the report that she was on her way to Cheyenne. That was another lie."

Middleton made parole in just under four years and returned to his hard-won turf on the Nebraska Panhandle. He seemed bent on going clean, on starting fresh, on living his life on the square. For a while he managed a saloon and dealt poker, dusting off his newfound city manners in Nebraska towns such as Valentine and Gordon and eventually Chadron.

By the time the Great Cowboy Race came along, he was trying hard to fit in. Even the *Chadron Democrat* was amazed to report that "Middleton was walking the streets of Chadron looking as bland as a Sunday School missionary." Others found him more like a "mild Methodist circuit rider." He sought signatures on a petition to get himself appointed Chadron's night police watchman. But some wag at a city council meeting blurted out, "Hell, you can get a petition to hang a man!" The appointment was voted down. But Middleton did manage a temporary job as a "special" night watchman, assisting the town constable "in times of need."

The new Doc Middleton craved acceptance in the emerging new West, even as his outlaw past shadowed him around town. At Billy the Bear's gala wedding in Chadron a year before the cowboy race, Doc presented the couple with an expensive silver spoon and vase. He signed the wedding registry, rather properly, as "D. C. Middleton."

With nine horsemen about to tear off for Chicago, all the smart Chadron money was riding on Doc Middleton to win. None of that, however, meant another hometown favorite was counted out.

Joe Gillespie sat on his horse, Billy Schafer, next to the others, the biggest cowboy, the strongest of them all, and the oldest at forty-three. Josiah Bankston Gillespie's brother was a well-respected Dawes County physician; his niece was Temperance, the beautiful bride of Billy the Bear. Gillespie had ties rooted deep in Nebraska soil and branching throughout the Chadron community. He was known affectionately as "Old Joe" for his gray sideburns and white handlebar mustache as well as his raw, rugged Western determination. In any challenge he undertook, Old Joe aimed to win.

He was born on an Iowa farm near the Mississippi River, two miles north of Farley (where he and the other riders would come tearing through in a week or so). In the 1870s, his father sold out and brought the family to the North Loup River Valley in eastern Nebraska. Young Joe, tall and big-shouldered, lean and handsome, took to breaking wild horses. He won some government contracts working as a teamster and surveyor and relaying the U.S. mail out of St. Paul. He opened a livery barn in Ord in central Nebraska.

But that kind of life was too quiet for Gillespie, and he soon turned up in the Chadron area and a Dawes County settlement called Coxville. He farmed and ranched near Crow Butte. He sold horses to the U.S. Cavalry at Fort Robinson and for some time drove a stage line through Sioux lands from the fort to the Pine Ridge Agency in the Dakotas. For a while he ran a sawmill. Family legend said he supplied relief horses after the disaster at the Little Bighorn. He was a Mason and a Methodist and an Odd Fellow, and his politics were rigid. He voted straight Republican until America entered the First World War. Then he tended toward the side of the Democrats.

Like many young men who answered the call to "go West," Gillespie was eternally restless. Yet he did one day manage to stand still for a formal indoor photograph. At twenty-one, he posed leaning against a studio prop, decked out in a heavy coat and broad tie, white shirt, dark vest, and starched trousers. He did not smile. His expression instead seemed one of angst, as if he could not

Another regional favorite, Joe Gillespie was the oldest to ride and also was hailed as the "cowboyest" of them all. (Gillespie family photo)

wait to tear off those city duds and rush back out onto the open range.

Gillespie was always taking new turns in life. At forty-eight, he enlisted as a private in the Second Nebraska Volunteer Infantry before the Spanish-American War. Even when he was much older and living in a small central Oklahoma town, he helped patrol the county as a deputy sheriff.

"Joe was always a horseman," though, recalled the *Cedar Rapids Journal* in Iowa when the native son came racing to Chicago in the summer of 1893. "And to find him in this race is just what one would expect. He has been in so many counties in Nebraska that there seems to be no place where he is not known."

Some called him "Indestructible Joe," a man "totally unafraid of anything," and he steadied the dapple gray Billy Schafer in line in front of the Blaine Hotel, waiting with the other cowboys for the roar of the Colt .44. He wore spurs with knotted rope ends tied around his boots, designed to tickle his horse's flanks and nudge them faster. For race day, he sported a gray laced shirt, brown trousers, high-top boots, and a flat sombrero to keep him cool under the mid-June sun. He also packed a pair of pistols.

"Gillespie talks in a glib manner on various topics and does no bragging," reported a Chicago paper, which caught up to him as he raced through Illinois. Although he weighed 185 pounds, "he is the lightest in his saddle of any of his competitors."

For sport he would gallop through scrub grass and hunt wild coyotes, challenging himself not just to shoot at his prey. That was too easy for Indestructible Joe. Instead he kept his guns holstered, whacking the coyotes with the heavy end of his riding quirt. Sometimes he would stand on their chests to stop their hearts if, as he said, "I think they have need of additional treatment."

His toughness was legendary. Billy the Bear recorded in his diary an encounter in 1887 when a Chadron town marshal bothered Gillespie about something. The marshal, Timothy Morrissey, born in New York to hardy Irish immigrants, was no softy, either; he had come to northwest Nebraska leading a team of oxen, and he had walked the last 135 miles from Valentine to Chadron. His was the first board shack to be put up in the new city. The day of the encounter with Gillespie, the county fair was under way, celebrating rural farmers, and a number of horse races were lined up in honor of what was left of the fading cowboy era. Then, around 5:30 p.m., wrote Billy, "quite a disgraceful affair was indulged in by the marshal of the day Timothy Morrissey who, forgetting the duties of a peace officer, engaged himself in a free fight with Joe Gillespie. But happily he got just what he deserved, for Joe drew blood on Ireland's pet in the twinkling of an eye."

Joe's wife, Anna, was a notably tough lady, too. She was small but not to be tangled with, their grandson Harold Comer said. "She wasn't afraid of the devil himself," Comer recalled, adding that one time "some gunfighter was going to kill a kid; he had him backed into a corner. I was told that she went up to him and took his gun and slapped his face." Anna Eliza Cook Gillespie was Canadian-born and educated in an Iowa seminary, and she taught youngsters in a small-town schoolhouse before marrying Joe in 1873 in Dubuque County. Soon afterward, they moved to Nebraska and produced seven children. They had gone there to join Joe's father, Andrew Gillespie. Also out west was Joe's older brother, Dr. Andrew Jackson Gillespie, a respected physician and school superintendent in Chadron and Dawes County.

Joe was among the first of the cowboys to toss in for the Great Cowboy Race, over the misgivings of his wife. "She said a man with a family should stay home instead of gallivantin' off on a thousand-mile race," he later told his granddaughter Ora Fay Gillespie Niegel. "Seems like when I heard of it, I couldn't keep from going. Everybody said my size was against me. Hundred and eighty-five pounds is a lot of tallow for a horse to carry so far."

Some in his family thought he initially registered to help guide another cowboy—possibly Doc Middleton—through the difficult Sand Hills, where the ground shifts and water holes pop up, tough to spot from the back of a flying horse. But Old Joe decided to ride those hills himself. He would cross the Mississippi and he would set his sights on Chicago. He aimed to show these younger boys what an older cowhand was made of. When Billy Schafer grew tired from days and nights tearing up the countryside, Gillespie would jump out of the saddle, grab the end of the horse's tail, and run behind him. The horse would have a lighter load, and Gillespie's boots would wear through. "He would get off and just hang on," insisted Harold Comer. "He'd just let him drag him sometimes." By the time the race was over, Old Joe had dropped thirty pounds.

He treated his horses well, and he earned their respect. He was especially fond of Billy Schafer and would not sell the horse for any price, even when he was offered $1,000 after the race. "Billy Schafer was talked about like he was family," Comer recalled. "I was six or seven before I realized Billy was a horse."

With the Great Cowboy Race about to launch on the evening of June 13, Gillespie said he did not care much for the prize money, the fame and notoriety, or even the leather-tanned Montgomery Ward saddle. It would be enough for him just to steal a peek at a big city such as Chicago, cast his eyes on the World's Columbian Exposition, and meet Buffalo Bill.

"Of course," admitted Old Joe, "that prize Colt .44 looks pretty good to me too."

Also eyeing that revolver was young, untested, red-headed James Stephens. The pistol was just the prize he craved to carry back to Kansas so that he could grow old in the saddle, spinning stories of how he had raced a thousand miles as a genuine American cowboy.

Single and not at all interested in settling down, he had ridden from central Kansas and hit Chadron a few days ago. He was twenty-five years old, short and thin, and at five feet four inches the smallest of the nine competitors. He was so green-looking that many in

James "Rattlesnake Pete" Stephens, a small man who rode tall in the saddle, hung this oil portrait of himself mounted on General Grant in his tiny barbershop in central Kansas. (Reno County Historical Society)

Chadron figured they had to cowboy him up a bit. He just did not look Western enough bouncing around town in a ten-gallon white hat, dusty flannel shirt, and fancy off-the-rack trousers from a South Halsted Street store in Chicago.

So they gave him a new nickname, "Rattlesnake Pete," and that helped make a cowboy out of Jim Stephens. It gave him a swagger around town, and soon he was firing up cigars and swilling drinks in the Second Street saloons. His horse, General Grant, had been a wild pony on the Plains, so that helped toughen up his image, too. Part of the trick was to feed the horse well. For that, Stephens kept some dried beef hidden in his saddlebag. For dessert, he told the horse.

He was born James Harold Stephens on April Fools' Day 1868 in Adel, Iowa, near the North Raccoon River. His older brother, Frank Stephens, was the first in the family to relocate to the Kansas prairie, near Ness City. Jim followed. He worked his father's horse ranch and broke horses for the U.S. Army; more than likely, they were remnants of Custer's doomed 7th Cavalry. He wore his long, thick mustache precisely trimmed and combed, and he was so small in the saddle that he often leaned back and hoisted his shoulders high. It made him appear larger and more like a cowboy.

Stephens saw the race as a perfect way to advertise his father's ranch. A little publicity could go a long way. "Times were tough and western horses were pretty cheap then," he recalled later. So he tied his bedroll on General Grant and rode out to Chadron. Stephens had tamed the mustang in a week; what was another week and a half's ride to western Nebraska?

New to Chadron, he bunked in a spare bedroom at Sheriff Dahlman's house. The sheriff's wife, Hattie, an Easterner educated at Wellesley College in Massachusetts, knew the Old West well; for a while she had lived on the Pine Ridge Indian Reservation, before the Ghost Dance. She took the rattles from six dozen dead snakes and sewed them into Stephens's hat band. "They hung it on me in Chadron before the race began," he said years later. "They started calling me Rattlesnake Pete. [The name] was given to me by Jim Dahlman. He handed me my hat back with a belt of 72 rattles from rattlesnakes and dubbed me Rattlesnake Pete, and that name's stayed with me ever since."

In front of the Blaine Hotel, all saddled up and ready to ride, Stephens had high praise for the eight others, and he never forgot them. "They were really tough men," he would say. "I was just a kid."

Being Rattlesnake Pete, however, was both hard to live up to and hard to live down. The moniker had been bandied about around the country and pasted on a good number of other characters seeking their own fortune and a fearsome reputation. Even Buffalo Bill had a Rattlesnake Pete. His real name was William Henry Liddiard, a federal marshal, grocer, and implement dealer in Springfield, Nebraska. He toured with Cody's Wild West show for a spell. Liddiard was notable for his handlebar mustache and was known in the Marshals Service as rather "quick on the draw." He was buried in Springfield's Ball Cemetery, but he apparently refused to lie still. For years his ghost was said to haunt the Nebraska graveyard, upholding the law in the spirit world.

More Petes showed up over the years. As late as 1935, an impostor rode in on a roan horse for the annual Days of '76 celebrations in Deadwood, South Dakota. He climbed down and strutted bowlegged along Main Street's crooked gulch, carrying on about hunting buffalo and shooting Indians. He claimed he personally had witnessed Wild Bill Hickok taking that bullet in the back of his head during a Deadwood game of stud poker in 1876. He tossed about a fair number of names, too, old pals such as "Poker Alice" Ivers and Jack McCall.

But he went too far when he claimed he was the Rattlesnake Pete who had raced to Chicago in 1893.

"I'm the cowboy who rode the horse from Chadron to Chicago in the World's Fair," he lied. "I rode in 14 days and three-quarters, registering my horse every 60 miles. It was a thousand miles and I got a thousand dollars for it. I was the only cowboy who got it." A journalist asked him whether he would do it again. "Just show me the color of your thousand dollars, pardner. Let me feed this pony and I'll be in Chicago a week come next Monday."

Four years later, another stranger, born August "Gus" Robson but passing himself off as yet another Rattlesnake Pete, barged into San Francisco with long hair, a thick beard, and a cowboy kerchief wound round his neck. He appeared "wild and woolly, spry and rarin' to go," despite his seventy-seven years. He said he had ridden with some of the best—Buffalo Bill, Calamity Jane, and Wild Bill. He said he also was Teddy Roosevelt's personal barber when the former president had hunted wild game in Africa. He claimed he still shaved with the same razor he had used to "whack off" Roosevelt's whiskers.

Even back in June 1893, many in the press confused James Stephens with another oddity named "Rattlesnake Pete" Gruber of Oil City, Pennsylvania. He often modeled in a suit of 125 rattlesnake skins and kept live snakes in his local barroom. "Naturally," noted one paper, "it had a depressing effect on business."

But Jim Stephens wore his nickname proudly. For years after the race to Chicago, he worked as a small-town barber in central Kansas and hung on his wall a large painting of himself as Rattlesnake Pete astride General Grant (page 122). He was pictured sitting upright under a big white hat, his shoulders arched back, pistols at the ready around his waist. Someone wrote on a bottom corner of the picture, describing Stephens when the race ended as looking "jaded and sleepy." But, the note added, "Pete himself is lively as a cricket and feeling first rate."

Like any good cowboy, Stephens could be cranky. When the barbers' union went on strike in Hutchinson, Kansas, most of them steered clear of Stephens's shop; he scared them off. "I gave them a cordial invitation to come in but they gave it up," he said. "I set 'em on their heads. I'm not afraid of them." He also ran a barber school in a room above a saloon. When the boys in the bar got too loud, Stephens fired off a pistol and marched the drunkards to jail. "He

had a six-gun," recalled his nephew Bill Stephens. "One of those big, old-fashioned long guns with a pearl handle." When Stephens once appeared at the jailhouse door with a group of rowdies in tow, the sheriff cited *him* for firing a loaded pistol inside the town.

Recalled Jack S. Gellerstedt, one of many Hutchinson youths who loved hearing Wild West stories from the old trail hand, "I once asked if he had ever shot anyone. After all, my knowledge about cowboys was gained from the silver screen at the afternoon matinees and, mainly, cowboys in the movies shot people. He said he once shot a man in the leg, but for whatever reason I do not remember. Perhaps there was some disagreement. I don't have the impression he intended to 'do him in,' but just slow him down some." Upon reflection, Gellerstedt added, "But I don't think he was ever in a gunfight. That's romantic Old West stuff."

Rattlesnake Pete married Florence Lawson two years after the race. In sixty years of marriage, she always referred to him as "Mr. Stephens" in public; at home, behind closed doors, he was "Jimmy." The couple never had children, and so it fell to his nephews, nieces, and other town children to listen to his cowboy stories. He shared with many of the young lessons in life's difficulties. "He warned us many times if we wanted to take a toke, it would rot our stomachs," recalled niece Joan Pivonka. "He'd put a nickel in a glass of beer and say, 'See what's going to happen to you?' . . . He was just a very small, very feisty person. Tons of energy even for his age. He was using up all kinds of energy."

The remaining cowboys are largely lost to history, overshadowed by the outsized personalities of the better-known riders and one sly railroad surveyor. But they had their moments.

Emmett Albright owned a ranch in a section outside Chadron, which locals called "the Table." Earlier he had worked horses in Texas and then shifted operations to northern Nebraska. When he first showed an interest in the race, back in February, he rode to town and was photographed for the papers booted up and spurred, with a broad Stetson hat and a six-shooter on his hip, poised to rope and ride. He sat upon a "fierce looking broncho," and he called his horse Outlaw. For a while he and Billy the Bear were equal partners in a

Joe Campbell from Colorado rode penniless, bet others he would not be last to Chicago, and wound up with a small spot in Buffalo Bill's Wild West show. (Dawes County Historical Museum)

money-lending and business concern. When in town, he often stayed the night at Billy's home.

Joe Campbell rode a horse named Boom-de-aye or Boomerang and had his picture taken, too, waving from atop the big gray gelding. He came from a crossroads called Watkins on the Colorado Plateau. He had ridden from Denver in eight days in mid-May and hung around town to make sure the race would be a go. He would need but one horse, he said; he decided not to bring along a spare. He also rode penniless, his pockets empty, but he bet some of the Chadron sharpies $250 that he would not be the last of the nine to reach Chicago.

"Little Davy" Douglas was still in his teens and arrived with two horses, Wide Awake and Monte Cristo.

George "Stub" Jones rode the bay gelding Romeo and brought along a second gelding, a black named George, after himself. His uncle, the stockman Ed Lemmon of South Dakota, the so-called Dean of the Range from the Northern Plains, had selected his two horses. "My nephew was a small man, weighing 135 pounds," Lemmon would remember. "He rode a light stock saddle. He was hardened into the saddle and knew how to ride, both to save himself and just as necessary to save his horse." Lemmon knew what his nephew would need to pull through on a long-distance, two-week sprint: "The horse and the rider are tested to the limit of their endurance."

Last to saddle up was Charley "C. W." Smith from Hot Springs, South Dakota, the son of a liveryman. When he worked, he pitched hay or hunted professionally, often dressing in fancy buckskins. Smith also did a turn at the U Cross cattle ranch on the Cheyenne River in South Dakota, and he almost missed the race altogether. While heading down to Chadron, one of his two horses, Dynamite, was stolen and ridden fifty miles in three hours, he said, before it was recovered. Yet the horse appeared "none the worse for the experience."

Known locally as a tough character, Smith was black-haired and dark-mustached, yet despite all the hard riding and racing to come, he wore a well-laundered, long-sleeved white shirt. He rode in a pair of leather boots so sturdy that they survive today, stiffened but still intact, at the Dawes County Historical Museum. Over time he became something of a name to fear. "I gather he was kind of a rough guy," said Meg van Asselt of McPherson, Kansas, the granddaughter of the man who donated Smith's boots to the museum. "Horse Thief Smith. That's what everybody called him. And every time my granddad would start telling stories about Smith, my grandma would hush him up. She'd say, 'Oh, don't tell the little girls that.'"

So Long, Nebraska | 8

At last, in the middle of downtown Chadron, the Blaine Hotel clock struck the hour. Six p.m. had arrived. All nine riders were side by side, everyone's nerves on edge. The town square fell silent; only the horses shied. Chicago and Buffalo Bill lay far, far ahead. For the sturdiest man waited a pot of money, a golden gun, and cowboy immortality.

Sheriff Dahlman rose and walked to the front of the Blaine balcony. Everyone's eyes turned up to him. "All ready," he announced. He read the race rules. "There must be no jockeying en route, and everything must be conducted on the dead square," he warned. In a bow to the Humane Society representatives, he added that "a rider cannot have his horse drop dead at the goal line and gain a prize. He must see to it that his horse is in fairly good condition on arrival."

Dahlman reminded all nine riders about the inspection stations, though Berry, the noncowboy, did not officially qualify for the race and would not need to report his progress. The sheriff cautioned them all against pushing their horses too hard during the long days in the saddle. That was the compromise with the Humane Society officials, he said, and that is what would keep the sheriffs in Iowa and Illinois off their trail.

James Hartzell, a town shopkeeper, chief of the volunteer fire department, and a member of the race committee, stood and asked the cowboys to "be kind and take good care of your horses. . . . I know you will conduct yourselves as gentlemen and will, I trust, uphold the good name of Chadron and Nebraska." Shouting now, he announced: "Gentlemen, the time for the cowboy race from Chadron to Chicago is upon us." He raised high the Colt revolver, and it gleamed gold against the cobalt sky. He fired.

June 13, 1893: Nine riders line up in front of the Blaine Hotel in Chadron, preparing to race a thousand miles for the glory of the fading Old West. (Dawes County Historical Museum)

The roar echoed over the crowd, bounced off the rooftops and trees, and hung in the summer wind. The cowboys lumbered off at a jog trot, kicking up sand and dirt amid a shout of hurrahs. A thousand miles of stamina lay ahead; what was the rush? Some of them pranced their horses at first, bowing and waving their hats to the end of the street, then riding past the last of the town lots and onto the Panhandle flats. With a salute to the edges of the crowd perched atop a small hilltop, they slipped under the eastern horizon and vanished in a slow swirl of dust.

Wily Doc Middleton held back briefly. He promised to overtake them all, though. He might be the last to charge out of Chadron, he said, but the last would be first to Chicago. No governors, no sheriffs, and no Humane Society agents would slow, stop, or rein him in, not this outlaw.

"Who's afraid of a few bullets?" asked Doc. Then he trotted off after the others.

In the flat scrub grass, all nine riders spread out, settling into their saddles with bedrolls and canteens jolting about, kerchiefs tied tight around their necks, spurs jangling, the route map snug inside their belts. Their aims were the big city, the prize money, and that gold-plated souvenir from the Colt Firearms Company, notoriously nicknamed the ".44 cowboy equalizer."

But while they could not know it then (and maybe some never realized it later), they were also racing for something far more meaningful. Not for individual glory, but for the immortality of the Old West itself, to help ensure that the West would be remembered as young and hopeful and forever vast, a wild and boundless outdoors where a man on a racing, hooves-pounding, heart-galloping broncho sym-bolized one of America's greatest virtues: endurance. This was the lasting legacy of the Great Cowboy Race of 1893. It was run and won in the dying light of the American frontier; it was a last desperate dash across the country before a new century and a new nation pushed the Old West aside.

More trouble, however, lay ahead, the kind that could land the cow-boys in a county jail somewhere between the high grasses of west-ern Nebraska and the tall towers of Chicago. At the state capitol in Lincoln, the stack of letters to Governor Lorenzo Crounse contin-ued to pile up, demanding that he call back the cowboys even after Chadron had defied the critics and launched the race.

The latest demand came from Miriam Baird Buck, an animal rights advocate and influential force in the emerging women's suf-frage movement. From her home office in tiny Bellwood, Nebraska, she had been busy organizing county committees to push for wom-en's rights and, in a separate effort, to reverse her state's image as a lawless, boisterous frontier lagging behind the coming modern times.

"Some of the humane ladies of Nebraska have asked me to peti-tion your Excellency, begging that you use your influence to discour-age the 'Cow Boy Race' which threatens to disgrace our state," she wrote to Governor Crounse. "I am very glad to do this in behalf of those to whom so much is denied—the poor horses that can nei-ther share the sport (?) nor the prizes.... The poor animals we have always with us, and those in a position to show mercy will I sincerely believe receive the thanks of all enlightened citizens, whatever a few ignorant, misguided boys or men may think. Even they are said to be appreciative of the principles of justice, but doubtless they have so long been familiar with cruelty to the lower order among those of this vocation that their sense of right in such directions is dulled."

She ended her missive to the governor: "Hoping to learn that this barbarous treatment of man's noble friend is not to be allowed."

Governor Crounse did not stop the cowboys.

In Des Moines, Iowa, Governor Horace Boies telegraphed county sheriffs and granted them legal authority to arrest any cowboy overworking his horse. Be on the lookout for anyone violating state law by overriding their animals, he warned. "With this thought in your minds you will be able to judge your duty."

And on the first day of the great race, the reform governor of Illinois, John Peter Altgeld, was preparing to pardon three surviving anarchists involved in the Haymarket Square dynamite bombing. He also had just condemned the lynching of Samuel J. Bush, a black man accused of assaulting a white woman. Twenty-five vigilantes had hung Bush naked, then dragged him around the courthouse square in Decatur, the first home in Illinois of Abraham Lincoln. Now Altgeld was confronted with the cowboy race, headed directly to his state. Wasting little time, he announced he was siding with the animal rights advocates. He warned that any rough-and-tumble cowboys had better not breach the Mississippi River into Illinois wielding an overlathered whip or a bloodied spur. Fond of horses himself, Altgeld did not want the kind of brutality and embarrassment seen in the European race a year ago.

In a signed and formal statewide directive from his executive office in Springfield, the governor described this type of long-distance racing as "barbarous cruelty" and a "shock to humanity." He declared it "in violation of the laws of this state for the prevention of cruelty to animals." "I hereby call," the governor said, "upon all officers as well as upon all good citizens to see to it that no violation of our law takes place and that anyone guilty of it shall be promptly brought to justice. We will welcome the so-called 'cowboys' into our state and bid them come in all their glory and have thoroughly an enjoyable time while with us. But we cannot permit the laws of Illinois to be trampled under foot simply as a matter of sport."

Upstate, along the white-light promenades of the Chicago World's Fair and at the front gates of the Wild West show, the Colt pistol shot in Chadron was reverberating as well. John Shortall, the American Humane Association president and head of its Illinois state branch, was relieved that only a small number of cowboys were racing. Still, "there must be cruelty in a long race of this character," he suggested. "I fancy there will be."

Shortall was eager to hear the results from the first inspection stations, hoping to learn that the whip was being spared. "They may practice all sorts of cruelty to win, but we will be ready for them," he said. He declined to discuss how he would monitor the race, except to note that he "planned to send men to any given point, and you can depend upon it that as soon as these cowboys are found ill-treating their horses they will be arrested and punished."

A sign that he meant business turned up that afternoon in the Mississippi River community of Dubuque, Iowa. Oscar Little, an Illinois Humane Society agent, was scurrying about town asking for the county sheriff's office. He found it, and inside was a deputy named Pfiffner. Little told Pfiffner about the Illinois governor's decree and "what the sheriff of Dubuque County should do should the cowboys come through here." Agent Little then rushed off for smaller Mississippi River port cities in eastern Iowa where the cowboys might come barreling through—Bellevue, Clinton, and Lyons, all possible points for the riders to cross the river and tear into Illinois.

Buffalo Bill was feeling more pressure as well. In his second career as an American stage and folk hero, Cody had to wonder whether he was on the wrong side of this one. He clearly did not want any adverse publicity to dampen the record crowds he was drawing to his arena. Nor did he wish to upset a campaign by Chicago religious leaders to close the fair on Sundays. He was all for that. The Sunday closure of the fair exhibits and machine operations would make Cody's Wild West the chief attraction open on the Lord's Day. It also would help make him a millionaire.

He had already attached his name and with it his reputation to the cowboy race; with nine horsemen churning toward his show grounds, it seemed too late to turn them back. He was planning advertisements for the race in many of the big Chicago newspapers. The spectacle of cowboys racing to his Wild West arena promised to be good for business, and that was always good for Buffalo Bill.

Yet as complaints spiked over the potential for animal abuse, the former Army scout, buffalo hunter, and Indian fighter tried having it both ways. With a crush of skeptical journalists surrounding him in his tent, Cody insisted that it never was his idea to race horses this far or that fast. He claimed he had never really encouraged it at all.

"I knew nothing about the race until a month ago," he protested. "And I understand it was got up over a year ago. My only interest in it is an offer of $500 to the man that brings his horses to the fair grounds in the best condition. The prize I offer is not to the winner, unless his horses are in the best condition."

He was saying he cared more about the horses and less about the cowboys, suggesting that he would present his personal $500 prize and the Colt revolver not to the cowboy first to scramble up to his tent ground, but to the cowboy on the healthiest horse. A dubious sentiment, coming as it did from a Western idol who had in his own days worn down many horses chasing buffalo thundering across the frontier.

Protests be damned! Cody thought. He believed in the eternal cowboy spirit and the awesome strength of Plains horses. "Eastern people don't understand what our western prairie horses are like, and this cowboy race will show them," he said. "The prizes in the race are secondary in the consideration for the cowboys. What they care most for is the honor of winning the Great Cowboy Race. Of course, the man who finishes first and wins $1,500 and the Colt which was fired as the signal to start from Chadron will be satisfied with the monetary part. But the fame and honor will be dearer to him than all the money considerations. To win this, I am sure no one of them will resort to cruelty or unfair tactics."

Cody mentioned that Paul Fontaine and W. W. Tatro, "those two humane officers who were at Chadron to see the start" of the race, had stopped first to visit him in Chicago. They had asked him for a letter of introduction to race secretary Harvey Weir to attest that the Humane Society officers were noble men and should be heard out. Cody claimed he had waved them off, saying he and Weir "did not have a personal acquaintance." But he also shrewdly did *not* tell the press that his aide Nate Salsbury had privately written to Weir that Cody and the Wild West show would pull their sponsorship of the race if the Chadron committee could not assure that none of the horses would be injured.

Cody was pleased, however, that Fontaine and Tatro had reached a compromise in Chadron that was "sufficient to show everyone" that by the time the race was run there would be "no cruelty." The great showman was squirming a bit in his chair by now, anxious but expansive, agitated but chatty. Still, Buffalo Bill knew how to play a crowd, including these niggling reporters pushing in around him, trying to weigh whether the country's foremost Western champion endorsed the days and nights of hard riding of horses.

"No," Cody argued, "neither the eastern people nor the Europeans know what is in that little rough pony, without which the great development of the western country would have been delayed many years." He leaned back in his camp chair. He seemed, according to the *Chicago Evening Post*, to be "in an abstracted mood for a minute, thinking, no doubt, of some big spring round-up or a hard sweep across the Bad Lands after a recalcitrant band of Redskins."

He straightened up. "Why, this little rat of a horse can stand more pounding rides up hill and down dale than most people imagine," he said. "What would kill a Thoroughbred just puts a keen edge on the pony's appetite. In this cowboy race from Chadron to Chicago the hardiness of the western horse can and will be amply proved."

There was no need, he said, to call the race "brutal or apply any harsh epithets." It was time to stop asking Humane Society officials to intervene or the governors to issue arrest warrants. Unlike what had happened last year in the European death slog, the American cowboys would not push their horses to exhaustion.

"A cowboy knows the value of livestock," Cody cautioned. Together a man and his horse could withstand any long ride through any thunderstorm. "His horse is his best friend, the one that stands the long night's vigil on the plains with him and many times faces the norther [wind]. And of the two, the horse gets decidedly the best of it." The average cowboy, said Cody, "loves his cow-pony a great deal better than many people love each other."

He dismissed Thoroughbreds as promptly as he had brought them up, saying they would crumple with day-and-night riding. The Western broncho could cover fifty or sixty miles a day, "and can be ridden into this city without turning a hair." He recalled the past conflicts with the Sioux and the Cheyenne, when "horses were ridden day and night continuously without even a chance to take the saddle or bridle off or to groom them a bit.... Many a time have I had to throw the reins over my horse's head and let him get a few nibbles of bunch grass while I took just 40 winks. Then up to the saddle again without even a chance to give him a rub."

Ever the showman, Cody had swung the conversation back to himself. Nearby hung his new ceremonial saddle commissioned by a silversmith in Omaha. It came with russet saddle skirting, tanned California leather, "Hon. W. F. Cody" in silver letters inlaid in the seat, and a horn mounted with a silver crescent and an engraving: "World's Fair, Chicago, 1893."

Cody hyped his Wild West show, too, of course. "I ought to know the animal pretty thoroughly in my many years' service on the Plains and in the Army," he said. "And look at our horses in the show. They are cared for in the best manner possible and are sleek and fat. I defy anyone to find any cruelty in our treatment!"

He rose, stepped into an outer tent, and shook hands with Senator Edward "Ed" O. Wolcott of Colorado. The hair-slicked, mustached Republican was paying a social call on Buffalo Bill with his wife and a party of Washington women. Cody offered Ed a pull on a small bottle. But the politician demurred. Wolcott had spied the reporters in the other room and announced he had better run. But not without first proclaiming to Cody, "You've got the greatest show on earth! I never saw the like!"

Ed dashed off, and Cody glowed. He turned and delivered a final thought about the cowboy race. It will be, he said, "an honest, manly struggle," and he predicted it would be run in less than two weeks. "The first man should put in an appearance about June 26," said Buffalo Bill.

And so the cowboys raced. They dodged sheriffs and arrest warrants and governors' warnings and statehouse proclamations. Their mission was to stay focused in the saddle and to win the race. Or at least make it to Chicago. Or if not that, to one day tell their grandsons driving gas-choking tin cans in some crowded big city that they had once sat atop a living, breathing mortal being in the greatest adventure of their long lives. That for two weeks of one short, glorious summer across Nebraska, Iowa, Illinois, and two mighty rivers, they had endured the challenge of a lifetime. And how they had become one with their ponies, pitching and slapping in a creaking leather saddle, man and horse chasing a combined dream. How on those horses they could see and feel and smell each mile flying past them—the haunches pounding, the muscles burning, the piston-fired syncopation of the horses' heavy hooves. And above all, they could taste the sweat from the horses' bit and bridle as it splashed back wet and hot into their own windswept, reddening faces.

Oh, yes, the race was on. They were riding to reassert the grandeur of the Old West, defying the fair promoters who had dismissed cowboys and horses as relics of a bygone American past. With each thud of their horses' hooves, the cowboys engraved their own names in the dirt, grass, and trails their immigrant fathers had trudged a generation earlier to reach the West.

The first stop was twenty miles out at Hays Springs, Nebraska. That first night, the bunch of them, with big cowboy Joe Gillespie in a slight lead, thundered into the town one county east of Chadron. They hooted and bucked their horses and drowned out a welcoming party. They fed, watered, and rubbed their horses and hurried on to Rushville, Nebraska, another small railroad town with lamp lights twinkling in the night.

Charley Smith reached the town first, before the sun came up. He tethered his horse in a barn and collapsed into bed. He rose soon thereafter, gulped down breakfast, and rushed out of Rushville. But while Smith slept, Doc Middleton and some of the others tore through town and kept on racing; they did not stop. A small knot of Middleton fans had stayed up most of the night ready to cheer the outlaw on. He blazed right past them.

By 10 a.m. on Wednesday, the second day of the race, some of the cowboys neared the small hamlet of Lavaca, Nebraska, nothing more than a store and a post office. They paused for water and a nap. Time, wind, heat, and distance already were catching up with the riders, and despite aching backs they settled deeper into the saddle. Middleton, Gillespie, and Albright shook the others for a while and were first to Gordon, Nebraska, fifty miles from Chadron. They saddled up again and rode off. Reporters said it appeared the trio was in "cahoots."

Horses were watered at a farmhouse six miles south of Gordon, and some of the cowboys followed a path south of the railroad and the Niobrara River. Some carried "wire nippers" to snip fences and slice shortcuts.

Lagging well behind, George Jones reached Gordon at what townspeople remembered as "a slow walk." He rested for two hours, though neither man nor horse appeared fatigued. He then remounted and started again on a swinging trot, following the reliable Fremont, Elkhorn and Missouri Valley Railroad tracks. While the other cowboys pushed hard ahead of him, Jones decided that in the days ahead he would ride under the sun and at night sleep beneath a hotel blanket or a canopy of stars. He saw the race as one long haul, a test all about pacing and reserving his horse's and his own strength.

Wednesday night, Jones rested at a small country station seventy-five miles by train from Chadron, eighty-five by wagon. He slept well and seemed in no hurry. He rose late the next morning, at about 11:30. He stretched and started out by noon. At the next town he rode in again at a jog trot, clocking himself at seven miles an hour. His horse was fresh and pulling on the bit but not sweating at all.

Jones did not realize that Middleton had pushed well past him. "His only fear is that Doc Middleton's hard-riding qualities may defeat him," wrote a *Chicago Daily Tribune* correspondent. "Middleton insists on hard riding night and day, and he's probably the only man in the outfit who can stand such hardship. Yet Jones thinks this will kill Middleton's horse, or at least render it worthless before the end of the race." On Thursday, June 15, Jones trotted into Valentine, Nebraska. He arrived late in the evening, his horse apparently still not in the least fatigued. He stabled his mount and lumbered off to bed.

Other cowboys had swung south of Valentine and kept riding through. The lead kept shifting. Some of the cowboys stopped to rest and water, while others walked their horses a spell.

At Ainsworth, Nebraska, a small railroad crossing, the first to ride in on Friday were Joe Gillespie and James "Rattlesnake Pete" Stephens. They hit town at a quarter to one in the afternoon and hurried to Mosely's livery stable. Neither said a word, and soon a crowd gathered. Jokes were tossed around about "Old Joe" and Stephens's rattlesnake hat. Berry rode into Ainsworth, too, and put his horse Poison up in Hogan's stable.

"Doc Middleton!" rose up a shout, and the crowd rushed to another livery stable. Middleton waved but wanted everyone kept back. "Quite a number expressed confidence in the skill and nerve of Middleton, while others banked on Gillespie's pluck and big horse," reported the *Ainsworth Star-Journal.* "Stephens had his admirers too."

More cowboys filled more of Ainsworth's horse stalls. "Emmett Albright's physical condition is giving his friends some uneasiness," noted the *Star-Journal.* "His horse, on being mounted, pitched at such a fearful rate that Albright is unable to retain any food in his stomach. He hopes to tone the buckskin down."

Who might win? "So much depends upon the staying quality of the horses," the paper concluded; "the judgment and health of the riders, as well as accidents which may be absolutely unavoidable."

The next stop was Long Pine, Nebraska, 190 miles east of Chadron, where the first of the cowboys pulled in Friday night. Humane Society officials Fontaine and Tatro and race committee secretary Weir were waiting, just off the early train. Here was the first registration station.

"Talk about circus day," wrote the *Omaha Daily Bee*'s man in Long Pine. It had been nearly impossible to learn anything about the riders out on the road, and a crowd had grown tired waiting. They were about to return home when suddenly a local wag mounted a wild broncho. He pulled a big white hat over his head and led another horse bucking down the center of Long Pine. "Everybody in town who could walk rushed out to see him," the paper reported. But no one was fooled; he was not one of the cowboys.

Middleton, Gillespie, and Stephens reached Long Pine first. They charged side by side into town through the Long Pine Chautauqua grounds. At the house of a man named Dwinnell, Gillespie registered first, Middleton third. "They were all in good spirits and their horses in such good shape that the Humane officers could find no fault," said the *Daily Bee.*

The women of Long Pine swooned around the riders and clustered about the horses, pulling strands of tail hairs as keepsakes. "If [the horses] have any hair left when they reach Chicago, it will be surprising," another reporter wrote.

As the cowboys dashed off, Fontaine pronounced the horses fine, Middleton's the healthiest. Fontaine's only worry was that the cowboys "need sleep." Race secretary Weir wired back to Chadron: "Gillespie, Stephens, Middleton in.... Horses satisfy humane men." He added, "Nothing has been heard from John Berry or Smith since they left Gordon."

Berry turned up in Long Pine later that night. He and several of the riders had torn through the Sand Hills, trying to avoid the small towns and big crowds that surrounded the hills. The Sand Hills were a more direct, if treacherous, route. Berry the railroad surveyor would know that.

Three days in the saddle had flown by, and the cowboys' determination continued to trigger objections around the country about animal cruelty. "A shame to American civilization," complained the *Toledo Blade* in Ohio. "An idiotic and cruel spectacle," argued the *Minneapolis Tribune*. The *Milwaukee Journal* suggested that the cowboys should trade their horses in for bicycles and "wheel" the rest of their way to Chicago. The *Lawrence (KS) Journal* dared the riders to rein in their horses: "If the men who ride are real cowboys they will bring their horse through without turning a hair, and there will be no cruelty of any kind." The *New York Tribune* wanted the race shut down altogether. Three days was too much; they had seen enough. "The cowboy racers appear to have made up their minds to run the gauntlet of the laws against cruelty to animals. We hope that their finish line will be just inside the doors of a strong and well-guarded jail."

Undeterred, the cowboys pushed on. Rattlesnake Pete Stephens made Newport, Nebraska, on Saturday, June 17, and he headed straight for Barber's barn. He treated General Grant to a mix of oatmeal water and feed. Stephens slept soundly, but just for an hour, under his white hat with a blue-ribbon band and the seventy-two rattlesnake tails. (The *Chicago Evening Post* called it "a hideous looking ornament.")

Middleton and Gillespie roared up behind him. They fed their horses oatmeal water and dined at the Lee Hotel. Desperate for a few hours of sleep, they fell into bed and did not awaken until midnight. Gillespie had come into Newport riding one horse and leading another. "His horses look well," noted the *Evening Post*. Middleton seemed "very tired, but his horses are all right." Many in Newport pushed in around him, recalling that the outlaw "knew every foot of ground in the county." The other riders were feared lost in the Sand Hills or "laid up for repairs."

The cowboys who were currently in the lead—Stephens, Gillespie, and Middleton—vanished out of Newport at first light on Sunday, June 18. Fontaine and Tatro waited at the second inspection station in O'Neill, Nebraska. When the cowboys arrived and their horses had been inspected, the Humane Society officials announced that the riders had "thus far won the approval of all concerned."

Stephens still held the lead; hot behind him charged Middleton and Gillespie. A local cornet band serenaded all three. Crowds smothered in close to see them ink their names into the race register book. The men stabled their horses and took supper at the Hotel Evans. Middleton recognized many of the faces in the crowd. He and his old outlaw gangs once had terrorized this pocket of northeast Nebraska. Yet many in O'Neill still were awed by the former bandit and horse thief. They hoped Doc would win; they considered him the obvious state favorite.

But Doc felt nervous; he was agitated and jumpy. He barked at the crowds to push back. He wanted to be left alone to think and concentrate on the race. The hours and speed and fortitude, the wind and saddle burrs were wearing on him. So he told them that in the days ahead he might start "slipping" through the larger towns under the cover of night, anything to get around the finicky crowds and the fussy women pinching his horse's tail.

O'Neill residents could see that Rattlesnake Pete was wearing down, too. He was coughing and pale, and they guided him to a doctor's office for a bottle of syrup and an extra prescription for refills for along the line. All three leading cowboys, Gillespie included, "were kept pretty busy taking special care of their horses, of which they seemed very proud," the local paper reported. Tired and torn, stiff-legged and bent, they sat down to dinner together, not letting any of the trio get out of sight.

Soon they were up and again in the saddle and clearing out of O'Neill, flying along the road east, battling the dust, sucking the wind, giving their horses the reins. Berry, the railroad man, missed them by just minutes. He roared into O'Neill next, but secretary Weir would not let him register, since he had been disqualified in Chadron. Some in O'Neill now jeered at Berry. They ridiculed him as the "Silent Man." When he left O'Neill, John Berry walked his horse Poison.

In the rear limped some of the others, straggling in after 6 p.m. Sunday and early into Monday morning. Douglas had taken sick and abandoned the race back at Atkinson, Nebraska. He was out. Mike Elmore, who owned Douglas's two horses, caught up with him. He

Doc Middleton poses with his horse. All the smart money in Nebraska rode with the reformed outlaw to Chicago. (Nebraska State Historical Society)

hired a buggy and purchased some extra harness gear, vowing that he would chase after the rest of the cowboys and by "hook or crook" beat them all to Chicago. But that was the last anyone saw of Mike Elmore and his buggy.

Other riders wandered into O'Neill nearly broken. Smith had sprained an ankle when his horse threw him, and Albright had lost time, he said, trying to maneuver around "a small lake in the road."

Deep in the O'Neill crowd, circuit judge and future congressman Moses P. Kinkaid pronounced himself "well pleased" so far. He said he was "confident" one or more of the riders would make Chicago in fairly decent shape atop a fairly healthy horse.

Late that Sunday night, with the three leading cowboys and their horses having cleared out of O'Neill, Fontaine and Tatro issued their first official Humane Society progress report. They asked the townspeople along the route to stop crowding the cowboys, pulling the horses' tails, and slowing them down. "We desire to have the public understand," they announced, "that so far as the race committee has made us a committee to judge of any over driving or cruelty and to lay off any horses what we may determine require it, the racers be allowed to go their way unmolested between register stations. All horses are examined at each register station by us. No over driving or cruelty will be allowed. The riders have thus far won the approval of all concerned and we trust no trouble will occur."

Few in the press in Nebraska and around the nation bought it, and many locals resented the Humane Society officials' interference. The writer of the "No Man's Column" for the *O'Neill Frontier* newspaper complained that Fontaine and Tatro had "made themselves the laughing stock of the West.... They have but little idea of this great West and underestimate the people who inhabit it. Instead of the boys being received with hisses and cries of shame, they have been greeted by brass bands and escorted through the different towns along their route in a manner that would have flattered a Roman conqueror."

The Nebraska columnist praised Middleton in particular, recalling an incident in a local barn where Doc was having one of his horses shod, and a blind man guided by a small boy wandered in begging for money. Middleton reached deep in his pockets and handed the man some cash "with generosity which is characteristic of all typical westerners." Tatro, however, "had not a cent" to share, even though his organization was well funded and said it cared deeply for animals. He offered nothing for a suffering fellow human being. The world, lamented the columnist, "must be a hoodoo."

In Iowa, the *Cedar Rapids Evening Gazette* also defended the cowboys and condemned the Eastern critics still railing against "cowboy cruelty" and warning that "each and every cowboy may land inside a jail." The *Gazette* listed other problems in the United States, saying there were far too many to "whimper over the woes of five or six ponies" on a horse race. Twenty-two people in Washington had been "killed through official neglect," the paper pointed out. "A dozen inmates of a 'sweat shop' were roasted in New York for lack of decent care of human life, and every daily paper from the East is filled with tales of want and crime and woe." To naysayers and critics, the paper advised, "Seek out a cave in some vast wilderness with bathroom attached and soak your heads. The West has no time for sickly sentiment."

Seventy more miles east lay Wausa, Nebraska, the third inspection station, with the registration book and the Humane Society agents waiting in the Saxton house. Again Middleton, Gillespie, and Stephens all arrived within five minutes of one another. Gillespie was first to hitch his horse to a side railing, but just by a neck ahead of the others.

A telegram projecting their arrival had been sent to Wausa overnight, and by 3:30 in the afternoon Monday everyone had lined up to welcome the three leading cowboys. A cheer escorted them in; this would be the last registration checkpoint in Nebraska.

Gillespie and Stephens scarfed down supper and rested briefly. Middleton stood guard in the stable, warning the townsfolk to stand back. All three riders scribbled their names in the registry book. They drank thirstily, watered their horses, shook off their clothes, kicked at their boots, and refilled their canteens. In no time they wobbled back to their horses, saddled up, and were gone.

Now barely speaking, the three of them rode tightly together, bunched up like ornery cattle. Gillespie, Stephens, and Middleton: the old man, the rattlesnake, and the outlaw, unable to shake one another. Each man eyed the others closely, their blouses soiled, their pants starched and hardened, their feet sore. Each man's face was burned summer brown, their lips chapped and cracked and, occasionally, bleeding. Still they strained over their Western bronchos, heads to the wind, unwilling to slow their horses.

Late in the evening of Monday, June 19, the seventh day of the race, they came upon a wooden boat landing on the Missouri River. They smelled the water before they saw it, and Gillespie, Stephens, and Middleton reared back, slowed their horses, and then staggered onto the ferry. Their heads sagged and their eyes burned. Their hips were badly bruised. More than ever they wanted to pull off their stiff, cracked leather boots. Instead they clutched the reins of their mounts and gripped the barge railing. They held on.

In the descending twilight, amid the lapping of a thick, brown, swirling current, the ragged cowboys floated toward the far shore.

Through the shimmering mist they could make out a line of lanterns flickering on the other side. The cowboys lifted their hats in salute. The crowd, about fifteen hundred strong, answered them back with a loud roar, a welcoming hurrah.

So long, sweet Nebraska. Howdy, Iowa.

In God's Land | 9

The cowboys came tumbling off the wood-and-iron *Vint Stillings* river ferry, a twelve-year-old flatboat, and the captain blared his whistle, urging the thick Sioux City, Iowa, crowds to move back from the landing gate. Doc Middleton unloaded first. He pulled off his heavy boots and knocked them dry. He hiked up his damp trousers and straightened the soiled kerchief round his neck. When he plopped his broad white sombrero back on his head, it sent up a swirl of trail dust. He petted his horse, the only one he had left.

The outlaw had abandoned his second horse, Romeo, on the other side of the muddy Missouri. Romeo had begun to limp, and with a strained hind leg gave out at a small place called Coleridge, one of the last spots in Nebraska. Now Middleton and the two other leading cowboys had crossed the river and planted their boots and horses' hooves deep in the river muck of what Iowans and others boasted was "God's Land."

"We came over from Coleridge today," Middleton announced, explaining how they had barreled through the falling dusk and the last of Nebraska to the water's edge and town limits of Sioux City. Everyone crowded in to see what had washed ashore, men in their farm overalls and town suits, women in aprons, some in house dresses, and gangly mobs of jumpy children. Some lifted their lanterns to shine light on the cowboys; others reached out to slap at the saddles and finger the creased leather. For hours they had been waiting along the embankment, and now here were the first three tattered cowboys trying to gather themselves up, soothe their horses, and find their way into town.

"As near as I can tell, we made about 64 miles," Middleton said, river foam lapping at his boots. "We came along at an easy jog, leaving at 5 o'clock this morning. I stopped several times on the road and fed four times during the day."

The cowboys were eager to shove on; their squinty red eyes scanned the crowd and strained past people's heads for the first road into the Sioux City business section. They longed for a barn to stable their horses, a hotel to sign the race registration book, and above all a cool bath and a warm bed. Night was upon them.

Middleton had looped his long brown beard under the handkerchief he tied around his neck. "I am a little tired," he confessed, asking the spectators to hold off on the handshaking and backslapping. "But not so much. I will get over it with a good night's sleep. My horse is in good condition and I believe I am a winner, even if I have but one horse left to finish with." He explained how his other horse had gone "lame" in Nebraska, and though Doc had pushed Romeo to Coleridge, a near eighty-mile stretch by itself, "I decided to leave it there and go on with one horse."

Gillespie pulled himself back up on his lead horse, Billy Schafer. His second horse brought up the rear. Both seemed relatively fit, and the old cowboy itched to keep riding. A reporter for the *Sioux City Journal* elbowed through the crowd and eyed Old Joe carefully. He found him "well along in years and quite gray, but he appeared fresh and chipper as could be." Gillespie's pair of horses seemed "in splendid condition," the reporter noted, "and appeared as full of life when brought from the boat as though they had just come from the stable."

Stephens was mounted on General Grant. With his second horse in tow, he jogged slowly over to Gillespie. He did not speak much. What he wore on his head, wet and soiled but still fixed tightly into the hat band, is what drew the eyes of the crowd. "He did not appear much fatigued," the *Journal*'s reporter wrote of Rattlesnake Pete, his crown of snake tails gleaming under the lantern lights. "He is the youngest of the three men and the lightest. He has both of his horses with him."

But all was not sitting well for Stephens, the novice cowboy from central Kansas. His second horse, he complained, was "not just exactly right." And Stephens was so exhausted that at times "I can't seem to see across the street." A *Chicago Daily Tribune* reporter was ready to count Pete out. "Stephens got up looking badly, evidently suffering from the heat," he wrote. "One of his horses is not in good shape from an attack of colic." He predicted that Stephens would have to abandon it soon. "And horsemen generally think that Stephens will be unable to reach the Mississippi with the other horse alone, as it is an inferior animal."

Humane Society inspectors Fontaine and Tatro headed up the Sioux City greeting party. They carefully examined the horses just off the river ferry ramp and eyed them again as the horses trotted onto the foot of Water Street. "They are in splendid condition and show every evidence of having received the best of care," Tatro announced. He was, he said, genuinely amazed. "I have no complaint to make. And the riders in the race have acted very fairly." But he predicted that Stephens would "lose a horse" before he reached the next big stop in Galva, Iowa, fifty-five miles ahead.

Nebraska was done, but Iowa stretched on, with its black, broken topsoil and emerald cornfields, the occasional barn or distant homestead, some days just a railroad junction or farther on a small town square. More than four hundred miles had been covered since the opening pistol shot had rattled the rooftops in Chadron.

Tonight, the race was nearly half run. At 8 p.m., Middleton abruptly mounted his remaining horse, Geronimo, and dashed past the crowd. He flew through the railroad yards and turned toward the Union Railroad Depot Hotel on Douglas Street, which had newly opened to accommodate railway passengers. Gillespie and Stephens hurried after Middleton. The Sioux City reception party mounted, too, or hopped aboard buggies or sped off on foot, chasing after the cowboys. Nearly trampled, several young boys scampered up a telegraph pole.

At the hotel, race secretary Weir opened the registration book and flipped to the pages for the three men to sign. The crowd nudged in as the cowboys bent over the big book and inked their names, noting the time and the date as precisely 8:12 p.m., Monday, June 19, 1893.

The cowboys then lumbered back outside and led their horses to a barn four blocks up at Seventh and Douglas streets, owned by veterinary surgeon Dr. J. J. Millar. The crowd scurried there, too, and jockeyed for a glimpse of the horse stalls filling up.

With their horses bedded down for the night, the cowboys stumbled a block back to Sixth and Douglas and the Hotel Oxford, a three-story turreted structure that had begun life as a roller-skating rink and later housed a Unitarian church. Now it stood out as the city's signature inn. The cowboys were wobbling on buckled knees and calloused feet. The crowd trailed after them.

The hotel lobby filled up quickly. Landlord Hunt, a local musician, entertained everyone for a while. Many of the locals spilled into the hotel bar, eager to shake hands with some of the cowboys and, with a bit of luck, win a word with Doc Middleton. But the cowboys were spent. They climbed slowly up the stairs, one heavy boot step at a time. Each of them collapsed into a bath but later slipped back downstairs for dinner.

Middleton took a moment to send a telegram to his fans in Chadron. "We arrived here at 8 p.m.," he dictated. He was, he confessed, "short one horse." But no mind, he advised his hometown. Doc Middleton was "still in the ring."

Shortly before 10 p.m., they trudged back upstairs, this time to bed. Middleton, Gillespie, and Stephens had now ridden for seven days and nights, from Chadron on the western Nebraska Panhandle to the Iowa state line. Their heads hit the pillows like rocks dropped into the rolling Missouri River, and the three of them sank into sleep.

Downstairs in the rowdy hotel saloon, Tatro held court. Surprisingly, he thought the horses looked better that evening than when he last had examined them in Nebraska. He was eager to see how they showed up at the registration stops ahead, in Galva and Fort Dodge, Iowa. Iowa would be flatter and make a more pleasant ride, many of the men drinking in the hotel bar predicted, a lot smoother than the Nebraska Sand Hills and the Niobrara River range. "They've passed the worst portion of the route," one fellow argued.

From out in the street, rumors swirled into the bar about some of the other cowboys. Davy Douglas had dropped out, it was said, though Weir claimed no official word of that yet. Joe Campbell was hopelessly lost somewhere in Nebraska; Weir could not confirm that either. Emmett Albright and Charley Smith were thought to be four hours away from Sioux City, still thundering across what was left of eastern Nebraska. Those drinking in the bar, enjoying what remained of this amazing night, doubted that they could stay awake long enough to greet any more cowboys.

The unknown was the railroad man, John Berry. While Middleton, Gillespie, and Stephens slept, Berry hit Covington, Nebraska. He napped outdoors, as the town was little more than a post office, and the post office was being closed down. He expected to reach the Missouri River around 8 a.m. Tuesday morning, cross over, and strike for the Illinois line. With good fortune, the wind at his back, and his horses strong, he might catch up with the three lead cowboys at Galva.

More dark whiskey was poured in the Hotel Oxford saloon, more glasses downed, and more eyes glazed over. The cowboys snored upstairs while the men in the bar below chewed over which was the healthiest horse and who the hardiest cowboy. Which horse would fail in Iowa? Which cowboy would win Chicago?

The Western broncho ponies seemed in rather good shape, still able to carry the heavy leather saddles. One horse's mane was elaborately groomed, and the bar patrons hooted over its pompadour hairstyle. Middleton's horse was a charmer. "He rides a powerful bay," enthused one man, "powerful from fetlock to ear tip." Yes, the man said, "that horse was keen and wide awake as if fresh from the stable."

Old Joe Gillespie had been a sight, too. His lead horse, Billy Schafer, looked handsome and strong. Gillespie had not even ridden his spare horse yet, it seemed, and he had told some of the crowd back on the riverbank that he hoped to ride Billy Schafer clear to Chicago. In four days' time, he expected to be sitting in the Wild West show stands, if not performing in the arena there. Of this Gillespie seemed certain: he would be first to shake Buffalo Bill's hand. "Can you beat that!" echoed one of the men, whistling across the barroom.

Stephens had looked particularly tired, his eyes splotched, his head hung low. His second horse still suffered from an apparent bowel disorder. That horse might not be much longer for this race, they all guessed.

As the men drank, a reporter headed back to Dr. Millar's livery stable for another look at the horses. The veterinary doctor stood guard, still training a sharp eye on the horses. "They're in unusually good condition," he said, marveling at how well all five so far had held up.

Weir was darting back and forth between the saloon and the stable. He said that if John Berry made it to Sioux City, he still would not let him register. But he would accept a formal affidavit on Berry's behalf if the railroad man rode up to the registration book and announced his presence. "So far the race has been very fair and very satisfactory," Weir told the saloon gathering. "The only difficulty experienced was with John Berry. He mapped the route to be followed, and his familiarity with it caused the other riders to protest against his being registered. The protest was sustained."

Otherwise, the Great Cowboy Race was holding up. "The weather has been splendid and the roads good," Weir said. "The first night out the riders were delayed some by a storm in the Sand Hills, but since that time no difficulties have been experienced. There has not been any cruelty toward the horses on the part of the riders yet, and I do not believe there will be. So far as Messrs. Fontaine and Tatro have expressed themselves to me, they are satisfied with the way the horses have been used and have no cause for complaint." The two Humane Society officials had "carefully examined the horses at each point," Weir said. "I am of the opinion that their presence at the registering points has been rather a benefit, for if there has been at any time a disposition on the part of the riders to abuse their horses, they have served as a check on it."

The chief concern now lay with the cowboys. Would they last the backstretch? "Who knows how long they're in the saddle each day?" Weir said. "You could estimate it by railroad miles but that would be incorrect. Best estimate is they are riding from 55 to 65 miles a day."

That night, Weir sent his own telegram back to Chadron. "The big three, Middleton, Stephens and Gillespie, crossed on the same boat at 8:05," he wired. "Middleton left one horse at Coleridge."

Tatro told the bar patrons that he and Fontaine largely agreed the horses were running fine. But he was not completely pleased. "I cannot say that everything is satisfactory to us so far, or that we are dissatisfied," he explained. "Since the race started I have given five warnings, and they have been complied with so far as I know. The last place I saw the horses was at O'Neill on Saturday. When the horses left Chadron they were improperly shod. At O'Neill, I required Doc Middleton to have his horse reshod and I superintended the work. I warned the men there against depriving their horses of sleep. Several of the horses went to sleep standing in the street while the riders were registering. The men promised to comply with my warnings and give the horses more rest."

He had a final word about Doc Middleton. He said the outlaw had bragged to a Lincoln, Nebraska, newspaper that the Humane Society officials favored him above the others to take first place. The top Chadron money was wagered on him, Middleton had said; now the Humane Society sided with him as well. Not true, said Tatro. In clear, flat words, Tatro stressed, "I wish to deny the statement and to say that we are not favoring anyone."

The whiskey at last ran low, the time swung late, and the men wandered off for home, tipsy and shaking their heavy heads, their shoulders sagging at the end of a long night in Sioux City.

George Thorndike Angell, founder and president of the Massachusetts Society for the Prevention of Cruelty to Animals, was not pleased at all. Twenty-seven years ago, he had become alarmed when two horses were ridden to death in a forty-mile race over rough country roads. Now he feared the same fatal course or worse for the cowboys and horses racing to Chicago and likely ruin. To the influential *Chicago Inter Ocean* newspaper he addressed a new letter of protest, urging the cowboys to tie up their bedrolls and call it quits. Sioux City at the Iowa border was far enough. They had covered a week now; it was time to head home, Angell said.

He was met with derision. "Any more words from him could cost him his life," threatened an unidentified member of the Chadron race committee. "Ranchmen are not in the habit of being checked in their plans. If he does not shut up, his head will be blown off his body."

The *Chicago Record* also expressed concern. In an editorial, the paper warned that while the horses might appear fine today, they could be dead before reaching the finish line. "Certainly none of the powers of these horses or riders has been taxed" so far, the paper observed. "They may not be for many stages yet. But isn't it more than possible that in the last stretch between the registering station in DeKalb County [Illinois] and this city, all the cruelty possible may be practiced upon overtaxed horses?"

Dawn the next morning poked the three leading cowboys out of bed and into their boots. With spurs jangling, they clunked down the stairs, out the door, and into the morning sun. Gillespie and Stephens whisked out of Sioux City first, although Stephens still did not look well, and one of his horses appeared to be still struggling with colic. He purchased some whiskey for his horse and stuffed it in his saddlebag in case the condition became unbearable, and up ahead a second doctor prescribed a bottle of medicine to slow the horse's lungs, which were in danger of hemorrhaging from all the jolting over hard roads.

Middleton had hoped to have his horse Romeo, the one he had left in Nebraska, shipped by rail to Sioux City. But a telegram arrived reporting that the horse was "too badly used up" and unfit to be moved. "Cord of horse's leg very badly swollen," the wire advised Doc. "Hardly able to get it out of barn. Would not advise shipping." His backup horse, Geronimo, the one that had carried him to Sioux City, was no gem either; it looked, Middleton confessed, "pretty well tired out."

So Doc needed time to think. If fate was kind and old Gillespie and young Stephens lost a horse, too, that might put him back on equal footing down the road. The flat patches of Iowa, unlike the loose sand of the northern Nebraska hills, might make one of their horses turn a hoof.

But Middleton realized he was losing both time and ground. Gillespie, old but strong, a working cowboy with both horses bearing up well, was emerging as the front-runner to Chicago. His horses were performing magnificently. "Why, if I had those horses I would choke the rest of them to death with a thousand yards of rope," Middleton told some of the locals in Sioux City, who were wondering why he had not left town yet.

Doc stayed put and kept on thinking, lingering around town, searching for some way to get ahead of Gillespie and Stephens. He recalled how back near the Boiling Springs Ranch, not far from Chadron, when the three of them were resting, he had tried to wake quietly and sneak out ahead of the others. "But they were too sharp for me," he recalled.

Middleton concluded that the only sure way to make Chicago with two horses would be if he shipped at least one of them east by rail. For a man who had spent much of his life on a horse on the open

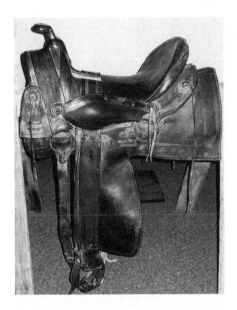

Doc Middleton's tough-as-leather saddle. (Minnilusa Historical Association, Rapid City, South Dakota)

range, the whole idea of coming in third or even last on one or more crippled horses or huddled inside a railroad train car seemed repugnant. "As long as I have one horse and he has four legs, I'm in," he insisted. He thought he might be able to "pick up the leaders" in the race closer to the other end of Iowa at the Mississippi River, but for now "we'll just set a while."

Berry, Albright, and Smith turned up in Sioux City a little after 10 a.m. on Tuesday. Albright seemed ridden out, his voice strained and hoarse. Smith was worried that one of his horses was playing out. Both men had their horses reshod, and it was an hour before they left Sioux City. Berry lost no time registering his late arrival; he was not allowed to sign his name in the official race book anyway. No legal affidavit awaited him, either. So he paused only long enough to water his horses and rest, and to hear Tatro predict that Stephens would lose one of his two horses on the road to Galva. Fine, Berry thought. That would just leave Gillespie as the cowboy to beat. Berry announced he was going to make Galva by nightfall, "with or ahead of Gillespie."

Middleton saw it the same way. "Old Gillespie stands the best show now to win, in my opinion, and I don't count Stephens in the race because he is petered out," he told reporters for the *Sioux City Journal*. Of the other cowboys, Doc said, "I think the race now is between Gillespie, Jones, and Albright. And one of Smith's horses can't go much farther."

Middleton saw Weir and the Humane Society officials off on the train to Galva. He stayed the next day, too. He finally left Sioux City, admitting by then it was unlikely he ever would reach the other end of Iowa and the Mississippi River. He would ride a bit longer, though, he thought, because a cowboy does not quit. Yet Doc knew that his race was effectively over. Once the odds-on favorite in all of northwest Nebraska, he now for all practical purposes was out of the running.

When Middleton stopped in Galva, the other cowboys were well ahead of him, yet still he kept up appearances. He asked William and Mary Harrison whether he could water his horse and sleep in their barn. They offered him a bed in their house, but Doc said no. He would just sleep with his horse. In the morning, he offered to pay the Harrisons, and now they said no. So the former outlaw tossed the couple's three-year-old son Bill an 1892 quarter and then galloped out of town, hurrying as if he still had a shot at winning the race. Ninety years later, the Harrisons' daughter, Laura Penrod, said of that quarter, "We've kept it all these years."

That left Gillespie and Stephens leading across central Iowa, the elusive Berry straining to catch up. And Iowa, Tatro told reporters, could well decide the winner. He reiterated that the horses needed to be reshod, rested, and fed more, and with Middleton all but bowing out, he predicted that only a half dozen or fewer of the cowboys would make it to Buffalo Bill and the World's Columbian Exposition. "I do not think that more than six horses will be in the race when Chicago is reached," he said. "Stephens, Jones and perhaps Gillespie will reach the city. The rest will have to stop."

He recalled the Humane Society's efforts to cancel the race before it began and warned that the next week's riding could bring out the worst. "We made a hard fight in Chadron to stop the race," he told Sioux City's citizens at the train station. "But it was a foregone conclusion. So we were appointed a committee to look after the cowboys, and if in my judgment I held that a horse was unfit to go further I was given the privilege of having him laid off. The cowboys agreed to the proposition, so that we will have to go through with them.

"It will," Tatro predicted, "take us nine or ten days yet to reach Chicago. Now we are in God's land."

Correctionville, Iowa, loomed ahead, thirty-three miles east of Sioux City. A small crowd gathered there after a telegram announced they should expect Gillespie and Stephens soon. The two cowboys charged in around 6:40 in the evening. "It was extremely hot and the horses looked jaded," reported the local paper. "Though all were in fair condition except Stephens' brown horse which had the appearance of being nearly exhausted."

Few let them leave without first saying a word about Doc Middleton. Where was the famous outlaw? Gillespie and Stephens had no idea. For all they knew, his last horse had given out past Sioux City. Their concern was for some rest, dinner, and a chance to cool their horses. At midnight they rose and rushed out for Galva.

As they rode off, most in Correctionville agreed that Rattlesnake Pete Stephens would never last and that Gillespie would win Chicago. Stephens was not holding up in the June heat, and his second horse still was dealing with colic and abdominal pain. Many thought the horse would never make Galva and certainly not the Mississippi River.

Berry pulled into Correctionville just after Gillespie and Stephens cleared out. "He came in on a good round trot," the paper reported, "his horses looking fresh and vigorous." He ate, slept, and then rose up at 3 a.m.; he too rushed off for Galva.

In Galva, the crowds had already waited hours and into the night for any dust cloud, hoof thumps, or other sign of cowboys. But blacksmiths grew sore from firing their anvils to signal what turned out to be false alarms, and everyone went home long-faced and sleepy. They left behind streamers, flags, and colored lights strung around town, now drooping in the still night air. Even secretary Weir went off to bed in Galva without any word of the cowboys approaching, though he left instructions to be awakened the moment they arrived. The few hotel rooms were filled, so country people who had come to town to greet the cowboys bedded down for the night in haystacks in the local livery stables.

Gillespie and Stephens thundered in at 6:45 a.m. on Wednesday morning, June 21, waking half the town but showing no mood, time, or patience for any welcoming reception. They registered in a hurry at the Commercial House, Gillespie aching from a splitting pain in his side, Stephens worried over his ailing horse. To everyone's surprise, Berry arrived just an hour behind them. His two horses, people said, looked "fresh and lively."

All three men took breakfast together, and they all cleared Galva by 10:30. Other cowboys trickled in much later, some staying for dinner. None rode out until later that evening.

Tatro remained in Galva only long enough to issue another official progress report; then he and Fontaine and Weir boarded the train for Fort Dodge, Iowa. "I am well pleased with the way the horses are standing the trip," Tatro announced. "They look fresh, if not better, than when they left Chadron."

His words made the papers as a new letter arrived at the Illinois Humane Society in Chicago from a Deadwood, South Dakota, rancher. He defended the strength of the Western broncho but urged the humane officials to stop the cowboys and end the race without another mile in the saddle. "There is no horse grown on the face of the globe hardier, truer, trustier or more until-death faithful than the broncho of the great ranges," wrote the "prominent citizen," who identified himself only as "J. H. B."

Unknown to the riders, more of the nation's newspapers were calling for the cowboys to be reined in and the American Humane Association to be discredited if the horses were not spared.

Grand Rapids (MI) Eagle: "If the Humane agents along the route do their duty, several of the 'cowboys' will rest behind prison bars long before they reach the World's Fair city."

Boston Journal: "The cowboy race from Chadron, Neb., to Chicago is certainly senseless and probably will be brutal. It demonstrates nothing but human idiocy and recklessness."

Milwaukee Evening Wisconsin: "If the cowboy race proceeds to a finish, the Humane societies of the states of Iowa and Illinois ought to hang their heads lower than the heads of the fagged ponies."

Kalamazoo (MI) Telegraph: "The affair is wholly disgraceful."

Gillespie, Stephens, and Berry wore on, oblivious to the rest of the world, their eyes straining, shoulders bent, knees gripping. They aimed for Fort Dodge until heavy rains slopped the gravel into mud and the prairie into puddle. They had been expected in by 7 p.m., but the storm forced them to find shelter around Pomeroy, Iowa, twenty-five miles short of Fort Dodge.

"A cold wind was blowing," Gillespie years later told his granddaughter. "I was so cold I could hardly sleep all night, so I got out as soon as I could see and started on. I wrapped my blanket around me Indian style because I hadn't brought a coat in order to save weight. Pretty soon it started to rain, and that was the coldest rain I ever saw in June. It rained pitchforks and bull yearlings until the ground was knee-deep in mud; sticky, gooey mud that almost pulled the horses' shoes off. Somewhere in that sea of mud John Berry got ahead of me again."

For those waiting in Fort Dodge, several false sightings had claimed that the first of the cowboys was drawing near. Many in town were disappointed to learn Doc Middleton would not be riding with them. It was not until Thursday morning that a trample of hooves sounded and blacksmiths banged on their anvils.

Stephens arrived first, nearly unrecognizable except for the rattlesnake tails sewn deep into his hat. He pulled in around 8 a.m. with only one horse; he had abandoned his backup, failing with colic and belly trouble, in a farm pasture. Stephens had the lead now, and he headed straight for secretary Weir. He signed the registration book at the Haire Brothers clothing store downtown. He walked General Grant to a box stall at Colby's barn and hurried off for a bed, breakfast, and a cup of coffee. He tried to appear jaunty and spry, but his knees locked and his legs buckled as he stumbled down the center of Fort Dodge. "I feel lively, I feel first-class," he tried to say, holding his chin high.

Twenty-five minutes later, Berry rode into Fort Dodge. He did not bother even trying to register and instead promptly delivered his two horses, including his lead horse, Poison, to Newberry's barn for a feeding and rubbing and a few hours' rest. Everyone by now knew his background with the railroad and his laying out of the race route. "But I've never gone over it before," he insisted, snapping at those who suspected he had memorized the route.

Gillespie clocked in around noon. He stalled his horses at Colby's and tossed down a meal. He staggered off in search of a hotel room and a nap. His horses looked "tired and on the lag," reported the *Fort Dodge Chronicle*. Old Joe was down to 179 pounds now. He had dropped twenty pounds since he had waved goodbye more than a week ago in Chadron. The *Chronicle* called him "a man well along in years. He is a typical cowboy."

People poured through the gates at the Colby and Newberry stables for much of the morning and over the noon hour. But many of the young boys came away shaking their heads. They had hoped to be dazzled by some tough-looking cowpokes with leather holsters and sizzling six-guns. Instead they had seen weary, droopy-eared horses and worn-out sidekicks. This was the West? "The men thus far seem to suffer more than the horses," agreed a special edition of the *Fort Dodge Post*.

The three leaders saddled and bridled their horses, kicked into the stirrups, and prepared to trot off. "The riders think that Fort Dodge is just about half way on their trip," the *Post* noted. "They are making about 60 miles a day."

Berry was first out, gone by 11 a.m. and coping with a badly sprained ankle often too sore to hold in the stirrup. Stephens and Gillespie headed out two hours later. Stephens was not faring so well either; he and General Grant "looked tired and sleepy," observed the *Daily Citizen* in Iowa City.

Yet Tatro pronounced the horses well enough to keep pushing on, not "over driven" or mistreated, especially not Berry's. "Fine fettle," he said of the railroad man's two horses. "There has not been any sign of cruel treatment of the horses," Tatro told a gaggle of newspaper reporters from around Iowa and Chicago. "In fact, quite the reverse is the case, and they are well cared for and are not being over ridden. A stop is made every night, giving both the horses and men a good night's rest, and stops are made during the day for from 3 to 5 hours."

Tatro said the men were starting to "walk their horses each day" and that "as yet, there's been no need for me to ride with them and inspect them." But he added that "this will be done if found to be necessary. It has been reported that when they reached DeKalb, Ill., the start of the home stretch to Chicago, they will be ridden for all that is in them." At that point, he said, "we will ride along with them."

Berry held the lead to Webster City, Iowa, twenty miles beyond Fort Dodge. He breezed through without a word. Gillespie and Stephens arrived two hours later. They cooled and fed their horses, ate supper, and hurried to catch up.

Now lead riders Berry, Stephens, and Gillespie were caught in a midday downpour outside Iowa Falls. So they rested again and waited it out; when the air dried and the dust calmed, they slogged on another fifty miles to Cedar Falls.

There, about ten miles still short of Waterloo, Gillespie and Stephens came upon a small traveling circus run by a Missouri entertainer named Colonel William Preston Hall. At the sudden sight of the cowboys, the circus fans spun their heads, and the quick-thinking ringmaster offered Gillespie and Stephens $10 each to romp around his ring. Could they thrill his fans with their "cowboy skills," maybe throw a lasso or two, maybe rope a calf?

Gillespie remembered it this way: "While I was waiting for my horses I wandered around town a bit to see what excitement I could dig up, and I found a circus, a little one-horse, one-ring affair. They had a mule that couldn't be rode, so I rode him. Nearly broke their hearts."

He and Stephens were nearly broken themselves, hungry and tired and knowing that if they dallied around the circus and put a few tricks on the crowd, Berry would take the lead. It was 6:40 in the evening on Friday, June 23. The sun was fading when they had limped into Cedar Falls. The last nine miles had been a slog of mud and heavy rain.

But the thrill of a circus and cheering fans sparked something in Old Joe Gillespie. He seized the chance to show off his Western bravado in the circus arena; it also would give his horses a needed rest. So he climbed atop that bucking trick mule and bounced around the circus lot, gripping the mule with one hand and waving his other, his hat flying, his spurs jingling, his battered backside bruising all over again. Stephens ripped off his rattlesnake hat and jumped into the ring, too, not to be out-cowboyed by the old Gillespie. After two performances, it was pushing 10 p.m. when finally they called it a night. Only then did Old Joe and the younger Rattlesnake Pete collapse at the circus gates.

Gazing down at the two worn-out figures, crumpled and exhausted, a local newspaper reporter wrote that "if the Humane Society were to extend their investigation to *human* cruelty, it would be much more viable than to animals."

Gillespie and Stephens managed to get back on their feet. Gillespie fed fresh grass to his two horses; they did not care much for hay. He stumbled off to bed at the Calumet Hotel. Stephens rubbed down General Grant and fed the horse ground oats, stirring in plenty of oatmeal. He spread his bedroll on a blanket of straw and curled up next to his horse in the livery stable.

He instantly fell asleep. And as the stars flashed across the eastern Iowa sky, Rattlesnake Pete dreamed that he and General Grant were prancing around not in a small-time traveling circus in a tiny Iowa town, but in the majestic Wild West arena in Chicago. He dreamed he was sipping champagne and cradling a "solid gold revolver" and that Buffalo Bill Cody was paying him $500 a night for the privilege of starring in his greatest season of all next to the Chicago World's Fair.

When he awoke, Stephens was startled to find a reporter bending over him in the stable, eyeing him closely, wondering how that particular smile came to Stephens's sunburned, weathered face. So Pete told the reporter about his dream. "I was enjoying all the good things in and about the White City," he said. "I had the honor of being the greatest cowboy in the world. With 42 rattles taken from my hat placed in a silk one, together with 100 additional rattles."

He sat up, dusted off strands of hay, and chased away a spider. He reached for his big hat. Morning had come, so Rattlesnake Pete saddled up General Grant and met Gillespie in the middle of town, and the cowboy duo cleared out of Cedar Falls. Next stop: Waterloo. The reporter was quite impressed. "I think that 'Pete' will win," he wrote.

They ripped past Manchester, Iowa, a little after noon and were stunned to learn that Berry had already flashed through. The night before, he had kept on riding while Gillespie slept in the Cedar Falls hotel and Stephens dreamed of Wild West glory. He stopped just long enough for a few cups of milk at a farmhouse window, lit up by a night lamp. He paused in Manchester to feed Poison and his second horse, rested for three hours, and then put Manchester behind him.

Berry was first to Waterloo as well, and he hardly stopped there, either. Stephens and Gillespie came in a half an hour behind him. Tatro and Fontaine awaited them, so Stephens and Gillespie had to stop to register and lose more time for the inspectors to examine their horses. Time was precious, more precious than miles now, and Gillespie already was thinking he should have bypassed the circus comedy in Cedar Falls.

In Chicago, Buffalo Bill was dealing with his own troubles. He knew he needed a winning cowboy on a fine, healthy horse to dash up to his arena gate amid the roar of cheers and hurrahs. He needed to reinforce the notions of cowboy resolve and Western broncho invincibility. And Cody did not want any of his fans jeering at a mistreated, abused horse or sneering if the race collapsed into a fool's endeavor. Nor did he want his record attendance numbers to fall during the summer season of 1893, his best Wild West ever.

So Cody dispatched his adjutant, Major John Burke, to Waterloo to make sure that at least one of the cowboys stuck to the saddle and lasted to Chicago. Burke's task was to shepherd the race through its final leg, from the last segments in Iowa to Cody's showroom door.

Burke wasted no time. Fresh off the train in Waterloo, he immediately agreed with Tatro and Fontaine that the horses were holding up well. The race must go on, Burke stressed, and at least one of the cowboys must make it to Chicago.

A Chicago journalist left the Waterloo railway depot, too, with a bicycle in tow. He said he was going to follow the cowboys on the final laps to Chicago, pedaling after them. He said he would help keep the race honest and record whatever he saw. That was not particularly good news, for Cody, especially if those last miles turned up some bad news, like a twisted hoof on a beaten horse or one of the cowboys cutting corners and cheating.

"Colonel Cody could put himself at a very much better enterprise than that of encouraging the cowboy race," warned the *Omaha World Herald*, speaking for many in the country who were increasingly outraged that the race had gone on for ten days with no end in sight. "The chances are the horses will simply be run beyond their strength." The paper contrasted the image of fading cowboys with the glorious future predicted in the impressive exhibits and new inventions at the World's Columbian Exposition. The cowboys, argued the *World Herald*, should have no place at the Chicago fair, no role in what the next American century would bring. "It may be characteristic of a portion of the West, but the people at the Fair do not want to see everything that is characteristic of this country. Only that which is best."

Surprisingly, Doc Middleton was now back in the race, too, albeit well behind. He had ridden out of Sioux City on his one good horse, pursuing one last chance at the cowboy prize. He was several days behind the leaders, and he knew that. Yet like the dwindling American frontier, Doc's long shot encapsulated withering Western stamina. Somber, slow, taking his time, he journeyed on. He had not yet given up on Chicago.

Far ahead of Doc, the race now seemed Berry's to win. If he were not eligible for the Colt and the Montgomery Ward saddle and the cash prize money, at least he could savor the honor of being first at the Chicago fair. So he, Poison, and his second horse wore on across the northeastern pocket of Iowa, pointed toward that father of all American rivers, the mighty Mississippi. Past Jessup and then to Independence, Iowa, with that pesky Chicago reporter frantically pedaling on his bicycle to keep up, Berry flashed like lightning across the countryside. He stopped briefly in Independence to reshoe both horses and briefly nap, and then he was up and off once more.

Berry was racing on his own now, well ahead of Gillespie and Stephens, letting them stop and eat and register and lose time with amateur circus stunts. His eyes were fixed squarely on Chicago, tears burning his cheeks, his arm muscles aching, his inner thighs rubbed raw. His sprained ankle kicked at his horse, and he urged Poison on.

Dubuque, Iowa, would be next. And after a high bluff, the Mississippi River.

By late Saturday on June 24, clusters of boys and old men started gathering on the corner of Eighth and Main streets in downtown Dubuque, the last stop for the cowboy race in Iowa. News bulletins were tacked up on tree trunks and lamp poles proclaiming the arrival any minute of the cowboys. Members of a club for teenagers called Young America stretched along city streets, craning for any glimpse of trail dust or the thud of pounding hooves. "Cowboys on the Brain!" screamed the headline in that day's *Dubuque Herald*.

Cody's man Major Burke waited in Dubuque, too. He had taken the train from Waterloo and hastily checked into the Julien Hotel, a stately brick-front inn built in 1839, seven years before Iowa even became a state and just a leisurely seven-minute stroll to the precipitous river bluffs.

He tried to swat down ugly gossip that he was spying for Buffalo Bill. No, Burke said, adamant and angry, Cody had not put the fix in. "Neither Cody nor myself are interested in the race," he protested, as far as money and Wild West show gate receipts went. "Only as Western men and rugged riders."

Burke had brought with him a personally selected veterinary surgeon, and the two said they would independently examine the horses when Gillespie and Stephens made it to Dubuque. They had every intention of keeping the horses healthy for Chicago. From what he and the surgeon had learned already, Burke said, "the horses are in tiptop shape and will go through alright."

Burke also scoffed at attempts in Iowa by animal rights activists to end the race before anyone crossed the river. The Iowa Humane Society had posted rewards of up to $800 for any proof of horse mistreatment or other evidence that could justify arrests. Reports were being mailed and wired to Des Moines, but now those efforts seemed too late. The clock was ticking down on Iowa. Only Illinois could stop the cowboys now.

And up and down the Illinois side of the Mississippi River, determined Illinois Humane Society agent Oscar Little was scoping out towns such as East Dubuque and Galena, two logical spots for the riders to breach the big river. At Galena he met with Sheriff Louis Homrich, a monument and marble dealer and twice-elected county lawman. He asked Homrich to stop the race if any cowboys or Berry tried to avoid the law. Stop them even if their horses looked healthy, he demanded. He had the paperwork in his pocket, Little told the sheriff: "I will furnish the warrants for the arrest of the cowboys."

Then he hurried to East Dubuque, fifteen miles upriver. He examined the so-called High Bridge, the long span linking the two Dubuques from Iowa to Illinois. If the cowboys rode through here, the bridge would be their sure route over the Mississippi.

Little was inspecting other Illinois riverbanks for other potential sites to cross the water by barge, ferry, or flatboat. He waved his stack of arrest warrants and passed them around to sheriffs, police chiefs, and other Illinois lawmen. Everywhere he went, he said he was furious that Fontaine and Tatro had let the race go on for so long, that they had allowed things to get so far out of hand. "They never should have sanctioned this race," he told the Illinois sheriffs.

But others warned Agent Little that it might not be prudent to interfere. He might be asking for real trouble. Too much money had been invested, people said. Too much time had been spent racing across the country's midsection. Too many miles had been ridden, and the new skyscrapers of Chicago beckoned too close to stop the cowboys now.

Then Little was handed an urgent telegram reporting that Berry, with Gillespie and Stephens closing in behind him, should come flying across the river and into Illinois tomorrow, Sunday, June 25, probably sometime in the morning.

The telegram advised Little not to put his life at risk. "Cowboys are noted for shooting," the wire cautioned. "It would be well not to stop them."

Across the River and into Illinois | 10

Church bells tolled in Dubuque that Sunday morning as a small man on a big horse came barreling in on the north Cascade Road. Atop a raw-boned stallion and leading a bay horse, he was first to reach the city hosting the final inspection station in Iowa. All that would test the rider now, all that he had yet to conquer, was that big rolling river, the Illinois prairie, and the glistening shores of Lake Michigan.

When his horse's hooves hit the pavement and the Sunday bells rang out, all of Dubuque fell still. Heads turned, and unwashed breakfast dishes were set aside. The churches emptied, and Sunday school sessions were canceled. City streets high on the river bluffs filled up, and everyone scrunched in to welcome the front-runner. The Great Cowboy Race had come to town.

Spanning the Mississippi River was the High Bridge, a creaky iron-and-wood structure strung together six years ago. It had seemed strong enough to handle most anything so far: heavy wagons and buckboards; horses, cattle, and oxen hauling rich river produce and timber, bricks, and Mississippi River limestone from Illinois and Wisconsin, all brought into downtown Dubuque to expand the bustling port city. The bridge rested atop seven concrete piers sunk into the banks and the riverbed. It stretched some 1,700 feet across the Mississippi, its shoulders bearing the surest and fastest route into Illinois.

Dubuque's citizens had not seen anything like the cowboy race before, at least not since the celebration in 1887 when the bridge was formally opened. On that day, five hundred floats had promenaded down the river, while high above a procession of residents and horse-drawn carriages filled with dignitaries tested the bridge's endurance. Bands played, a drum corps rolled, and banners streamed from the seven pylons and downtown lamp poles. A local military outfit called the Governor's Greys, including Yankee veterans from Civil War campaigns in the Midwest and Tennessee, performed in matching uniforms, firing volleys up and over the river heights. The bridge company handed out thousands of commemorative bronze medals.

German and Irish Catholic immigrants, many unskilled and unschooled, had landed here by midcentury for jobs in Dubuque's growing manufacturing center, its beer-brewing houses and boat-building plants. Their muscle built the High Bridge, and this Sunday their hands were joined in prayer when the first of the horses' hooves sounded and the church bells pealed.

Everyone rushed outside. The first of the cowboys was here. Even if he was not a cowboy.

John Berry came roaring into Dubuque at 9:30 that morning aiming for the High Bridge, and there was nothing Oscar Little or anyone else could do to stop him. Berry was small, thin, and red-mustached. On his head bounced a "home-sick hat," a Chicago reporter recalled. His $3 trousers were ripped in the back, and another Chicago reporter wrote that Berry disappointed nearly everyone because he did not appear anything like a dusty trail cowpuncher loping in off the range. "Not much like the typical cowboy of the eastern imagination did this rider look," complained the *Chicago Herald*. "Nor was he rigged out in buckskin, jingling spurs, broad hat and revolvers. But he is riding the race under protest, and he says he don't care a lasso's lunge whether he is ever called a cowboy if he wins the race. And he stands a good show to win."

Berry was the first rider whom Dubuque had set eyes on after days on the lookout for the first of the horsemen. Both their patience and their expectations were running thin, and John Berry, the railroad man, was going to have to do. "Dubuque has been afflicted for two days with a violent attack of insomnia waiting for these cowboys," lamented the *Herald*. Yes, Berry would do.

He had ridden twenty-three miles in the past four hours, up and saddled long before dawn after a six-hour rest at Farley, Iowa. Now he led his horses straight to a stable and swathed their legs in alcohol-soaked bandages. He headed over to the Julien Hotel, slipped on a dinner jacket, and sat down to a plate of broiled chicken.

John Berry atop his horse Poison. Together they challenged eight cowboys in racing from the Nebraska Panhandle to the Chicago World's Fair. (Courtesy of William McDowell)

Cody's man Major Burke heard all the commotion and burst out of bed in his Julien Hotel room. He hurried downstairs to the dining hall and started teasing the waitresses noodling around Berry, trying to get his attention. Berry soon left the restaurant without speaking to either the women or Major Burke. He took a room in the hotel and slept for ninety minutes.

Oscar Little rushed over to the livery stable and peered at Berry's two horses. He thought them rather healthy, tired but able, though Poison seemed "feverish."

By noon Berry was up and out of bed and back on Poison, and with his second horse in tow headed east toward the High Bridge and its gateway to Illinois. He did not wave and did not look back. He picked up speed and flew up the ramp and onto the bridge.

A large crowd chased after him, practically carrying him across the river and into Illinois. Men followed on horseback, in buggies, and on bicycles, others running on foot, women waving at the bridge railings, children jumping and screaming. The bridge creaked and groaned, but it stood the weight. Pedaling furiously after them came the persistent Chicago reporter on his bicycle, determined to follow the leader to the finish line.

Berry did not care much for the attention. In his last miles in Iowa, he had flown past farmers waiting at gate posts, ignoring them as he flashed by. He picked out shadows in farmhouse windows, figures peeking through curtains as he blazed past. This morning, nearing Dubuque, he had tipped his hat to a dairy farmer. The startled farmer spilled a pail of milk and then urged Berry on as he thundered past.

He may have been disqualified at the start of the race, but John Berry now held the lead—if not by much. For just as he hit the High Bridge, James Stephens came tearing into Dubuque. With his rattle-tail hat and dusty flannel shirt, he slowed up on his only horse, General Grant. In the middle of the street, he fed it oats and reached into a saddlebag for a horse treat of dried beef. He noticed the town was eerily deserted, and he guessed that everyone must have gone to church.

Soon, however, the bridge crowd, filing back into town, spotted Stephens. They chased after him as he led General Grant to the Noonan Brothers livery stable and then found Tatro and Fontaine at a local home near the High Bridge. He signed the registration book.

People trailed Stephens to the Julien Hotel, delighted as he swaggered into the dining room with full cowboy gusto, like a Western rascal out of a Buffalo Bill dime novel. He clomped around in his hard-heeled boots, and many giggled. He sat down to eat, and they applauded. Rattlesnake Pete glanced contemptuously at the restaurant menu. "Bring it all," he barked to the waitresses. "And get me some fried rattlesnakes soon's you kin."

Stephens pulled out of Dubuque around 2:30, two hours behind Berry, crossing the High Bridge and starting his last leg through Illinois. That was about the same time when Joe Gillespie burst through the doors of the Julien Hotel, with his broad shoulders and a week's growth of white whiskers.

"Where's the secretary? I want to register," he hollered. "Been hunting all over and can't find out where I've got to register. And I want a map too. I don't have a map on this road." Old Joe's spurs clanked as he rushed off to meet Tatro and Fontaine and sign the registration book. He stayed in Dubuque the longest, three and a half hours, clearing out around three in the afternoon. His horses appeared the "sorest," some thought, and he hoped to give them plenty of rest. Berry was far ahead somewhere in Illinois with Stephens chasing him, and Gillespie wanted his lead horse, Billy Schafer, to be strong enough to catch up.

Charley Smith dragged in next, suffering from dysentery. He had rested near a small Iowa country creek and dipped his hat in the murky water for a long slurp. It laid him up for two hours, and in Dubuque he visited a doctor before leaving. He looked "quite weak," observers said.

Doc Middleton rode in on the morning train. His race was done by now; he was just following out of curiosity and in an effort to preserve his name and reputation, and perhaps a seat inside Buffalo Bill's arena. He breakfasted at the Julien, and then he and his horse boarded the next train east through Illinois. He would continue to Chicago, if only to watch.

At Dixon, Illinois, Doc stepped off the train incognito, trying to claim his name was Charles Colby. But he soon was recognized and obliged again to explain how he had dropped out of the race and was riding the Illinois Central to Chicago to meet the others. A Dixon veterinarian examined Middleton's horse and pronounced it fit enough to ride, "in sound condition and showing no signs of ill usage or hard driving." But Doc said no; he would ride the rails.

Other cowboys, still far back in Iowa, were harder to track. The owner of a small stable west of Dubuque claimed that Emmett Albright had stopped long enough to secretly ship his two horses on an Illinois-bound railroad boxcar. The stable proprietor said that Albright had started off for Dubuque but after about a half mile ducked into a side road and doubled back to the Illinois Central yard. A woman named Mrs. Hennessy of Manchester, Iowa, said she helped guide him to the tracks. And an Illinois Central Railroad agent said that another cowboy, "a stranger calling himself Johnson," had shipped two horses from Manchester on an "Extra" no. 53 train east as well.

None of that much mattered now. Iowa was history, and riding the rails was cheating. Now the race was all Illinois, five horses, and three men: Berry, Stephens, and Gillespie, riding amid flat country and summer crops until pastures would give way to the bricks, sidewalks, and towers of Chicago.

From Dubuque, Galena was fifteen miles downriver, and Berry tore through there in the afternoon, still well in the lead. He looped east toward Council Hill and for a while followed the Apple River before calling it a night. The next registration stop would be Freeport, reachable sometime tomorrow, on Monday.

Oscar Little had not given up. The scrappy Illinois Humane Society agent hired a buggy and a matched team at East Dubuque and hurried off on the Hazel Green Road for Freeport. He had noticed Berry's horse Poison flashing through there and he still thought the horse "feverish." He wanted a better look at Freeport.

Stephens pounded after Berry, though three hours behind. Gillespie hurried after Stephens, an hour behind him. So it went until Freeport, where townspeople and county homesteaders were staying up much of the night pestering passing wagons and buggies with the same question: "Are they coming?"

Illinois rolled on, trees and small river hills, the horses passing over creek beds and through dry brush, the land crooked and hilly across the state's northwestern hinge. The tiny towns flew by, settlements barely holding on anymore, with perhaps a church, a dry-goods store, a grocery, a coal chute, and a cluster of homes. Otherwise it was all farms, fences, and farmhouses.

At a small railroad junction called Lena, Dave Young broke up bundles of fine straw in his barn and spread it out to await the racing horses. He hoped they would stop at his place, where for thirty years he had provided stable accommodations for wayfarers traveling the old Illinois roads. Tonight he hung a lantern high on an elm pole in front of his barn, signaling for one or more of the cowboys to pull in for a while. None did.

At Elroy, a dot of a town with little more than a post office eight miles before Freeport, a country crowd gathered to wait out much of the night, straining for a glimpse of a cowboy or two stopping to water or eat and maybe rest. None showed.

Not until Freeport, on the Pecatonica River, were the men at last seen. At dawn a hundred or more people lined up in front of the Frazier and Moritz livery stable. Some suspected they may have missed the cowboys overnight, that some of them might have sneaked through town and secretly slept over at the Clifton House hotel. But the hotel manager denied any such rumors, and so people idled around town until the sun peeked over the prairie and the first horse and rider approached Freeport.

At 7:15 in the morning, Berry leaped off Poison and stumbled inside an already opened saloon. The men inside turned and stared at the "hatchet-faced, sunburned, long-haired" straggler bursting into the darkness of the bar. Some of them jeered. Berry ignored their snickering and complaints that he was not a real cowboy. He ordered not a cold beer or a Scotch whiskey like any hardworking cowboy, but instead a tall glass of cold lemonade. Then he let his critics have it.

"Of course I am in the contest," Berry told those cradling their drinks in the saloon. "And the people in Chicago will shout for me." In twenty-four hours or less, he predicted, he would ride triumphant through the streets of Chicago, 130 miles yet to go, and into the arms of Buffalo Bill. "I'm out for blood, that's what I am," he declared. "I have ridden this race under the same conditions and hardships as the others. I am distinctly in the race. The others are all against me and don't want me to get in first. But I shall give them a case of disappointment. I hope to shake hands with Buffalo Bill before Joe Gillespie or Smith or Rattlesnake Pete get into Cook County."

He scoffed at Gillespie (too old) and Rattlesnake Pete (too odd). He thought that George Jones, far in the rear but carefully trotting his horses, saving their strength, might be a bigger worry. "Jones is the man I am looking for to give me a tussle for the finish," Berry said.

Oscar Little turned up in Freeport that morning, too. The Humane Society agent requested that Sheriff James McNamara and the chief of police inspect Berry's two horses. But the lawmen saw no reason to arrest Berry, even for the "feverish" Poison.

Berry took a few precious minutes to hustle over to the Stephenson County courthouse. He found Tatro, Fontaine, and Little inside, and he put the three of them on notice that he, John Berry, the leader in the cowboy race, was the first rider to reach Freeport, daring them to write that down in their book. Then he scrambled out of town. It was five hours more to Byron, Illinois. Berry stopped four times along the way, slowing for water and to sponge off his horses.

Gillespie was slowing, too; the old man was wearing out. For a while he leaned well over his horse's shoulders. Once he fell asleep and tumbled out of the saddle. Other times he hopped off Billy Schafer's back and held onto the horse's tail, saving its strength while he ran behind it.

At Byron, Gillespie promised he would overtake the front-runner. He no longer worried about the others; for him, Berry alone was the man to beat. "I will have John Berry in my hunting sack by tomorrow noon," he promised.

Gillespie already had passed Stephens somewhere after Dubuque, believing that Rattlesnake Pete was "riding his horse to death." Said Old Joe to reporters, "He'll never catch us. I flatter myself I know how to use a horse." He was big and brawny, the toughest of them all. He napped briefly, then tossed down three sirloin steaks and a small loaf of bread.

Before he dashed off, he sent a hastily worded telegram to C. H. Weller, a Sioux County, Nebraska, saloon keeper and horse-racing confidante. "Berry makes a hard fight for first money," Gillespie fretted. "I say he is not in the race." Gillespie was gone before Weller could reply. He would have advised his friend to ignore the disqualified railroad surveyor.

When Rattlesnake Pete hit Freeport, he drew a crowd of reporters; they caught him hopping off General Grant and shaking "his serpentine hat band." He described taking a short nap alongside the road. Just before falling asleep, his saddle under his head, he had heard a buckboard wagon passing by. Tucked low inside was John Berry, he claimed. A buggy clopped past him, too, Stephens said, carrying Gillespie.

DeKalb, the last registering station on the cowboy race to Buffalo Bill's tent ground, was just under seventy miles past Freeport, and Berry made the ride in twelve hours and twenty minutes. He arrived just short of ten at night, crumpling off his horse. He begged the crowds to stand back; he worried that someone might still poison Poison. He briefly rested near his horse, one watchful eye on Poison. Then he was up and gone an hour before midnight.

Gillespie and Charley Smith rode into DeKalb together; they rested an hour and then hurried off after Berry. Stephens hit DeKalb next. He tried to sleep and rest General Grant. He hoped to be out by three in the morning. But when he tried to saddle and bridle his horse,

General Grant would not budge. "He's absolutely unable," Stephens admitted to reporters. They would have to stay put a while in DeKalb. So he lowered his rattlesnake hat over his head and slept through the night in the barn with General Grant. In the morning, he would start for Chicago.

From DeKalb, it was sixty-five miles to Chicago. There were two routes, which both led to Buffalo Bill's Wild West show. The most direct was the township line to St. Charles, Illinois, and then the old St. Charles Road, which entered the big city at Lake Street. The other choice was to take the same path to St. Charles and then a cutoff on the Geneva road to Turner, then Wheaton, and then back to the old St. Charles Road.

Some said the difference shaved off about five miles. Others said it saved only two miles. But in a long-distance race like this one, which was coming down to the wire, any last-minute shortcut could win or lose it. Chicago was that close.

Chicago | 11

In the summer of 1893, seventeen-year-old Mable L. Treseder and her mother arrived by train from Wisconsin for ten glorious days of shopping and dining in Chicago and to take in the World's Columbian Exposition. From the Union Depot, they were driven by coach to a pleasant, two-story hotel off Michigan Avenue, where, she later wrote, "no street cars were allowed to run, and tall buildings were residences of wealthy people." They climbed two flights of stairs, turned down a long hallway, and came to a small room with a bed, dresser, an assortment of chairs, and a large Brussels carpet.

In the morning, they set out to discover the great city and the wonders of the Chicago fair, a magical achievement that heralded America's future and with each sunset flared into a blazing city of white lights. "We were up early and anxious," Mable remembered.

Later, after returning home to Viola, Wisconsin, a rural community eighty miles from where the cowboys crossed the Mississippi, she began a travelogue. She bent over a table near a window with plenty of farm sunlight, writing thirty pages in all. But over the years the manuscript lay neglected on a shelf, gathering dust in the family home until 1943, when her son Sheldon T. Gardner rescued the memoir.

By then the first page had been lost, so her story begins on page 2. Fifty years had passed since the Treseders had explored the fabulously big city. In that half century, one world war had come and gone and the nation was mired in another. A searing economic depression had devastated millions of families, and blowing, billowing dust had buried the Great Plains, even as unbelievable new inventions modernized American life. The Wild West had come to an end, and Mable, who had graduated college, taught, and married the school superintendent in Vernon County, Wisconsin, had died in 1934. She had titled her travelogue simply "A Visitor's Trip to Chicago in 1893."

Page 2 begins with mother and daughter riding south in a jarring train car filled with all types of tourists bound that summer to enjoy Chicago, see the fair, and thrill at Buffalo Bill's Wild West show. Declared Mable with the irrepressible spirit of youth: "We had a jolly time."

On their first morning in downtown Chicago, she and her mother were astonished by the clamoring, clanging, bustling, noisy, whirling metropolis. The devastating Great Chicago Fire lay a generation behind the city, twenty-two years back, and the old fur-trading post on Lake Michigan had grown into a grand crossroads about to top two million people. High-rise buildings scraped the sky, electric elevators replaced steep wooden stairwells, and streetcars scurried about, ferrying passengers no longer bothered by the smell, the labor, or the groaning of workhorses.

In 1893, the old American West was dying, while Chicago was being reborn. Where the frontier was settled, Chicago was adding new factories, smokestacks, and the soot and slime of the slaughterhouses. While the Old West represented what the American frontier had been, Chicago was leading the nation forward. And while the West was past, Chicago was progress.

"I hardly know what to say of the city," wrote Mable, remembering how Chicago's ambition had daunted her and her mother. "It was worse than the confusion of tongues at the Tower of Babel. Noise and confusion existed all day and all night long." They visited the furniture and dry-goods stores in the center of the city: the Hub, the Boston Store, the Bee Hive, and Siegel and Cooper. They purchased two new dresses in Lloyd's third-floor ladies' fashions department, where everything was so hectic that "we found the store nearly as full as the Hub and the poor clerks looked as if they were ready to drop."

Here at the birthplace of the ascending American skyline, Mable and her mother crowded into the elevator at the Masonic Temple, at 302 feet high one of the world's tallest commercial buildings. But they stopped at the seventeenth floor, three flights from the top, to "rest," she recalled. Peering down on the streets below, they could make out "people as small as little children." Mable's mother became "so dizzy" she refused to ride the elevator another inch higher. So they stayed a while longer, "looking out over the city, and getting our brains a little more straightened we began our descent." She wrote, "It was even worse than going up, and that anyone knows is bad enough. It seemed as if the floor of the elevator was drawn from under our feet and there we stood in midair. Then we had a falling sensation."

Shortly before 8 a.m. on another morning, they were off again, this time to visit the fair with eight companions. "After walking three blocks we took the elevated and after riding three miles, which took but a few minutes, we were left safely on the ground and our car started on its round after the many, many passengers it was yet to transport to the busy shuffling fairground."

They toured Louis Sullivan's Transportation Building, examining everything from the smallest covered carriage hitched to a tiny stuffed colt to the largest locomotive engines in Europe or America. They viewed a Mexican cart, a Russian sleigh, and a Japanese sedan, along with a 2,400-ton steam hammer forged in South Bethlehem, Pennsylvania.

Solon Spencer Beman's Mining Building included a Utah boulder weighing three thousand pounds, bottles of water collected from the Great Salt Lake, and "a Statue of Liberty carved from rock salt whose pure whiteness made it a beauty," Mable wrote. They strolled past a miner's cabin from New Mexico, gold nuggets from Washington State, some "bottled petroleum" dug out of Wyoming, and an 8,300-pound sheet of copper melted and pressed in Michigan.

Phonographs in the hall delighted the crowds with New York band music and a chorus or two. One song especially charmed the Treseder party:

I've got a cat and I'm glad of that
But daddy won't buy me a bow-wow.

They ventured past mock Penobscot and other Indian villages and cave dwellings, and a sample of what the vast Chicago stockyards looked and smelled like. "Cattle were standing in an immense large shed or barn," Mable wrote. "As we women folks were not interested here, we passed on.... But the men tarried."

The women glided through Machinery Hall, the Agricultural Building, and the Fisheries and Horticultural displays. But the Manufactures and Liberal Arts Building, designed by George B. Post, was what most dazzled Mable. Covering more than thirty-four acres, with a glass roof that mirrored the clouds, it "to me was the nicest building of all." She ogled Japanese robes valued at $1,250 apiece, a parlor ceiling embroidered in silk in "a most beautiful room," and a carved-soap replica of a ship that had sailed the Atlantic to Spain in fifty-seven days. Swiss lace covered the walls, and wood carvings were set out on shelves. Nearby were Chinese pottery, a brass bed post, and "one of the prettiest and queerest things" of all: a woman's wrap sewn together with prairie chicken feathers.

Mable discovered the "most laughable exhibit" in the U.S. Government Building. It was filled with leftovers from the U.S. Post Office's dead letter section. Among the lost items were thimbles, snakes and a horned toad, love letters and pressed flowers, wedding cakes, dolls, false teeth, skulls, bones, butter bowls, and fish. Here too were housed a medallion worn by Benjamin Franklin's daughter and a tree stump pocked with Civil War bullets from Virginia's Spotsylvania County Courthouse.

Separate buildings were dedicated to each of the forty-four states, and Illinois's, as host to the great fair, seemed the grandest of all. Here was honored the country's first "lonesome prairie," Lincoln's law office in the state capital in Springfield, and "a picture, statue or design of Illinois welcoming the nations of the earth," as Mable put it.

Chicago was, of course, the biggest star of all. Once a dreary collection of swamps and sluggish cabbage fields, Chicago by the summer of the Great Cowboy Race was creased with more than 76,000 miles of railroad tracks veering in from points west alone. Seven passenger depots handled thirty railway companies. The Chicago River roiled with lumber, grain, and shipping barges. On the South Side were hotels, stores, and public buildings. The North Side featured the Halsted Street shopping district. The West Side housed gritty manufacturing plants.

Stitching these neighborhoods together were almost 400 miles of street, cable, electric, and elevated lines. The cable car speed limit was set at nine miles an hour, a dizzying thirteen in less populated areas, and its progress echoed down upon Chicago, wrote New York journalist Julian Ralph, with "such a racket of gong-ringing and such a grinding and whir of grip-wheels as to make a modern vestibuled train seem a waste of the opportunities for noise." Ralph added, "The whole business of life is carried on at high pressure." There were no red lights, green lights, or railroad signals, only the tinkle of a bell within the operator's reach.

The urban horse, used for ferrying passengers and goods, was fading away. Their numbers had dropped by 20 percent over the last two decades in Chicago. Not only was the horse no longer practical, it was too expensive—$1,900 a year to maintain a "motorized delivery wagon" compared to $3,000 to board and feed a horse. The open carriage may have delighted picnickers on a trot out to the country, but it clashed with the city's cable-run trolleys, taxis, and buses. The automobile was still down the road in the future, but throngs at the fair were drawn to the display of a German petrol-powered motorcycle. It would replace the horse, too.

The famous Chicago "L" had opened just a year earlier in 1892, and it chugged on steam from Twelfth Street to Jackson Park, the site of the fairgrounds. It was a short jog, and some scoffed at it as the "Alley L" because it carried passengers over some rugged back lots. But it stayed.

The city's population had soared past a million in 1890 and in twenty years hence would be more than twice that size. More than six million hogs were slaughtered and meat-wrapped each year, and the beef-packing lots were generating nearly $5 million in profits. The Chicago Board of Trade, the Masonic Temple, the Auditorium Building, and the Unity Building shot up as towering steel, iron, and brick giants hovering over the spreading city below.

Urban renewal pushed Chicago in new directions. At Twelfth Street and Michigan Avenue had once stood the offices of John Alexander Dowie, a balding, long-whiskered Scottish preacher and faith healer, a curiosity of old Chicago. Now the elegant Hotel Imperial stood there, and gave its guests off to see the fair a commemorative ticket aboard the spinning Ferris wheel directly above a lush and crowded beer garden.

Setting the Ferris wheel in motion was a feat in itself—two heavy piers were sunk in the ground, and the base supported three dozen cars sturdy enough to hold forty tourists apiece in midair above the city and the whitecaps of Lake Michigan. It was designed like a bicycle wheel, another sign that the horse was history in a city packed with wobbling bike riders—so many that for a while the city enforced a ban against bicycle races in Lincoln Park. By 1893, "wheelmen" were far more popular in Chicago than cowboys. "Wheel mania," many called it.

"During the lovely summer evenings," recalled Edith Ogden Harrison, the mayor's wife, "before every Astor Street home on our block, one could see the trim bicycles awaiting the cessation of an early dinner for the owners inside the houses, for it was a foregone conclusion that everyone took a ride after dinner in the cool of the evening." Riders numbered in the hundreds at first and soon thousands, and private schools offered bicycle riding lessons. The fad became a hobby, then a sport, and finally sensible transportation.

Equally crowded that summer were the grand palaces of the fair's White City and its mile-long Midway Plaisance. Teams of construction workers and other blue-collar laborers built them by day, at night journeying home to the squalid tenement districts. The fair, the stockyards, and the booming construction industry provided jobs, which gave rise to local labor unions. Most of these workers were German and Irish immigrants, and most would never leave Chicago. In the downtown Loop, hotels and restaurants staffed up with young maids and waitresses. Just a month previously, in May 1893, four hundred women had joined in solidarity to form the Waiter Girl's Union No. 1.

The same laborers built the private palaces for those who now reigned over the new Chicago—from newspaper baron Joseph Medill to Potter Palmer, who plotted State Street and lived on Lake Shore Drive in a brown sandstone and gray granite mansion with a tower and turrets, which the poor called the "Palmer castle."

The twenty-two years between the Great Chicago Fire of 1871 and 1893's Great Cowboy Race would be recalled as "the most crowded and dynamic" the city ever saw. The rise was nothing less than meteoric, a growth of nearly 268 percent in that two decades' time, with 150 square miles added to the city's territory and pushing it in every direction up, out, and past the lakefront. Beyond the central business district, the company town of Pullman, named after George Mortimer Pullman and his Pullman Palace Car Company, debuted as the swankiest, wealthiest sliver of Chicago, home to clergymen and company executives in red brick and terra-cotta homes.

The great fire had leveled the city, but it also kindled the start of modern Chicago and the new America it helped invent. In October

An 1893 souvenir photo from the World's Columbian Exposition. The fair highlighted the coming American century and discounted Buffalo Bill and his cowboys as relics of the past. (Library of Congress)

1871, either an anxious cow or a gambler down in his poker chips knocked over a lantern in the O'Leary family's barn off DeKoven Street; two thousand acres and eighteen thousand structures burned down. More than ninety thousand people were left homeless, and some three hundred lives were lost.

"All gone but the wife and babies, and *pluck*," is how the breadwinner of one family put it, determined to find work as a house and sign painter. Said the venerable *Chicago Tribune* in a down-but-defiant editorial: "CHICAGO SHALL RISE AGAIN."

And so it did. The 1893 Columbian Exposition and its bright White City would become the crown jewel of the new city and a model for the new century. "We shall be sending our youth by the hundred thousand to sojourn for a season within her borders," Ohio evangelist Washington Gladden wrote of young tourists such as Mable Treseder flocking to Chicago. "Chicago is burning to show us her tall buildings and her big parks."

"If a thing of beauty is a joy forever," wrote William T. Stead, a British editor, "then that vision of the White City by night, silent and desolate, was well worth crossing the Atlantic." "In Chicago," wrote Giuseppe Giacosa, an Italian playwright, "I knew that American life flourished abundantly: enormous factories, interminable streets, amazing shops, deafening sounds. And then there was the Exposition ..."

More than $14 million in gate receipts was collected at the fair. More than twenty-seven million people visited, by far the largest attendance of any international exposition up to that time. The Chicago fair was three times more popular than the 1876 fair held in Philadelphia to mark the centennial of American Independence. On one day alone, "Chicago Day," October 9, near the end of the fair, more than 760,000 people shoved through the turnstiles.

They came in droves, by rail, by water, by bicycle, by wagon, by horse, by foot, as families, as couples, and as strangers. The train stations overflowed with passengers and piled-high baggage, the walls ricocheting with the shouts of those packing into the new modern city.

Lucille Rodney walked to the Chicago Fair. She departed Galveston, Texas, on May 16, and if she could reach the Columbian Exposition by August 1, $5,000 would be hers, the result of a wager with the Elite Athletic Club of Chicago. Her husband, G. B. Rodney, followed along as an escort in a horse and buggy.

She averaged twenty-three miles a day, forty in good weather. She wore out eight pairs of $5 English walking shoes and dropped twenty pounds in the first two weeks. Just twenty-eight years old, she followed the railroad trestles and registered at local train stations. Despite a broad-brim straw hat and her long black hair, the fair-skinned Lucille became deeply sunburned.

"Oh, the dreadful trestles. I don't like them," she told reporters in Dallas. "One lady on the way asked me if I crawled on them. I told her no, but I don't like to cross them." Once a dog bit her husband. She stopped at farmhouses for meals "because we can drop them a note by a passing freight train and when we get there they are fixed for us."

A native of Manchester, Iowa, Mrs. Rodney announced at the halfway point that "if I am successful on this trip, I am going to walk from New York to San Francisco." "If you do," piped up Mr. Rodney, "you will go without me."

She lost seven days to summer storms in Kansas. She slipped on a rock in Missouri and sprained her hip. Some rural hooligans tried to mug her, but she scared them off with a "small, trimmed and well-loaded revolver." She bruised her hip again outside Decatur, Illinois.

Ten days later, on July 31, twenty-four hours ahead of time, Lucille Rodney entered Chicago in triumph. She marched straight to the pink granite and red brick Polk Street depot and slipped in under the twelve-story clock tower. Her feet had covered 1,346 miles, no small feat of endurance.

To savor the day, she skipped the world's fair and instead hurried off to Buffalo Bill's Wild West evening performance. In the stands, the weary walker conceded to reporters that she was tired and spent. "The heat was fearful," she said, "and although the people along the road were as kind as they could be, the hardships I had to undergo were terrible."

Dignitaries also flocked to Chicago from exotic points around the globe, among them the duke and duchess of Veragua, the Austrian Archduke Franz Ferdinand, the raja of Kapurthala, and Prince Komatsu Yoharito of Japan. Most stunning of all was the Spanish *infanta,* Princess María Eulalia, escorted by beloved Chicago Mayor Carter Harrison along the grand colonnades and around the parks, the exhibit halls, the water fountains, the state pavilions, and the Midway Plaisance.

Washington lawmakers and the president of the United States were on hand for official duties. The governor and mayors presided over special Illinois State Day ceremonies. Journalists from the world over streamed into Chicago to profile the fair.

The fair had opened on May 1 after meat-packing executives pledged millions to cover the city's expenses. It was designed to commemorate the four hundredth anniversary of Christopher Columbus's New World landfall, and in 1891 Chicago had beat out New York, Washington, D.C., and St. Louis to host the extravaganza. In two years' time, Jackson Park, on the edge of Lake Michigan, was transformed into a gleaming city, to the eye a floating palace, to the city a bridge to the future.

Part of it was sideshow: beer-drinking elephants and giant stuffed mastodons, Indian relics and curiosities from the past, much of it housed in the exhibit buildings that Mable Treseder loved touring. But beyond the sixty-five thousand displays in two hundred buildings, the fair offered the American public its first peek at the coming twentieth century, and that is what fascinated them most of all. Here they previewed how life in America would be lived.

Battery-run boats floated fairgoers around the lakes and lagoons, and a "movable sidewalk" transported them along portions of the fairgrounds. The fair's railroad, the first to use high-speed electric engines, chugged in and out. Drinking fountains constructed with Pasteur filters offered oases from the blistering summer sun. Long-distance telephone calls could be made on the spot, Thomas Edison's Kinetoscope peep shows flickered behind curtains, and a machine flashed images along telegraph wires strung around the fair.

In the Court of Honor's Electricity Building, orchestra music was piped in from New York through a giant phone amplifier dangling from the ceiling. According to the fair's chief electrician, John P. Barrett, "Light and power here reach their greatest development since the world began."

Along with the German motorcycle, there were many prototypes of other modern conveniences to come, including the dishwasher and the fluorescent lightbulb. The first souvenir postcard was presented at the fair; so was a commemorative stamp; so were commemorative coins. The first box of Cream of Wheat debuted, as did the first stick of Juicy Fruit chewing gum. Pabst Blue Ribbon beer, voted "America's Best" at the fair, was popped open and poured down. Legend has it that the fair introduced America to Cracker Jack.

Speed, above all, was the rage. Mulji Devji Vedant, a Brahmin writing in the *Asiatic Quarterly Review*, recalled spending hours marveling at new state-of-the-art motor engines for "carriages, ships, cycles, etc. etc." One engine, he wrote, "is reported to be capable of running nearly a hundred miles per hour."

The fair brought fresh hopes of money yet to be made. Richard Sears sketched out the copy for the cover and inside pages of his 1894 mail-order catalog while visiting the fair, inspired by all the splendor and profits pouring into Chicago. It would be his largest issue, a whopping 322 pages long. On the Midway, Scott Joplin played a new piano music called ragtime. In the corridors, pickpockets weaved in and out of the crowds tapping their feet.

There also lurked a dark side of the fair. As the cowboys raced to Chicago, the state's newly elected governor, John Peter Altgeld, came under political fire for commuting the prison terms of three convicted anarchists in the Haymarket Square bombing. Talk of his impeachment intensified. In defending the pardons, the governor said that not only would the public weather the scandal, but that Chicago and Illinois would rise above it. "While our institutions are not free from injustice," Altgeld argued, "they are still the best that have yet been devised." He assumed the electorate would come to appreciate his grant of mercy, but in the end they chose otherwise. The governor did not stand for reelection. In 1899, he ran for mayor of Chicago and vaulted to the lead as the early favorite, yet he finally came in a humiliating third, with a mere 15 percent of the vote.

A serial killer was also loose that summer in Chicago, and two days before the fair closed, a disappointed office seeker murdered the immensely popular Mayor Harrison, gunning him down at his home after he had helped to spearhead the exposition. He was beginning his fifth term at city hall.

Outside the fair, evangelists such as Dwight Moody staged lakeside tabernacles and cashed in on the tourist dollars. Inside the city, "Chicago May" Churchill roamed the streets as a petty thief. At night, she and other prostitutes reaped a gold mine of business off fairgoers, laborers, the rich, and the not so rich. Born Mary Anne Duignan in Ireland, in Chicago she dubbed herself "the Queen of the Crooks." But becoming a crook and prostitute first required some time spent learning the tricks and some firsthand schooling in the trenches. "The first big crooked job I did in Chi," she later wrote, "was with Dora Donegan. It turned out to be a big one for me. I pulled a john into the Sherman House. After I got him there I didn't know how to land him. Dora came to the rescue. She saw that I was too modest in handling the prey. I lacked brass. She bawled me out for 'not playing square by the gentleman.'"

When the fair closed that autumn, it had proved the most successful endeavor of its kind. Its ambition and ingenuity were boundless. The new century would belong to America "by the right of might," and there lay the theme of the World's Columbian Exposition.

For academics, the fair provided a venue for six thousand lectures to nearly seven hundred thousand fairgoers. One of the most significant was presented offsite, not connected to the fair at all, and was delivered by a young Wisconsin university professor before a gathering of the American Historical Association.

Frederick Jackson Turner was a junior faculty member in Wisconsin, and three years earlier, in 1890, he had read with great interest a bulletin issued by the superintendent of the U.S. Census. It had concluded that the American Western frontier had been chopped into so many small settlements that a frontier line no longer existed. Therefore, the bulletin advised, "westward movement cannot any longer have a place in the Census reports."

Many in Chicago considered Turner an upstart from a small Midwestern school. Just thirty-one, he was short, thin, and a mere 130 pounds, easy to pass unnoticed on a busy Chicago street or the fair's parade grounds, and difficult to make out on an academic stage. He had been born during the first year of the Civil War in tree-lined Portage, Wisconsin, and grew to manhood watching most of his own hometown's frontier wither away—the old immigrant covered wagons rolling through town, the Ho-Chunk and Winnebago peoples pushed aside by Army soldiers. The one time his hometown ever witnessed any real Wild West gunplay was when a pair of feuding Irish immigrants fired at each other on a startled street. The man who survived was hung.

The village of Portage, in the bower of the Wisconsin River Valley, served as the perfect laboratory for the young historian. He could stay home and fish in the marshy Fox River and still study the vanishing West. The evidence was unfolding all around him. Farmers and shop owners in Portage gradually took the place of old-time French fur trappers, explorers, and Indian traders. A third of the town came from somewhere else, usually from back east or preindustrial Germany or the highland tundra of Scotland and Wales. What he saw was a changing landscape, what he called "the rapid Americanization" of the country.

In the summer of 1893, Turner was to address the World's Congress of Historians and Historical Students. A heat wave was smothering Chicago, up to 97 degrees all week, and two people collapsed and died from heat stroke. As he took the stage at the Art Institute, at the foot of Adams Street between the downtown Loop and the lake, the *Chicago Times* observed that "never in the city's history was a day more insufferably hot and continuously scorching."

His audience was tired, uncomfortable, and distracted. Many historians had attended an afternoon performance of Buffalo Bill's Wild West show, and that alone left them exhausted. They also were stunned to learn that more bodies had been discovered in a cold-storage plant, the latest work of the serial killer. Thus attendance for Turner's address ran rather light, in fact "very light," as the *Chicago Herald* reported.

Turner suffered his own misgivings and struggled with nerves and stage fright. He had arrived by train from Madison, Wisconsin, and took a room at a University of Chicago dormitory. There he walled out the world, writing and editing his essay, which was due to be presented in just two days. "I am in the final agonies of getting out a belated paper," he lamented in a letter to a friend.

He missed the first addresses at the historical meetings, still adding and scratching out words, dropping lines, penciling over paragraphs from his essay. He briefly visited the opening session and then he rushed back to his dorm room and locked the door.

Turner's turn would come on Wednesday evening, after he passed up the chance to join the others at the Wild West show. Before some of the nation's most eminent historians, he rose and addressed the audience. He decided not to read all fifty pages of his paper; it was too hot, the room was stuffy, and everyone was far too tired. So he summarized in capsule form what would become known as his monumental "frontier thesis."

The idea had been taking shape in his mind for several years: the concept that the frontier had developed an enduring American character, borne on the shoulders of pioneers and cowboys, and that it had created "a new product that is American" all unto itself. "Up to our own day American history has been in a large degree the history of the colonization of the Great West," Turner said in his remarks. "The frontier is the outer edge of the wave—the meeting point between savagery and civilization."

The settling of the frontier and the closing of the Wild West marked the first major turning point in American history, in his analysis. "Now, four centuries from the discovery of America, at the end of a hundred years of life under the Constitution, the frontier has gone. And with its going has closed the first period of American history."

And as the West ended and the frontiersman and the cowboy were ushered out, Turner inscribed their epitaph: "To the frontier," he said, "the American intellect owes its striking characteristics. That coarseness and strength combined with acuteness and inquisitiveness; that practical, inventive turn of mind, quick to find expedients; that masterful grasp of material things, lacking in the artistic but powerful to effect great ends; that restless, nervous energy; that dominant individualism, working for good and evil, and withal that buoyancy and exuberance which comes from freedom—these are the traits of the frontier."

When he finished speaking, there was no discussion, no questions posed from the audience. He sat down in silence and watched the room empty, everyone heading for the exits and the last of a cool breeze off Lake Michigan.

But his idea soon spread, and "it remained the creed of nearly every American historian," according to Turner's biographer Ray Allen Billington. "The nation embraced the Frontier Thesis as the gospel, and rewrote its textbooks to glorify the pioneer above the industrialist or the immigrant."

The frontier was finished, the wilderness tamed, the buffalo slaughtered, and the cattle drives no more. The Old West was gone, even as the leader of the Great Cowboy Race came roaring into Chicago.

The Finish Line | 12

By 9:30 in the morning on June 27, Chicago had been awake for hours. In the stockyards, men poked and prodded the beef and hogs, the flies were getting to the cattle before the knives could, and the butchers' aprons were running red. The smokestacks were stoked, the chimneys billowed, and the ash was drifting for miles over the lakefront. The shops in the Loop were open, and business was brisk. The Alley L was up and chugging, young boys chasing its shadow under the tracks. Hammers banged and pounded at the construction sites, more steel and brick going up, the hod carriers lifting their burdens skyward.

In his tent next to the fair, Buffalo Bill prepared for his matinee and evening performances, presented at 3 p.m. and then 8:30 p.m. as the summer sun sank: cowboys and Sioux warriors fighting it out, a stagecoach heist, twirling lariats, and above all the great Cody himself. Twice today, as on every day, he would fire at whirling clay pigeons and knock them out of the air.

Outside the tent, a group of Sioux Indians, Russian Cossacks, Arab Bedouins, and Uhlan lancers, part of the Wild West show's colorful lineup, were startled to spot a small, lean rider nearly falling off his horse. His white shirt was pasted with brown blotches of sweat, his yellow trousers were heavy with muck, and his small hat was partly shredded.

Several of the Wild West actors tried to lower the man out of his light cow saddle, reaching for his shoulders and legs, struggling to get a hand underneath him. But the man pushed them away, his thin rain slicker and rawhide whip slipping out of his hands.

Buffalo Bill popped his head through the doorway and rushed outside. He cracked a big smile. Stretching a long arm out to welcome the rider, he tried to greet the man in what reporters racing to the scene called "a mighty hand grab." The rider's hand went limp. "Look after my horse, boys," he whispered. "Please." Then John Berry slumped out of the saddle and collapsed onto the hard ground marking the finish line of the cowboy race, crumpling at the feet of Buffalo Bill.

"Why," exclaimed Cody, "he's a little bit of a man! . . . You are the first man in," he bellowed. "You are all right, John. You are all right."

The finish line fell quiet. Some drew back to give the man air. But he did not speak or move or signal at all, and Cody leaned down to him. Should he congratulate the rider or praise his horse?

"I'm glad to see you!" Cody shouted. "How do you feel?"

Still the man said nothing, and two beefy roadies from the Wild West show carried him to the cool shade inside the mess tent. They laid him across Cody's couch.

Cody tried to spark some life in the man. He poured him some port wine, and everyone hushed as the rider tipped it back and drained the glass. Cody poured him another, and the man downed that one, too.

"What can I do for you?" Cody asked.

"Nothing," the man answered in a long, thin rasp. "Only look after my horse."

The horse, Poison, was led to a Wild West show stable by two of Cody's "bronco killers," support staffers named Tony Esquival and Phil Smith, who specialized in calming ornery and tired horses. They rubbed, scrubbed, and sponged off the horse's hide "in a fashion he had never encountered since the days he had to rustle a living off dry leaves on the Montana range," one journalist wrote. They oiled the horse's joints with liniment, flicking the tired, sore limbs and wiping out its parched mouth with a wet sponge and rag. They handled the horse with the care they would give a "sick infant," one observer said. Someone else, seeing the horse bury its head in a clump of hay, thought it was like watching "an elephant" eat.

For Cody, the scene was picture perfect. His newspaper ads had been screaming: "Expected Tuesday, at Buffalo Bill's Wild West. The contestants in the COWBOY 1,000-MILE RACE, an equine race, *Humanely Run! Humanely Won!* Under the Supervision of the Society for the Prevention of Cruelty to Animals. The Contestants and Steeds Will Be Introduced as They Arrive on Tuesday."

And now, as Chicago awoke this morning, he had hit the big bonanza. His show was smashing box-office records, thanks in part to the long-distance Great Cowboy Race. And the first rider to reach Chicago had just landed on the ground at Buffalo Bill's boots. After two weeks of protests, Cody needed a man on a broncho not ridden to death or otherwise terribly mistreated or abused. In this one brief moment on Tuesday, June 27, he had his man and his horse and, equally intact, his enormous American pride.

Many had seen Buffalo Bill's newspaper ads predicting that today was the day, and at dawn throngs already lined the brick-and-stone streets on the northwest edge of the city. Soon a shout went up from a small boy who had shimmied up a telegraph pole. "Here he comes!" cried the boy. "Hurrah!"

John Berry, the noncowboy, was nearing Cottage Grove Avenue. He turned onto Seventy-first Street. Poison spooked as a cable car clanged by, but Berry steadied the horse and urged it on. They swung past Madison Street … California Street … Ashland Avenue … and finally mighty Michigan Avenue. He followed the waving arms guiding him the last few blocks toward Sixty-third, and he could tell it would be smooth sailing from here to Jackson Park, the fair, and the Wild West campground.

The crowds broke up. Chicago residents, fairgoers, and tourists, thousands of them, rushed on foot and bicycles after the small figure, sunburned and weathered, stooped and spent, clinging to his saddle horn, swaying but bravely hanging on to his horse. He seemed "the sorriest, sleepiest" man they had ever seen. His soft white hat was ripped, his cotton shirt torn at the throat and drenched in sweat, his dun-colored pants held together by frayed suspenders and a leather belt cinched around his waist. His face blazed crimson, his cheeks were swollen, his eyes were two narrow slits.

In Cody's tent, Berry lay on Buffalo Bill's sofa and panted, trying to catch a breath. The cook fired up the kitchen stove and served him a breakfast tray of half a fried chicken, warm biscuits, and hot coffee. Berry took one glance at that steaming plate and shoveled it down.

He next stumbled off to check on Poison, finding his horse head deep in a pail of oats. He hobbled back to Cody's tent and finally described how much he had suffered in the past twenty-four hours. For a man of few words, Berry said a bucketful.

"I left DeKalb last night at 11:05 p.m. on Poison, and I kept pounding along as fast as I could without hurting the horse," he began.

"When we reached Turner, we got a telegram from DeKalb stating that Smith and Gillespie were just two hours and 30 minutes behind. So I knew I had the race sure. I fed and watered between Elburn and Lodi. We took the straight St. Charles Road and struck Maywood about 7 o'clock this morning. I had the comfort of seeing the smoke of this great place and then began to get nervous. I was afraid for the horse when we struck the pavement for fear he would break down. He ain't used to pavements, you know."

He paused to let his stomach rest and digest his breakfast. "I rode the last 150 miles in 24 hours," he related. "Sore? Well, I should say I was. I don't feel much like sitting down, but I am so sleepy that I can't talk. I have had no sleep for ten days to amount to anything. But I feel in fairly good shape. Except sleepy."

He turned to Cody's adjutant Major John Burke and asked whether he had discovered any spur marks on Poison at Cody's stable. No, said Burke, beaming. Not a one.

"Some of the riders say I rode in a wagon," said Berry. "But they are liars. I have ridden on my horses, Sandy and Poison, all the way."

From the start of the race, Berry said, he had felt outnumbered. "There was a combination put up to beat me. The rest of the riders got out in front of me at the start. But I think I did a wise thing. While the rest kept a rapid pace I walked my horses half the time the first two days. I did not catch the leaders until I reached Iowa Falls. From there we kept pretty close together."

From across the Mississippi River and on through Illinois, "I was in the lead and they had to follow me. They have not caught up with me yet. Yes, I am glad to win, for it is an honor.... I left Freeport at 9:15 yesterday morning, and here I am at 9:30 today. Of course I am glad it's over."

Berry fell back on the couch and scanned the faces. "But I am able to go on and do some more riding," he said. He rolled his head back and closed his eyes. Two more words slipped past his lips: "If necessary."

They helped him over to the Hotel Columbia, next to the Wild West grounds. They booked him a room. Just before he fell asleep, he noticed again the narrow eyes, the smirks, the thin faces glaring down at someone they suspected had cheated. "I won the race fairly," Berry insisted. "I do not care whether the stake money is coming or not." As he started to drift off, desperate for sleep, he seemed to protest once more: "I haven't closed my eyes in ten days and ..."

Through the hotel room window and out in the street, Poison's owner, South Dakota rancher Jack Hale, who had rushed to Chicago by train, defended his rider John Berry. "John rode for me as a friend and cares only for the glory of the thing," Hale proclaimed. "I have known him for 20 years. He's a capital rider and a man of great endurance."

Some suggested that Hale had fixed the race to draw national publicity for his South Dakota ranch. If one of his horses was first to Chicago, that would work wonders for his stock farm. Others recalled how Chadron had hoped a local rider would win because it was their race, after all, and they believed a man and a pony from outside the Nebraska Panhandle should not be given any real chance to beat the home team. Chadron town leaders had initially demanded that if any of Hale's horses were going to be allowed to race, he would have to let local favorite Doc Middleton ride Poison.

Not true, Hale said. There had been no such offer, no such demand. He admitted that his friend John Berry was no cowboy desperado like the wily Doc Middleton. "He's not one of your bad men," said a now angry Hale. "But he's an all-round Westerner who can ride, box and wrestle with any man.

"I entered my horses for the race and trained them without any idea who was going to ride," Hale told reporters. And he considered Poison the pride of his herd. "There," he said, pointing toward the Cody stables, "is a horse that is nearly Thoroughbred. His dam is an old race mare that has won a great many races through the Northwest under the name of Trade Dollar, and his sire was a Kentucky bred horse of excellent breeding. It takes a horse of great courage to stand such a ride, and this can only be found in horses that have been bred for racing for many generations."

He insisted that Poison's initial rider had fallen ill and that Berry simply stepped up to ride in his place: "At the last moment John Berry volunteered, and I knew he was safe to ride. That made trouble for him and me. The Chadron people said Berry was no cowboy and knew the route too well. So finally Berry rode under protest. But I don't think that protest will hold good when he gets back to Chadron after his splendid ride."

Hale further claimed he had collected a "batch of letters" written by "certain Chadron folks" that proved some of the Nebraska town leaders had been in cahoots to fix the race for one of their own. But Hale was not yet ready to produce the sealed letters. When he did, he promised, "they will show up bad."

⊶ ⊰◊⊱ ⊷

Emmett Albright trotted into Chicago ninety minutes behind Berry, riding in with both horses looking quite well and Albright rather fresh himself for a man supposedly long in the saddle. He leaped to the ground and strutted about the sidewalk, searching for Buffalo Bill. He led his horses to Cody's tent until they reminded him that to officially cross the finish line he had to ride, not walk, over it. So Albright gamely swung back on his lead horse, snapped the reins, and galloped across the last few feet of the Great Cowboy Race.

"I think I have won," Albright claimed, now sprawling across Cody's comfortable couch in the Wild West mess tent. "I am the only man who brought in two horses. I am awfully tired," he said, "for I have been sick and vomiting since I left Chadron and I have not slept for five days and have not eaten anything since yesterday noon. I did not feel tired until this morning, when I began to let down. The excitement carried me through. Nerve can do a great deal. I can't tell where I passed the other boys, but I know I passed them last night somewhere. You can hear great things on the road. I heard that I had no horses, was dead and everything else. I could have beaten Berry, but I knew he was riding under protest so I did not try. I think I get the first money."

Many considered Albright, too, ineligible. They had heard stories that he had shipped his horses by rail a good part of the last jaunt from Dubuque and that his speed was the speed of freight trains on the Illinois Central. When pressed, the cowboy sheepishly admitted that much of this was true. He had slithered off with his horses on a night train to steal some time and beat the others. He tried lamely to excuse it by saying he believed some of the other riders were "shipping too."

Major Burke did not care to hear another word; he quickly dismissed Albright outright. "Albright," he scoffed, "is the comedian of the outfit."

More people pressed in along the finish line, newspaper reporters especially. They wanted answers, and they wanted to hear from Cody. Two riders had arrived in Chicago that morning by hoof or by rail car and more were yet to follow, and already the results of the cowboy race had descended into chaos. Who gets the prize money? Who wins the golden revolver? Who rides home on the new Montgomery Ward saddle?

First to be settled was the matter of the horses. Minneapolis Humane Society official Paul Fontaine, fresh into Chicago, too, said the riders he had seen "have acted the part of gentlemen.... They have taken better care of their horses than they have of themselves. And we have no cause to complain or take any action whatever.... It was constructed satisfactorily in every way."

His colleague John Shortall, president of the American Humane Association and the Illinois Humane Society, accompanied by a contingent of veterinary surgeons, made the rounds of the Cody stables, examining the three horses already in, thumping their knees, listening to their lungs, inspecting their flanks for cuts, bruises, or bleeding.

As Cody watched them weave through his stalls, the famous frontiersman declared there was a lot more to the Great Cowboy Race than just the first-prize money or a saddle or a gun. "It will show the world what the native American horse is worth," he said. "European nations are watching the result of this race with interest. It is a test of the hardiness of the broncho, and after the wonderful result of 150 miles in 24 hours, and 1,000 miles in 13 days and 16 hours, there will be a rush for the American animal."

Look at this horse Poison, he continued, heaping on the praise. "Not a drop of water on him, except under the saddle." He declared that the horse was "good for another 100 miles, if necessary." The two Albright horses also were "in fine condition and could not feel better. They are out in the paddock now, kicking up their heels."

Cody could not have been prouder of the horses or any happier that the race had ended in triumph, he said, despite all the criticism, the nagging doubts, and the still unresolved questions. "Of course," he concluded, "on the entanglements of the riders and protests I am not in a position to decide. But I do say that the horses are in splendid condition. I was not surprised at that either, though, for it is just as I said. The cowboys know that their horse is their best friend and that its best endeavors can be brought out by kindness and care."

Major Burke of course backed up Cody; both were highly satisfied. He recalled how back in Iowa he had dubbed the riders "the Lemonade Brigade." "They don't drink anything but lemonade," Burke said. "Why, I bought a string of lemonade from Iowa to Chicago and the boys just broke me."

Burke called Berry's riding under protest a small "technicality," stressing that all eight of the real cowboys knew that he had worked with the committee staff in mapping the route. Nothing about Berry's past or railroad career was kept from anyone, Burke said. "It was agreed among the boys that none should know in advance the stopping places along the route. Berry, having some ability in that line, at the request of the committee did part of their clerical work, and the other boys in the race protested against it."

But these were questions for another time, Burke said. Right now "the principal thing was that their horses should come in good shape, and that the race has been one of honest endurance and skill."

More in the crowd rushed back inside the stables to see for themselves, and it took ten Chicago police officers to secure the stalls. Everyone laughed when an ornery Poison kicked and tried to bite Shortall. That alone seemed enough to pronounce the horse "animated" and still rather feisty. Cody sauntered in for a close look at the horses, and the police stepped aside. "They're as sound as a dollar," pronounced Buffalo Bill. "And not a bit tired."

To decide who should be declared the winner, Cody called a meeting at one in the afternoon and escorted a group of horsemen and newspaper reporters to his family dining room on the tent grounds. There they would try to sort things out. But first he filled their glasses.

"Gentlemen, a toast," he said. "I propose a toast to the Cowboy Race, which has demonstrated to the world that we raise in our Western country the hardiest and best horses for cavalry purposes to be found on the surface of the earth. During my travels in foreign countries, I have frequently been asked by army officers about the merits of our American horses for cavalry purposes, and have always maintained that they were superior to any others. This race will result in bringing thousands of dollars into the pockets of our Western horse-raisers, as well as in teaching the most enlightened methods of harboring an animal's strength for a long distance journey."

The group sat down for lunch, but suddenly more shouts were heard, and everyone dropped their silverware and hurried back onto Sixty-third Street. Joe Gillespie had come firing in, yelling at the waving fans and hollering "like a renegade Comanche." He yanked on the reins and pulled Billy Schafer to a near crash at the cowboy finish line. He leaped off the horse. "I'm the lightest rider in the West!" he shouted.

He had dropped thirty pounds over the past two weeks, and the next time, he vowed, he would race another thousand miles and do it within ten days. He had left his second horse with a farmer farther back, asking him to "hold and take good care of him until called for."

Many now insisted that Gillespie should be awarded the prize money, the saddle, and the Colt revolver. Berry, after all, had been disqualified from the start, and Albright had shipped his horses. Here now was Old Joe Gillespie, who would have ridden in first had he not lost precious time traipsing around on a trick mule in a small-town Iowa circus.

At many of the small towns in Nebraska, Iowa, and Illinois, overzealous fans had plucked hairs from Billy Schafer's tail, just like they did with Doc Middleton's horse. "I could cuss at the men," Gillespie groused. "But what can a feller do agin' a woman? And some of them were mighty attentive to the man who rode him." He held up from his saddlebag a knot of dainty handkerchiefs women had presented to him along the route, now keepsakes of his own.

But Gillespie's abiding affection this afternoon was for Billy Schafer. "He's the best horse I ever throwed a leg over," Old Joe told reporters. "Give him a little rest and two quarts of oats, and he'll throw off another 50 miles this afternoon."

Asked how he felt, Gillespie whipped out his quirt and kicked up some dust. "Hell. Give me some grub and another hoss and I'm ready to start right back to Chadron."

Gillespie led Billy Schafer to a horse stall and stretched out on a bed of mixed straw and hay next to his horse. But he was too riled up to sleep. His arms tucked behind his head, he rambled on about how he'd wound up confused in the Chicago outskirts and thought the

Joe Gillespie (*left*) and Charley Smith at the Wild West finish line in Chicago.
(Dawes County Historical Museum)

city larger than the whole state of Iowa. He knew he was floundering in those last few miles, so he stopped two young men on bicycles and asked for the shortest route to Buffalo Bill. He complained that the young men had sent him off in the wrong direction and then quickly disappeared down a side street. "Why, this here damn town stretches all over the earth!" Gillespie complained.

He soon jumped to his feet and headed over to the Wild West arena for a look around. That afternoon Gillespie, with a reservoir of leftover energy, was handed the reins to drive four mules in the matinee performance, and he stole the scene where a gang of desperadoes held up the Deadwood stagecoach. After the last curtain call, he wandered a while longer through the show grounds, soaking in all the lingering cowboy spirit, and only then did the oldest man in the race agree to lie still and nap.

Meanwhile, Charley Smith trotted in on Dynamite; he had left his second horse, Red Wing, at Malta, Illinois. He dismounted and marched straight for the Cody mess hall. He was forking into his second pie when some reporters approached and asked him how he felt, too. "I feel like a broncho," he replied, "and will bet my cash in hand and in sight that I can start out tomorrow morning and cover another 1,000 miles in ten days."

As the hours wore on, more riders straggled in, others wiring ahead that they planned to file formal complaints against John Berry.

Doc Middleton turned up on the afternoon train, finding the Cody tent ground in a state of confusion over who had won, who had lost, and who had not ridden fair.

That evening, Cody hosted a formal banquet at the Hotel Columbia just before the nightly performance of Buffalo Bill's Wild West. Sitting as guests of honor at the head table were Gillespie, Albright, Smith, and Berry too. Glasses were lifted for "the riders"; other toasts were sounded for "the riders who have not yet arrived." Some hailed Chicago and the World's Fair. Still more called out for Buffalo Bill.

A particularly elegant tribute was paid by P. J. Gilligan, an old-time Butte, Montana, pioneer. He praised "the cowboy and his habits," explaining that though the Western horseman was becoming a dying breed, he, for one, would always prefer to look back upon "the sunny side of the cowboy's life."

Gilligan's toast encouraged proposals for more cowboy contests. What about a race from Chicago to St. Louis, "with frequent changes of horses"? Why not ride from New York City to somewhere along the Rio Grande, a race "between Mexicans and cowboys"?

The toasts and discussions ran so long that Cody almost missed his evening show. He scarfed down his meal and dashed for the exit.

That night Buffalo Bill wired a telegram to his many supporters out west and as far back east as New York. The great showman assured them that things were under control in Chicago and that a decision would be reached soon over who had won the cowboy race and who had cheated. "The cowboy race ended on my grounds today," he wired. "Berry first, Albright second, others well up. I am the judge. Humane authorities perfectly satisfied, as horses are in splendid condition. Signed, William F. Cody." In the morning, he and everyone else assumed, some kind of agreement and middle ground could be reached, and a formal public announcement regarding the winner would be made.

On Wednesday, the race committee members and Buffalo Bill continued arguing over who was the legitimate winner. Berry had ridden into Chicago first, but he had been disqualified from the start in Chadron. Should he still be counted out at the end? Albright had been second, with two horses. But he had admitted to secretly shipping them by railcar for long stretches, a clear violation of the race rules. Gillespie had been third; his horses seemed fine, and he was incontestably a cowboy.

The committee and Cody next heard from the bike-riding *Chicago Inter Ocean* newspaper correspondent who had trailed several of the riders. He said that near Farley, Iowa, "by the light of the moon" he had spotted Gillespie riding in the back of a buggy, sound asleep. He said he had woken Gillespie, and old Joe had stammered that he merely was trying to snatch a bit of rest. He claimed other riders were hiding in wagons under the cover of night, too, and that he and Rattlesnake Pete were not going to let them win. "Pete and me have been riding square all along, but these other fellows are riding in hacks after night," Gillespie told the reporter. "And I propose to win this race if I have to ride a hack all the way."

The reporter said he later "came upon Rattlesnake Pete at a farmhouse feeding his horse. He was glum. He said he had seen Smith and Gillespie pass two miles out of White Oaks Springs, both riding in vehicles and leading horses." The reporter told more stories about other cowboys hiding in buggies, and he claimed that Albright was not the only man to secretly send his horses by rail. "At DeKalb I was told Monday morning that some of the riders had shipped their horses by train to Chicago, and others had tied [them] to vehicles and ridden in."

The committee considered a telegram from James "Rattlesnake Pete" Stephens, well back of the pack and still struggling to make Chicago. He had strayed off course and bunked at Ben Morse's livery stable in Rockford, Illinois. He slept there until about four in the morning, hoping to swing past Cherry Valley and then ride into Chicago, another eighty miles more. He wired that he planned to lodge a formal complaint against those he suspected had not ridden fair. He wanted a halt to any decisions on the prize money and other awards until his allegations could be thoroughly investigated and he himself declared the winner.

He pushed on to DeKalb and arrived there, the last registration station, at dawn. An inspector took one look at his horse, General Grant, and wired bad news to Chicago. "Rattlesnake Pete, the fifth of the cowboys to register here, arrived at 5 o'clock this morning," his telegram advised. "The horse was so badly used up that he may not be allowed to proceed. He claims that Gillespie, Smith and Albright have not been riding square and has entered a protest against the prize being awarded to either of them."

Meanwhile, Jack Hale, the owner of Berry's horse Poison, now threatened the committee with a lawsuit if his horse and rider were not declared the flat-out winners of the race.

Cody was just about worn thin. And yet that afternoon six of the "grizzled and bronzed" riders lined up out outside his Wild West arena. The grandstand seats were filled, the crowd roaring and pounding their feet as Cody came charging in. He pulled up to the center of the two-acre show ring and lifted his hat. He shook back his long gray hair and pointed his famous goatee heavenward. "I am here to introduce the gentlemen who have ridden the great race from Chadron, Nebraska, to Chicago," he shouted above the band music and the grandstand cheers. "They will ride the same horses ridden on their ride of 1,000 miles, so that you can see the condition of the horses after they have ridden this tremendous distance, averaging 73 miles per day. They illustrate that the western horses of America have more endurance than any other horses in the world."

At the drop of a white flag, Berry rode Poison through the north gate. Albright and Gillespie followed him in, racing toward Cody's uplifted arms. Smith, George Jones, and Doc Middleton roared in next. "Never felt better in my life," Doc teased the crowd. "Weigh as much as I did when I left Chadron."

They thundered into the ring on a final spree of high cowboy gusto, bursting with Western daring, all to the delight of the crowds come to see a real Wild West roundup. One after another they bowed their heads and steadied their horses. "It is the first time they have been in public," Cody said, apologizing in jest for the restless horses. "They are a little shy." But none, he said, was marked by spur or whip, and that drew polite applause from the Minneapolis Humane Society officials sitting nearby. Cody singled out Gillespie above the others. "Old Joe is old," he said. "But he is still in it. American men as well as horses can ride a thousand miles."

At the show's evening performance, after another tour of honor for the cowboy race riders, Cody announced that two more horsemen were due into Chicago, including Rattlesnake Pete. "They are still to arrive," said Buffalo Bill. "They are expected this evening or tonight. When they arrive the decision will be given as to the winner of this great race."

Dawn came on Thursday, but it brought no immediate answers. Rattlesnake Pete at last lumbered in that morning, and in the afternoon the race committee met yet again, this time in a small room under a staircase near the Illinois Central tracks, away from the pressing crowds.

Cody brought along Major Burke. Hale sat in as well, along with some of the other horse owners. For two hours they hashed over the complaints and heard the threats of legal action and the allegations of shipped horses and cowboys snoozing in buggies. They debated the race rules and conferred again with the Humane Society representatives. Fontaine and Tatro discussed their preliminary findings. "The race has been accomplished in every way satisfactory to the Humane Society," they concluded. They cited the horses' stamina as nothing short of "wonderful" and commended the cowboys for not overworking them.

Tatro added a mea culpa: "It started in foolishness and was foolish business all through," he said of the journey from Chadron to Chicago. "But it has been an educator of the people, showing them that the so-called cowboys are not a set of horned animals, all wild brutal men, and that the Humane Society discovered it was wrong in supposing that the riders would treat their animals badly." The race had ended, he said, as "a big success in every way."

When an attempt was made to formally disqualify Berry, Hale tossed down his receipt for the entry fee and read them the printed rules of the race: "This race shall be open to the world. No horses barred." It said nothing about excluding railroad men who helped draw the race route. Hale argued that the map had been published in two newspapers two days before the race anyway. Berry, Hale insisted, "had ridden square."

The committee members debated and adjourned for a while and then argued some more a little later, this time in Cody's dining tent. He sought some kind of compromise. Others suggested a pool to divide the money among the riders. Eventually they strode out of the tent and announced at the gates of the Wild West show that they had reached an awkward and confusing settlement, but one that might stick. It was just going to have to do.

Berry was declared the winner of the race, and he took home $175 from Cody's purse plus the fancy Montgomery Ward saddle. He received none of the $1,000 prize money from the Chadron race committee, though. While overall he won less cash, who could deny he

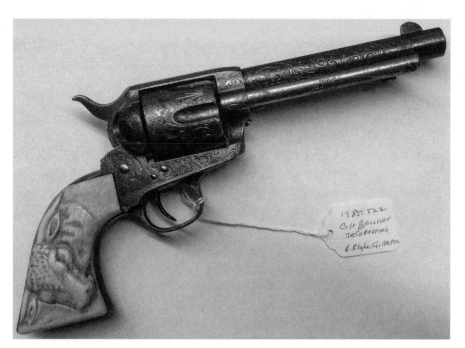

The biggest prize of all: the golden Colt revolver. It was fired to start the Great Cowboy Race, and Buffalo Bill himself awarded it at the finish line. (Dawes County Historical Museum)

was the first to Chicago? His official time was clocked in at thirteen days, fifteen hours, and fifty minutes.

Gillespie said he was fine with that arrangement: "He beat the race." Old Joe was awarded the largest share of the money because Berry had prior knowledge of the route and Albright had shipped his horses. Gillespie won $200 of the $1,000 in prize money from the race committee, plus $50 of the $500 that Cody separately had pledged.

Six others, including Rattlesnake Pete, took a slice of the remaining $800 in prize money and the $275 remaining from Cody's allotment. Middleton, Albright, and Campbell each were awarded the smallest amounts: $75 in prize money and $25 from Cody's share. In the end, everyone pocketed something, except Little Davy Douglas, who had dropped out of the race long ago.

There was one presentation left, nearly forgotten in all the ruckus over cash prizes, cheating cowboys, and a railroad ringer. Cody stepped up to Gillespie and placed the golden Colt revolver in Old Joe's hand. The money was fleeting, but that firearm was the grandest prize of all. Gillespie rode home with it.

The Agony Is Over | 13

"The agony is over, and we are glad of it," harrumphed the *Chadron Citizen*'s editors after six months of planning, two weeks of racing, and several days of grueling indecision that had ended with John Berry, the noncowboy, declared as winner of the Great Cowboy Race.

"What is the West good for anyway?" the editorial grumbled. "We pride ourselves on our cowboys with the long terrifying names, and they were a part of our very assets. And yet a man with a name which is almost as tenderfoot and respectable as any which serves as a sign for a shoe store in Rome, New York, has everlastingly walloped us at our own game. Our western heads are bowed in shame."

So the civic leaders of Chadron did what any spunky town far out on the High Plains would do: they proposed another cowboy race.

While the Chicago results were still under debate, a letter had arrived in Chadron from Cheyenne, Wyoming. It was signed by Emma Hutchinson, the Denver cowgirl born in a barn and now a champion rider. She had first wanted to ride against the men this June, but her backers had bailed out before she could reach Chadron. Now she pledged to ride alone from Chadron to Chicago and beat Berry's time. To many in Chadron and across the West, a genuine horsewoman in a saddle was more of a hero than a railroad surveyor.

Hutchinson's letter was addressed to race committee secretary Harvey Weir. But Weir was still stuck in Chicago, sorting out the mess over the race money and awards. So the Chadron postman walked over to the courthouse and handed the letter to William Henry Reynolds, the Dawes County court clerk and treasurer and the future Chadron mayor.

"I left Denver last Saturday noon; arrived in Cheyenne Tuesday morning at 10:30; will leave for Chadron next Tuesday," Hutchinson wrote. "I have two dogs with me and my horse looks fine and the dogs are making the trip splendid. I had to lay over here to do some business. I will be in Chadron a week from the day I leave Cheyenne, and then I will ride to Chicago. I have had so much bad luck I am going to let some of the Denver people see what I am made of, and from Chadron I will beat the winner's time in to Chicago."

Reynolds forwarded the letter to Blanche McKenney in Kansas City, Missouri. Another long-distance female rider with her own Wild West show, McKenney had been reading about the Great Cowboy Race in the daily papers; she was following it closely. She had been trying to get word to Hutchinson to suggest that the two of them race for a $1,000 purse. But her idea was a short race, maybe just a mile long, or at the most twenty miles around a local track.

With Hutchinson already riding to Chadron, Reynolds thought he might be able to raise money for a wager and put something together for the two cowgirls, if Chadron and the American public had not already had their fill of cowboy stunts.

Hutchinson arrived in Chadron in the middle of July. She brought her two dogs, her cowboy hat, and her bifurcated skirt. She decided to rest a spell, soon extending it to a week while she ventured around town mulling McKenney's challenge. Some in town suspected that her supporters might be getting cold feet again.

"I shall start just as soon as I complete arrangements," Hutchinson said to those who asked, especially to those hoping for another cowboy race. "But I can't tell you now who my backers are or the details of my arrangements. I have a challenge from Blanche McKenney of Kansas City to contest with her for any amount of money from $500 to $1,000. Or more. But she is in position to obtain extra fine horses, and of course I'll not accept her challenge as it stands now."

Hutchinson countered with her own proposal. She suggested she and McKenney choose horses "from a bunch" corralled in the Chadron area and race them right there. Then, she said, "I will accept her challenge." McKenney said no, however, and the deal fell through. So Hutchinson swung up on her Denver horse and rode home. That was about the last anyone in Chadron ever heard from her.

In Chicago, the press was wasting no time evaluating the thousand-mile trek from Chadron, and editorial writers were quick to deride the Great Cowboy Race as more a sprint for money than any legitimate Western triumph. "It was supposed that the race would be an honest trial of the endurance of men and horses," carped Chicago's *Inter Ocean*. "It proves to have been a tricky scramble for lucre."

The newspaper complained that James "Rattlesnake Pete" Stephens had drank his share of both whiskey and the prescription medicine that he picked up for his ailing horse General Grant along the race route. It claimed he even had shared some of the whiskey with the horse, thinking that it might give General Grant an extra kick and hurry them toward the finish line. But, noted the paper, Rattlesnake Pete "would have fared better had he refrained from the cup that cheers and inebriates."

Was there a larger lesson to be learned from the Great Cowboy Race? If so, it was not only about money or a gun or animal cruelty. It was not about riders sneaking their horses onto train cars or cowboys foolishly riding a circus mule. Rather, it was something at the heart of what had transpired in June 1893 between a small Western town all alone near the Badlands and the glimmer and glory of the bright lights of the Chicago World's Fair.

"It is true that bronchos and cowboys can endure great hardships," reflected the *Inter Ocean*. "But we did not need to learn it again. The narratives of a hundred forced marches with General Crook, a thousand journeys across the Plains, myriads of perilous adventures on the frontiers had taught us this long ago."

The paper, like much of the press, judged Buffalo Bill Cody the overall winner—and loser—of the cowboy race. The contest had helped boost his Wild West grandstand attendance records. But for someone of his stature in what was left of the West, the gimmick seemed uncalled for: "His show is marvelous enough without the addition of one or two broken down bronchos and a few tricky riders."

On July 1, the Humane Society officials issued their final report, and they were magnanimous. Signed by John Shortall, head of the national and Illinois groups, the report thanked Fontaine and Tatro for inspecting the horses at registration stations and Agent Oscar Little for helping to keep the riders honest. The officials were grateful to the governors of Iowa and Illinois for threatening arrests. And they commended the cowboys for "their fair play and obedience to the law."

They said Buffalo Bill Cody would remain an "officer in good standing" of the humane societies. "Finally," Shortall wrote in summing up, "the nation is to be congratulated upon so universal an expression of execration of such cruelty as was promised at the beginning of this madcap, foolish proposition of a 1,000-mile race in mid-June over our hot prairies." Although the race offered not "the least value" to society, it nevertheless had been run with distinction.

Race committee secretary Weir, back in Chadron, returned the compliments. "You cannot speak too highly of Tatro and Fontaine," he told reporters. "They advised the boys and cautioned them and gave them several warnings, which were heeded, for the boys knew they were for their own good.... It was wrong in supposing the riders would treat their animals badly. I consider the race a big success in every way."

In Chicago, Cody dove back into his show program, preparing to make the second part of his season so spectacular that it would thrill even larger crowds before the Wild West and the World's Columbian Exposition shut down in the fall. He also sent word back with Weir for his old friend Billy "the Bear" Iaeger in Chadron, the cowboy race committee member who years ago had lost his feet and his fingers to a Wyoming snowstorm. Cody wanted "Billy's measure at once" on how the race turned out, and in return he would "send him the finest pair of artificial legs that money can buy." Commented the local *Dawes County Journal* in Chadron: "The only big winner in the cowboy race was city clerk Iaeger."

Few of the cowboys stuck around the big city; most were restless to move on. Joe Campbell, a tailender in the race, however, accepted a $60-a-month salary to work a while for Buffalo Bill.

Emmett Albright also had a slow start getting out of Chicago. The day before the Fourth of July, he rushed into the police station on Harrison Street, forgetting his summer jacket and hollering in a frenzy that his horse Outlaw, the one he had ridden to Chicago, had been stolen. He had stabled the horse in Buffalo Bill's barn near the show grounds on Sixty-third Street before it went missing.

Other cowboys headed out of town, some back to Chadron, others riding deeper into the Old West. John Berry popped in and out

Posing at the finish line on Buffalo Bill's show grounds are (*left to right*) Joe Gillespie, Charley Smith, George "Stub" Jones, James "Rattlesnake Pete" Stephens, Emmett Albright, and Joe Campbell. (Dawes County Historical Museum)

of Chadron, but he said precious little. Always a quiet man, he was asked if he thought the race had turned out well. "Yes," he muttered, "a success outside of the frauds that were practiced." The man who was first to Chicago said no more.

Doc Middleton came home to Chadron with a bad cold. But he had been entranced with Chicago, and once back on his feet he talked a lot about staging his own Wild West show. He planned to start out in central Iowa and then dip south, hunting up venues in ballparks and fairgrounds. He rode up to Pine Ridge and interviewed some reservation Sioux, announcing first that he had twenty-five people ready to sign, then fifty-five, plus nine or ten head of "genuine buffalo." He also wanted to hire some Army soldiers and cowboys. He basically was following Buffalo Bill's model. He planned a re-creation of Wounded Knee and an attack on the Deadwood stagecoach. His biggest stars would be Thomas C. Clayton, better known as "Jerky Bill," a deadeye rifle shot who could ride any wild bucking horse and "stick to the saddle like a shadow at noon," and "Opportunity Hank" (real name Henry Atkins), an old-time Chadron area frontiersman, card shark, and all-around "fighting man."

His plans were ambitious, and Middleton did manage a few shows in a handful of small venues. But he never came close to rivaling the great Buffalo Bill. So Doc talked next to Joe Gillespie about the two of them racing each other in daily romps around a track in Chicago and getting their hands on some tourist money. That idea did not pan out either.

Gillespie had other problems. One was the ribbing he took from those unhappy he had not been declared the out-and-out first-place winner. "Lots of our old friends were disappointed that you were not first in the cow-boy race," his older brother William Moore Gillespie wrote to him. "But they said they knew you could have done better if you had tried and had the same chance as Berry did."

Before Old Joe left Chicago, he temporarily lost his prized Colt revolver. Around the middle of July, it turned up in a Chicago pawnshop, and one of Buffalo Bill's stable boys, Edward Crespon, was arrested. Crespon was charged with stealing and pawning the trophy and was fined $25. Gillespie had his pistol back, and he rode back to Nebraska with it safely locked up in his saddlebag.

For a time after the race, it seemed that every kid in America wanted to play cowboy. In Buffalo, New York, two teenagers from New Jersey hiding out in the Nickel Plate Road rail yards were cornered by police. One of the boys, Adolph Stander, was armed with a rifle, some fishing tackle, and a nickel-plated watch. He told the officers that they had run away from their homes in Newark "with the intention of joining the cowboys" who had raced to Buffalo Bill and the Chicago fair. Stander was sent home; the friend, however, escaped.

With the race over, Chadron, in contrast, grew weary of cowboys. A pair of new ones showed up shortly after the race, and they were hauled into police court on drunk and disorderly charges. They were found guilty and fined $3 each. They had settled into one of the old abandoned, burned-out homesteads near town, and they threatened to "blow the brains out of anyone who disturbed them." A night watchman and his sidekick grabbed their guns and clobbered them over the head with a cane. It was that easy now to subdue a rowdy cowboy.

Buffalo Bill's arena in Chicago seemed the only place left for any honest cowboy action. But everyone knew the country was changing and that Cody's lariats and Indian war whoops were essentially playacting. Nobody got hurt; no stagecoach was robbed; no Indian warriors scalped anyone. And Buffalo Bill never missed a shot. His Wild West had become a caricature of the real Old West. America's future now lay just past Cody's gate, inside the pantheons of the Chicago fair.

Doc Middleton, the "reformed" outlaw, closed out his life in 1913 in Douglas, Wyoming, twenty years after he had raced to Chicago. His attempts at going straight and cleaning up his image never really succeeded. In the end, he was arrested for selling rotten liquor and promoting a knife fight in his saloon, which locals called "a blind pig." That was Western slang for a bar that sold bottles under the counter.

Doc was fined $150 and court costs of just under $50, but when the old outlaw was unable to scrape up the money, they tucked him away inside the county jail. When he came down with an acute bacterial infection and pneumonia to boot, they moved him to the "pest house," a quarantined facility for the unwanted. It was a small building with just two spare rooms on a hill near the town cemetery. The rooms were not lit, and the watchman on his rounds had to swing a kerosene lamp to peer inside and make sure Middleton had not escaped from yet another jail. But Doc's eyes were nearly swollen shut from the erysipelas that left his face and legs splotched with red patches; his head burned with fever, and he could hardly see a thing.

One of his sons visited, and Doc hugged his boy and "wept like a child." He was about sixty-three years old, but no one was sure. His long, scraggly beard had been trimmed off long ago, his mustache had turned ashen white, his will had wasted away. He died in the pest house, and the county paid to bury him in an unmarked grave.

John Berry died the same year that Middleton did. He had ended up in Wyoming, too, and took up ranching with his wife, Winifred, along Skull Creek in the northeastern part of the state, outside the small town of Newcastle. The Berry ranch home in Wyoming had once been a lively, thriving affair. But that all gradually changed. "It was an old house, just an old two-story house, with a kind of high-pitched roof, shingled, like an ordinary homestead house," recalled his nephew David Howell. Berry's niece Doris Bowker Bennett would walk by the house as a girl, and even then the old place seemed empty and crumbling apart. "The ranch was a few miles down the creek from ours," she wrote in her memoirs in 1976. "I recall the house standing facing the road; the shell of it stands there today, its unpainted wood preserved by sun and wind."

For a while, Berry dressed in suits and ties and became a town debater. Never a cowboy and no longer a railroad surveyor, once a man of few words, he now debated a wide range of current events on the stage in the Newcastle public library, including the passing of the American West. One night he finished his argument on the question of who had been treated worse by the white man in America: the African slave or the native Indian? Berry spoke on behalf of the Indian. When he was done, he returned to his wooden chair and then sank to the floor. They carried him to a nearby sofa, just as they had done twenty years earlier in Cody's tent, and there he died.

After the Great Cowboy Race, Old Joe Gillespie loaded his family into a buckboard and wagon. They headed out of the Chadron area and turned south toward Indian Territory, which later became Oklahoma. He brought the fancy new Colt revolver and his beloved horse, Billy Schafer. This would be another long-distance journey: seven hundred miles in fifty days, August through October 1899. They treated Billy Schafer like one of the family, and they buried the horse next to what is now an Oklahoma asphalt highway.

"Well," Gillespie's wife, Anna, wrote in her diary upon leaving the Chadron area. "I feel as if I had said goodbye to old Dawes County with the debts and discouragement, its hot winds, droughts, and hard times generally, and intend to begin a new life."

In the new century, Joe Gillespie would settle for a livery stable, a blacksmith shop, and a deputy sheriff's badge. For a time he also farmed and raised livestock. Nearly up to the end, the old cowboy was still breaking horses and hunting coyotes with his riding quirt. He died forty years after the cowboy race, in 1933, a week shy of turning eighty-four. The Old West gradually vanished, but Old Joe never surrendered his cowboy spirit.

James Stephens, a.k.a. Rattlesnake Pete, lived the longest of the long riders. He hung around a bit in Chicago and Chadron but could not establish a foothold. So he saddled up General Grant and rode home to his family in central Kansas. He took a job as a town barber above a rowdy saloon and later opened a one-chair shop in his home on North Washington Street in Hutchinson, Kansas. On the wall he hung that large oil painting of himself sitting atop General Grant, arching his shoulders back to make himself look taller. He angrily denied drinking too much or pouring whiskey down his horse's throat during the race. "That's all wrong," he snarled.

Stephens never had children of his own. So when young boys came crashing through his door for a haircut or old men dropped in for a shave, they would settle into his chair and listen in wonder as he described barnstorming across the heart of America, through the Sand Hills and scrub grass and what little was left of the untamed prairie—one thousand miles of tough leather and hard riding to the bright white lights of the Chicago World's Fair. And how he'd worn a crown of seventy-two poisonous rattlesnake tails, and shaken hands with Buffalo Bill.

In his old age, he often drove around town in a big luxury Oldsmobile 98, a small man in a large cowboy hat sinking behind the steering wheel, speeding up and down the city streets like he was off to the races again. He died in 1957, just short of turning ninety. His hometown Kansas newspaper wrote of the last of the cowboys: "James 'Rattlesnake Pete' Stephens has ridden to that Great Range up yonder."

Postscript

"Broncho Charlie" Miller was a small, mustached man who over his long years carried the mail for the Pony Express, starred in Buffalo Bill's Wild West show, and once, in London, raced his horse against a man on a bicycle.

In the summer of 1931, at the age of eighty-one, he set out on one final cross-country Western adventure. He mounted his horse, pushed his long hair back over his stooped shoulders, and with trembling hands steadied his hat and rolled out of New York City. He was headed back west to deliver a packet of New York mail to San Francisco on his five-year-old brown mount named Polestar, "one of the finest horses I ever seen," he later wrote.

He left Manhattan with a police escort, and it took nearly a year before the clip-clop of Polestar's hooves was heard on the far shores. He passed the big steel towns in Pennsylvania, the St. Louis gateway, and the bulging Kansas City stockyards. "The hardest part of the whole trip was goin' through them big cities, with Polestar shyin' and buckin' and everybody starin' at me like they thought sure the circus had come to town," Charlie wrote. Worse, he recalled, was that "there was plenty of gasoline stations and automobile repair places scattered all along the route, but it was like findin' hen's teeth to find a blacksmith!"

Charlie and Polestar turned left for the warmer southern route. They stopped in Oklahoma to say howdy to old "Pawnee Bill" Lillie, relaxing on his Blue Hawk Peak ranch veranda, minding his Scottish shorthorn cattle, and recalling his own Wild West show of years gone by. "I had a mighty fine time there," remembered Charlie. "It was like the first downright breath of home and the hearty ways of the Old West."

In Texas, he sat down to Christmas dinner at a small cow camp: "sourdough bread and beans and good black coffee!" Through El Paso and Tucson and the Southern California desert, Charlie and Polestar rode on. "My horse's feet and legs was cut and bleedin' from the bitin' sand, and the right side of my face was just plain raw. That was the only time on the whole trip that Polestar wavered."

In Los Angeles, the clop of the horse's hooves echoed off the downtown streets. Charlie tipped his hat and in his teeth clenched Polestar's reins, getting the horse to kick a bit at all the car horns and stop the noonday traffic. Then it was up the Grapevine road and through the tassel-high wheat fields of California's Inland Valley to the Golden Gate and the blue waters of the Pacific.

Charlie promptly went looking for the mayor of San Francisco. He had a letter for him from the mayor of New York. To the crowd outside, he announced that he was none other than the famous Broncho Charlie Miller, once the "top man" for Buffalo Bill. Dirty and worn down from his long ride, he also was loud, boisterous, and undeniably eccentric, a relic of the Old West.

He soon went broke hanging around San Francisco and was forced to sell Polestar. All he netted was $75. He thought about trying to parachute on horseback from an airplane. He thought about making another cross-country trip, "in one of these here flyin' gasoline buggies." But he could not afford a car. And no pilot was going to fly any horse or crazy cowboy. Eventually he grew tired of the whole big city. "It costs too much for a plain broncho buster like me," he said. But there was no place left for him out on the Plains, either; they had long ago been fenced, farmed, plowed up, and paved over. "So," sighed tired old Broncho Charlie Miller, "I just moseyed along back East on the train."

Sources

1. The West of Our Imagination

During the summer of 1893, much of the nation was swept up in the excitement of the Great Cowboy Race, stretching from Second Street in Chadron, Nebraska, to Buffalo Bill's Wild West show next to the World's Columbian Exposition in Chicago. News of the nine riders and their horses flashed across the telegraph wires, landed on the front pages of the country's newspapers, and traveled across the thousand-mile route by anxious word of mouth. But like much of the Old West, these two weeks of racing across Nebraska, Iowa, and Illinois soon galloped into history. Over time, this remarkable feat of American endurance was lost in a twentieth century of unlimited progress and spectacular innovation.

Yet depictions of the cowboy race have resurfaced from time to time in magazine and journal articles, pamphlets, and other publications. It was from these sometimes obscure sources that I first began to learn of those fourteen days and nights of remarkable cowboy stamina.

Some of the best accounts are William J. Deahl Jr., "The Chadron–Chicago 1,000-Mile Cowboy Race," *Nebraska History* (Summer 1972): 166–93; *The Chadron to Chicago Cowboy Horse Race of 1893*, a forty-four-page booklet compiled by Rip Radcliffe to commemorate the Chadron Centennial (Chadron, NE: B & B Printing, 1984); Harry T. Sly, "The 1000 Mile Horse Race from Chadron to Chicago," a seven-page, self-published, undated essay on file at the Dawes County Historical Museum in Chadron; Harold Hutton, *Doc Middleton: Life and Legends of the Notorious Plains Outlaw* (Chicago: Swallow Press, 1974), chap. 15; "The Great 1,000-Mile Race from Chadron to Chicago!" *Sports Illustrated*, September 3, 1962; Walter Livingston, "Riders East," *Adventure Magazine* (December 1941): 65–73; "The Cowboy Race," *Harper's Weekly*, July 1, 1893, 633; R. C. House, "The Great Cowboy Race of 1893: Small-Town Nebraskans Tactfully Counter National Humane Societies' Intense Opposition," *Tombstone (AZ) Epitaph*, no. 11 (November 2001): 1; *Chicago Inter Ocean*, July 3, 1893, 1; and G. E. Lemmon, "Developing the West," a series of columns published in the *Belle Fourche (SD) Bee* in 1940 and 1941.

Undertaking further research, I discovered a good number of other books that feature the race. Among them are Walter Havighurst, *Annie Oakley of the Wild West* (New York: Macmillan, 1954), 174–79; Mari Sandoz, *The Cattlemen: From the Rio Grande across the Far Marias* (New York: Hastings House, 1958), 416–17; Ed Lemmon,

Boss Cowman: The Recollections of Ed Lemmon, 1857–1946, ed. Nellie Snyder Yost (Lincoln: University of Nebraska Press, 1974), 191–94; Clifford P. Westermeier, *Trailing the Cowboy: His Life and Lore as Told by Frontier Journalists* (Caldwell, ID: Caxton Printers, 1955), 355–58; Frazier Hunt and Robert Hunt, *Horses and Heroes: The Story of the Horse in America for 450 Years* (New York: Charles Scribner's Sons, 1949), 191–95; Addison Erwin Sheldon, *Nebraska Old and New* (Lincoln: University Publishing, 1937), 371–73; *Chadron Centennial History, 1885–1985* (Chadron, NE: Chadron Narrative History Project Committee, 1985), 32–33; Charles L. Curtis, *Horses and Riders: True Tales of the Old West*, vol. 7 (Carson City, NV: Pioneer Press, 1998), 60–61; Richard J. Walsh, *The Making of Buffalo Bill: A Study in Heroics* (Indianapolis: Bobbs-Merrill, 1928), 302–3; Don Russell, *The Lives and Legends of Buffalo Bill* (Norman: University of Oklahoma Press, 1961), 375–76; Robert A. Carter, *Buffalo Bill Cody: The Man behind the Legend* (New York: John Wiley, 2000), 372–74; and Henry Blackman Sell and Victor Weybright, *Buffalo Bill and the Wild West* (New York: New American Library, 1959), 233–37.

Additional journal and magazine articles were quite helpful. They include Laura Trowbridge, "The Fabulous Cowboy Race," *The West* (April 1968): 16–17, 48–50; Shelley R. Frear, "The 1893 Chadron to Chicago Cowboy Horse Race," *Old West* (Spring 1998): 12–17; Otto Wolfgang, "1,000 Mile Race," *Quarter Horse Journal* (1965): 90–92, 192; Walter Schmidt, "History's Most Grueling Test of Horse and Rider," *Challenge* (November 1955): 31–33, 70–76; "The Maddest Horse Race Ever," *Motor Club News* (March–April 1966): 3; "The 1,000 Mile Horse Race," *Outdoor Nebraskaland* (July 1986): 14–17, 54; Bernard Schuessler, "The Great Chadron to Chicago Horse Race," *Sunday World-Herald Magazine of the Midlands*, October 15, 1972; Raymond Schuessler, "The Great Horse Race," *Boys' Life* (May 1970): 66; and Robert Beasley, "The 1,000-Mile Race: A Newspaper's Publicity Gimmick Turned Out to Be the Longest and Toughest Horse Race Ever, from Chadron, Nebraska to Chicago," *Great West* (October 1968): 30–33.

For historical accounts by newspapers, see Elisabeth Hughes, "47 Years Ago a Railroad-Man-on-a-Horse Won Great Chadron-to-Chicago Classic," *Omaha World-Herald*, June 22, 1940; "Famous Thousand-Mile Horse Race Brought Nation-Wide Attention for City of Chadron," *Chadron (NE) Record*, September 4, 1967, 1; Bev Pechan, "The Chadron to Chicago Horse Race," *Rapid City Journal*, September 29, 2009; and M. Timothy Nolting, "Celebrating the Anniversary of the Chadron to Chicago Cowboy Race," *Chadron Record*, June 26, 2013.

Finally, this gem provided a surprising amount of additional detail: *The 1,000 Mile Chadron to Chicago Horse Race*, Diamond Jubilee official historical souvenir booklet (Chadron, NE, 1960).

The speech from Red Cloud was recorded by Charles W. Allen, a journalist from Chadron who knew the great Sioux chief quite well. It can be found in his book *From Fort Laramie to Wounded Knee: In the West That Was* (Lincoln: University of Nebraska Press, 1997), 143.

Army Captain Charles King's statement is quoted in Robert G. Carter, *On the Border with Mackenzie, or Winning West Texas from the Comanches* (Austin: Texas State Historical Association, 2001), 46–47, as well as in Robert M. Utley, *Frontier Regulars: The United States Army and the Indian, 1866–1891* (New York: Macmillan, 1973), ix.

2. The Harsh Land

The tragedy of the Haumann sisters is told in Sheldon, *Nebraska Old and New*, 347–51. Janice Hodges of Thedford, Nebraska, Retta's great-niece, also helped fill in more of the family history.

For more on the Sand Hills, see C. F. Keech and Ray Bentall, "Dunes on the Plains: The Sand Hills Region of Nebraska," a resource report published by the Nebraska Conservation and Survey Division, Lincoln, February 1971; and Solomon D. Butcher, *Pioneer History of Custer County, Nebraska* (Denver: Sage Books, 1965), 399–403. See also Kathryne L. Lichty, "A History of the Settlement of the Nebraska Sandhills," master's thesis, University of Wyoming, 1960.

Mari Sandoz was Nebraska's most celebrated pioneer historian; her father, Jules, helped map and settle the virgin grasslands. Of her many works, her most intimate is the biography of her father, *Old Jules: Portrait of a Pioneer* (New York: MJF Books, 1963). A good summary of her own life and other works can be found in Virginia Faulkner, *Roundup: A Nebraska Reader* (Lincoln: University of Nebraska Press, 1957), 382–86.

In "Nebraska," a feature Sandoz wrote for *Holiday* magazine in May 1956, she relived much of the state's history, seen through her own pioneer eyes as a young woman coming of age in the state's northwestern region. Here she tells of the "gradual climb toward the Continental Divide," of how an October afternoon "can be so lovely it stops the heart," and how she helped map out territory on the floor of her family's dusty cabin. She recalls, too, the old Sioux who sat by their front door, "visiting over his pipe," the Pawnee rainmaker, and the crush of white immigrants. As a young girl, she met Buffalo Bill Cody and thought him "the showiest showman of all time."

As Sandoz wrote the state's early history, Willa Cather captured it in literature. Raised in Red Cloud, on the state's southern end, she too lived a young girl's life on the open range. Her novels, particularly *My Ántonia* and *O Pioneers!*, are as rich as the state's topsoil. Her love of the land is recounted in Faulkner, *Roundup*, 124–30. Cather herself, in her essay "Nebraska: The End of the First Cycle," *Nation*, September 5, 1923, sadly conceded that the "splendid story of the pioneers is finished." More of her remembrances are found in Mildred R. Bennett, "Willa Cather and the Prairie," *Nebraska History* (Summer 1975): 231–35; and in the introduction by Elaine Showalter to *O Pioneers!* (New York: Everyman's Library, 2011), vii–xvii.

Daniel Webster's dismissal of the West is cited in Tristram P. Coffin, "The Cowboy and the Myth," *Western Folklore* (October 1953): 79.

For President Lincoln and the Homestead Act, see Paul W. Gates, "The Homestead Act," in *An American Primer*, ed. Daniel J. Boorstin (Chicago: University of Chicago Press, 1966), 386–92.

The pioneers' guide warning immigrants to "make up your mind to rough it" comes from "Tips for Stage Riders," printed by the *Omaha Herald* throughout much of 1877. It also is cited in Huston Horn, *The Pioneers* (New York: Time-Life Books, 1974), 195.

George Washington Franklin's diary was excerpted in the *Journal of the West* (January 1977): 37–39.

Thomas Jefferson Huntzinger appears in David J. Wishart, *The Last Days of the Rainbelt* (Lincoln: University of Nebraska Press, 2013), 51, 68, 70, 79, 82, 100.

Wallace Hoze Wilcock also can be found in Wishart, *Last Days of the Rainbelt*, 51–52, 55, 87, 97.

The value of newspaper sheets as winter blankets is mentioned in *American Agriculturist* (February 1862): 53.

For even more health cures and other medical miracles, see *A Treasury of Nebraska Pioneer Folklore*, comp. Roger L. Welsch (Lincoln: University of Nebraska Press, 1984), 356–59.

The Antelope County growth figures are from Everett Dick, *The Sod-House Frontier, 1854–1890* (Lincoln: Johnsen Publishing, 1954), 440.

The emergence of Haigler is reported in Wishart, *Last Days of the Rainbelt*, 60–61.

George Edwin Bushnell's "Trip across the Plains in 1864" is available online at http://freepages.genealogy.rootsweb.ancestry.com/~steelquist/GeoBushnell.html.

Cora A. Beels of Norfolk, Nebraska, was interviewed on August 27, 1941, by Wolfgang Schmidt for the *Pioneer Life in Nebraska* pamphlets, comp. by the workers of the WPA Writers' Program of the Works Progress Administration for the state of Nebraska.

Lucy Alice Ide's diary was memorialized as "In a Prairie Schooner, 1878," *Washington Historical Quarterly* (July 1927): 191–98.

Emily Towell's journey west was recorded in her diaries and published in Kenneth L. Holmes, ed., *Covered Wagon Women: Diaries and Letters from the Western Trails, 1875–1883* (Lincoln: University of Nebraska Press, 1991), 197–219.

Charles Moreau Harger's essay "Phases of Western Life" ran in *Outlook* magazine, January 6, 1894, 18–20. He also wrote "Cattle Trails of the Prairies," *Scribner's Magazine* (June 1892): 732–42. His work was followed by another *Outlook* essay, G. M. Whicher, "Phases of Western Life," January 13, 1894, 63–65, which described the "sameness" of the prairie.

Charles Morgan's story about pioneer women and their use or nonuse of gloves comes from Wishart, *Last Days of the Rainbelt*, 93.

Martha Gilmore Lundy's efforts to establish a town cemetery in Kit Carson County, Colorado, are also recounted in Wishart, *Last Days of the Rainbelt*, 105.

In 1929, Jules Haumont presented his "old settler" talk to the Daughters of the American Revolution at Broken Bow, Nebraska. It was later published as "Pioneer Years in Custer County," *Nebraska History* (October–December 1932): 223–37.

Henry H. Raymond's diary is preserved in the stacks at the Kansas Historical Society in Topeka. It also was excerpted in "Diary of a Buffalo Hunter," ed. Joseph W. Snell, *Kansas Historical Quarterly* (Winter 1965): 345–95.

The surprise encounter between Matilda Peterson, No-Flesh, and her piping-hot doughnuts has been told widely and with great relish, including in Everett Dick, *Tales of the Frontier: From Lewis and Clark to the Last Roundup* (Lincoln: University of Nebraska Press, 1971), 205–6; and in Horn, *Pioneers*, 219.

The plagues of grasshoppers and the frontier fight to contain them, including the stories of Herman Westermann and the Finch family, can be found in Alexander H. Wagner, "Grasshoppered," *Nebraska History* (Winter 2008): 154–67.

The *Wichita City Eagle* article, dated August 13, 1874, was cited in Horn, *Pioneers*, 216.

For more on the grasshopper menace, see "The Plains: Some Press Bulletins," Agricultural Experiment Station of the Colorado Agricultural College, Fort Collins, January 1908, 17–18; *Compendium of History, Reminiscence, and Biography of Western Nebraska* (Chicago: Alden Publishing, 1912), 92–93; and Dick, *Sod-House Frontier*, 202–3.

The blizzard of 1888 that so ravaged swaths of the frozen tundra covering Nebraska, Iowa, and Minnesota, as well as the Dakota Territory, is perhaps best told by David Laskin, *The Children's Blizzard* (New York: HarperCollins, 2004). Other accounts were gleaned from Faulkner, *Roundup*, 263–68; Bayard H. Paine, *Pioneers, Indians and Buffaloes* (Curtis, NE: Curtis Enterprise, 1935), 47; and W. H. O'Gara, comp., *In All Its Fury: A History of the Blizzard of Jan. 12, 1888* (Lincoln: January 12, 1888, Blizzard Club), 1947.

Robert Louis Stevenson's thoughts about the difficult West were offered in his 1879 article "The Plains of Nebraska" and were later included in his travel memoir *Across the Plains* (London: Chatto & Windus, 1892). They were further excerpted in Faulkner, *Roundup*, 401–3.

Howard Ruede's diary and correspondence were collected in *Sod-House Days: Letters from a Kansas Homesteader, 1877–78* (1937; Lawrence: University of Kansas Press, 1983). They also can be found in Martin Ridge and Ray Allen Billington, eds., *America's Frontier Story: A Documentary History of Western Expansion* (New York: Holt, Rinehart and Winston, 1969), 624–30.

George Washington Franklin's diary was, as noted earlier, excerpted in the *Journal of the West* (January 1977): 37–39.

The correspondence of Emma Robertson of North Bend, Nebraska, was published in "The Ranch Letters of Emma Robertson, 1891–1892," *Nebraska History* (Summer 1975): 221–29.

Frank H. Spearman's essay "The Great American Desert" appears in *Harper's New Monthly Magazine* (July 1888): 232–45.

The interview with Frank Grady of Raymond, Nebraska, was conducted on October 3, 1941, by J. Willis Kratzer for the *Pioneer Life in Nebraska* pamphlets, comp. by the Workers of the WPA Writers' Program of the Works Progress Administration for the state of Nebraska.

For more on the struggles of opening the West, see Cass G. Barns, *The Sod House* (Lincoln: University of Nebraska Press, 1970); Seth K. Humphrey, *Following the Prairie Frontier* (Minneapolis: University of Minnesota Press, 1931); Dee Brown, *Wondrous Times on the Frontier* (Little Rock, AR: August House, 1991); Everett Dick, *Vanguard of the Frontier* (Lincoln: University of Nebraska Press, 1941); Donald R. Hickey, Susan A. Wunder, and John R. Wunder, *Nebraska Moments* (Lincoln:

University of Nebraska Press, 2007); Charles Dudley Warner, "Studies of the Great West," *Harper's New Monthly Magazine* (March 1888): 556–68; and David Lowenthal, "The Pioneer Landscape: An American Dream," *Great Plains Quarterly* (Winter 1982): 5–19.

3. The Vanishing Cowboy West

Cora A. Beels shared her hair-raising stories of cowboy shoot-'em-ups in tiny Norfolk, Nebraska, in her August 27, 1941, interview with Wolfgang Schmidt for the *Pioneer Life in Nebraska* pamphlets.

The March 8, 1879, *Oakdale Pen and Plow* reported the cowboy violence in that small Nebraska town.

The troubles in the little Kansas towns of Winfield and Chanute are mentioned in Dick, *Sod-House Frontier*, 392–93.

The dark episodes in Kearney, Nebraska, are offered in Maud Marston Burrows, "The Last Cowboy Raid of Kearney," *Nebraska History* (April–June 1938): 126–27.

The Dodge City, Kansas, portrait appears in Joe B. Frantz and Julian Ernest Choate Jr., *The American Cowboy: The Myth and the Reality* (Norman: University of Oklahoma Press, 1955), 93.

Fred Horne's raucous day in court was reported in the *Chicago Tribune*, May 26, 1885.

The devilries of Curly Bill, Russian Bill, and Sandy King were captured in Ben C. Truman, "The Passing of the Cowboy," *Overland Monthly* (November 1902): 464–67.

David Love's memory of the wounded cowboy comes from John McPhee, *Rising from the Plains* (New York: Farrar, Straus and Giroux, 1986), 89–90. It also is cited in Frantz and Choate, *American Cowboy*, 68.

The artist Charles M. Russell's anecdote that cowboys are only "part human" and more of his frontier observations can be found in his memoir, *Trails Plowed Under: Stories of the Old West* (Lincoln, NE: Bison Books, 1996).

The Charley O'Kieffe cowboy memoir was published as *Western Story: The Recollections of Charley O'Kieffe, 1884–1898* (Lincoln: University of Nebraska Press, 1960). See also Welsch, *Treasury of Nebraska Pioneer Folklore*, xv, 307, 312–13.

Marshall W. Fishwick wrote "The Cowboy: America's Contribution to the World's Mythology," *Western Folklore* (April 1952): 77–92.

J. T. Botkin's stories were compiled in "Concerning a Day When Cowboys Were Cowboys," part of the *Collections of the Kansas State Historical Society, 1923–1925, Together with Addresses, Memorials and Miscellaneous Papers*, ed. William Elsey Connelley (Topeka: Kansas State Printing Plant, 1925), 493–96.

Cowboy slang was lassoed in Rudolph Umland, "Nebraska Cowboy Talk," *American Speech* (February 1952): 73–75. See also Mark H. Brown and W. R. Felton, *Before Barbed Wire* (New York: Henry Holt, 1956), 126–29; and Charles Wellington Furlong,

Let 'Er Buck: A Story of the Passing of the Old West (New York: Overlook Press, 2007), 235–42.

The best description of the cowboy's lot in life—who he was, what he wore, what he rode—remains Owen Wister, "The Evolution of the Cow-Puncher," *Harper's New Monthly Magazine* (September 1895): 602–16. Also top-notch are Frantz and Choate, *American Cowboy*; E. C. "Teddy Blue" Abbott and Helena Huntington Smith, *We Pointed Them North: Recollections of a Cowpuncher* (Norman: University of Oklahoma Press, 1955); Lon Tinkle and Allen Maxwell, eds., *The Cowboy Reader: The American Cowboy's Life on the Range* (New York: Longmans, Green, 1959); Philip Ashton Rollins, *The Cowboy: An Unconventional History of Civilization on the Old-Time Cattle Range* (Norman: University of Oklahoma Press, 1997); David T. Courtwright, *Violent Land: Single Men and Social Disorder from the Frontier to the Inner City* (Cambridge, MA: Harvard University Press, 1997), 87–103; John Bratt, *Tails of Yesterday* (Lincoln, NE: University Publishing, 1921); James H. Cook, *Fifty Years on the Old Frontier as Cowboy, Hunter, Guide, Scout and Ranchman* (Norman: University of Oklahoma Press, 1980); Solomon D. Butcher, *Pioneer History of Custer County, Nebraska* (Denver: Sage Books, 1965), 154–57, 167–72; Clifford P. Westermeier, *Trailing the Cowboy: His Life and Lore as Told by Frontier Journalists* (Caldwell, ID: Caxton Printers, 1955), 26–37; Jack Potter, *The Trail Drivers of Texas* (Nashville: Cokesbury Press, 1925); Matthew Johnson Herron, "The Passing of the Cowman," *Overland Monthly* (February 1910); Thomas Holmes, "A Cowboy's Life," *Chautauquan* (September 1894): 730–32; and Robert Sturgis, "The Real Cowboy," *Prairie Schooner* (Winter 1932): 30–38.

L. M. Cox was interviewed on November 22, 1937, in San Angelo, Texas, by Elizabeth Doyle as part of the Works Progress Administration's Federal Writers' Project. The session in which he discussed long-distance horse riding was titled "An 1880s Cowboy Speaks for the Record (1937)."

Julian Ralph's article "A Talk with a Cowboy" ran in *Harper's Weekly*, April 16, 1892, 375–76.

More on long-distance rider and rodeo champion Ed Richards can be found in Louis S. Warren, *Buffalo Bill's America: William Cody and the Wild West Show* (New York: Alfred A. Knopf, 2005), 402.

Ed Lemmon's reminiscences were published in *Boss Cowman*.

Cora Beels's quotation is taken from her August 27, 1941, interview with Wolfgang Schmidt for the *Pioneer Life in Nebraska* pamphlets.

Kansas City Mayor William S. Cowherd's speech was reported in the *Kansas City Daily Journal*, June 28, 1893.

The old trail driver's dismay that homesteaders were "the ruin of the country" can be found in Louis Pelzer, *The Cattlemen's Frontier* (Glendale, CA: Arthur Clark, 1936), 190. More on this old pioneer can be found in David Dary, *Cowboy Culture: A Saga of Five Centuries* (Lawrence: University Press of Kansas, 1981), 319.

The story of cowboys looking for work in New York City came from the *New York Sun*; the story was reprinted on May 25, 1893, in the *Kansas City Star*.

Red Cloud's speech at the Cooper Institute in New York was reported by the *New York Times* on June 17, 1870. It merited the lead story on p. 1 that morning. It is also included in George H. Hyde, *Red Cloud's Folk* (Norman: University of Oklahoma Press, 1967), 179–80.

The great chief's Fourth of July speech in Chadron was reported by the *Chadron Democrat*, July 4, 1889. It also is noted in Charles W. Allen, *From Fort Laramie to Wounded Knee: In the West That Was* (Lincoln: University of Nebraska Press, 1997). Addison E. Sheldon, superintendent of the Nebraska State Historical Society, further recorded the speech in *Nebraska History* (January–March 1929): 44.

The story of Red Cloud visiting the reservation post office is related in Allen, *From Fort Laramie to Wounded Knee*. It is further discussed in Charles Wesley Allen and Red Cloud, *Autobiography of Red Cloud: War Leader of the Oglalas* (Helena: Montana Historical Society Press, 1997), 1, 8–12, 196–99. Red Cloud is also discussed in a December 1907 profile by Warren K. Moorehead, "The Passing of Red Cloud," in *Transactions of the Kansas State Historical Society, 1907–1908* (Topeka: State Printing Office, 1908), 295–311.

The scavenger hunts for dried-out buffalo bones are described in M. I. McCreight, *Buffalo Bone Days* (Sykesville, PA: Nupp Printing, 1939); Lemmon, "Developing the West"; and Mari Sandoz, *The Buffalo Hunters: The Story of the Hide Men* (Lincoln: University of Nebraska Press, 1954), 357–58. She also gives figures on the thinning of the herds, 350–52. See further Wayne Gard, *The Great Buffalo Hunt* (New York: Alfred A. Knopf, 1959), 295–308.

George Bird Grinnell's essay "The Last of the Buffalo" was published in *Scribner's Magazine* (September 1892): 267–86.

Colonel McLaughlin's story of the final buffalo hunt is recounted in Lemmon, "Developing the West," 5–6. For more on McLaughlin's experiences with Indian people, see Jeffrey Ostler, "The Last Buffalo Hunt and Beyond: Plains Sioux Economic Strategies in the Early Reservation Period," *Great Plains Quarterly* (Spring 2001): 115–17.

A. N. Ward of Milford, Nebraska, claimed to the *Omaha World-Herald* that he had shot the last buffalo in the state in 1881. The paper published his account in its sports pages on October 2, 1910. In Kansas, a hunter named Wilson Schofield claimed the last buffalo kill in that state in October 1873. His story is documented in Adolph Roenigk, *Pioneer History of Kansas*, a 1933 self-published collection of tales from the frontier days, 98–101.

Edward Creighton's work stringing the telegraph is recounted in Christopher Corbett, *Orphans Preferred* (New York: Broadway Books, 2003), 115–20. Also of interest is Dennis N. Mihelich and James E. Potter, eds., *First Telegraph Line across the Continent: Charles Brown's 1861 Diary* (Lincoln: Nebraska State Historical Society Books, 2011).

Amos Ives Root was a cantankerous sort who had no love for horses, especially once the automobile screeched into town. From his home in Medina, Ohio, he published *Gleanings in Bee Culture*, and he unloaded his disgust for horses in his issue of January 15, 1904.

Professor E. H. Moore read his paper "The Cattle Industry in the United States" to the second annual convention of the National Cattle and Horse Growers Association meeting in St. Louis on November 23, 1885. The address was quoted the next day in the *Cheyenne (WY) Democrat Leader*.

The *San Angelo Enterprise* report was published on June 7, 1886, in the *St. Paul (MN) Daily Globe*.

The General William Tecumseh Sherman and Buffalo Bill Cody correspondence is contained in William F. Cody, *The Wild West in England*, ed. Frank Christianson (Lincoln: University of Nebraska Press, 2012), 130–33.

Buffalo Bill Cody's treatise "Famous Hunting Parties of the Plains" was published in *Cosmopolitan* (June 1894): 131–43.

The film crew working at the Pine Ridge Reservation to dramatize the Wounded Knee massacre was cited in the *Chadron Journal* on October 17, 1913.

The *Topeka Weekly Capital-Commonwealth* ran the column "A Fading Race" on April 25, 1889.

Paul de Rousiers's trip across the West is memorialized in his book *American Life* (Paris: Firmin-Didot, 1892), 187–88.

The *Kansas City Times* article also ran in the *Omaha Daily Bee* on May 30, 1893.

Enthusiasm for the Great Cowboy Race was quoted by riders Doc Middleton and Emmett Albright—juxtaposed with the reality that the West was no longer what it had been just "a few years ago"—in the *Chicago Daily Tribune*, April 13, 1893.

For more on Robert Porter and the Census decision to no longer recognize the frontier, see Gerald D. Nash, "The Census of 1890 and the Closing of the Frontier," *Pacific Northwest Quarterly* (July 1980): 98–100. See also Porter's official report: Department of the Interior, Census Office, *Compendium of the Eleventh Census: 1890* (Washington, DC: Government Printing Office, 1892).

Ray Allen Billington is the premier biographer of Frederick Jackson Turner. His keynote work is *Frederick Jackson Turner: Historian, Scholar, Teacher* (New York: Oxford University Press, 1973). He further highlighted Turner's groundbreaking study in "Frederick Jackson Turner: The Significance of the Frontier in American History," in Boorstin, *American Primer*.

Emerson Hough wrote "The Settlement of the West: A Study in Transportation," which ran in *Century Illustrated Monthly Magazine* (November 1901): 91–107.

Ray Stannard Baker's autobiography, *American Chronicle*, was published in 1945 (New York: Charles Scribner's Sons). His essay "The Western Spirit of Restlessness" was published by *Century Illustrated Monthly Magazine* (July 1908): 467–69.

Doris Bowker Bennett's memories of the fading West and her uncle were included in *A Girl in Wyoming: 1905–1922*, her memoir privately published in 1976. She described the once pristine Western landscape on p. 100 and mentions her uncle, the cowboy racer, on pp. 26–27.

The Cody newspaper interview ran in the *Columbus (OH) Evening Dispatch*, September 4, 1907.

For more on the vanishing Wild West, see Zack T. Sutley, *The Last Frontier* (New York: Macmillan, 1930); Allan Nevins and Henry Steele Commager, *A Short History of the United States* (New York: Modern Library, 1948), esp. chap. 15, "The West Comes of Age," 335–57; Lawrence H. Larsen, *The Urban West at the End of the Frontier* (Lawrence: Regents Press of Kansas, 1978); Richard White, *It's Your Misfortune and None of My Own* (Norman: University of Oklahoma Press, 1991), 613–30; Henry Steele Commager, *The American Mind: An Interpretation of American Thought and Character since the 1880's* (New Haven, CT: Yale University Press, 1950), 41–54; Robert M. Utley, *The Last Days of the Sioux Nation* (New Haven, CT: Yale University Press, 1963); Ralph K. Andrist, *The Long Death: The Last Days of the Plains Indians* (New York: Macmillan, 1964); Emerson Hough, *The Passing of the Frontier: A Chronicle of the Old West* (1921; New York: United States Publishers Association, 1970); D. M. Kelsey, *History of Our Wild West and Stories of Pioneer Life* (Chicago: Thompson and Thomas, 1901), esp. 392–437; and Dan Elbert Clark, *The West in American History* (New York: Thomas Y. Crowell, 1937).

Significant magazine articles on the end of the West include Chauncey Thomas, "The Frontier Is Gone," *Golden Book* (November 1928): 594–96; Will C. Barnes, "The Passing of the Wild Horse," *American Forests* (November 1924): 643–48; William Trowbridge Larned, "The Passing of the Cow-Puncher," *Lippincott's* (August 1895): 267–70; Woodrow Wilson, "The Making of the Nation," *Atlantic* (July 1897): 1–14; Frank Norris, "The Frontier Gone at Last," *World's Work* (February 1902): 1728–31; William R. Lighton, "Where Is the West?" *Outlook*, July 18, 1903, 702–4; Rev. Thomas L. Riggs, "The Last Buffalo Hunt," *Independent*, July 4, 1907, 32–38; Harold Peyton Steger, "Photographing the Cowboy as He Disappears," *World's Work* (January 1909): 1111–23; Bernard DeVoto, "The West: A Plundered Province," *Harper's Monthly* (August 1934): 355–64; Jeffrey Ostler, "The Last Buffalo Hunt and Beyond: Plains Sioux Economic Strategies in the Early Reservation Period," *Great Plains Quarterly* (Spring 2001): 115–30; and John Cloud Jacobs, "Last of the Buffalo," *World's Work* (January 1909): 11098–100.

Also of interest is the opening address by Gurdon W. Wattles, president of the Trans-Mississippi and International Exposition in Omaha, printed by the *Omaha Daily Bee* on June 2, 1898.

4. Buffalo Bill Goes to the Fair

The bible on the adventures and Wild West career of William F. Cody remains Don Russell, *The Lives and Legends of Buffalo Bill* (Norman: University of Oklahoma Press, 1960). Other fine works include Robert A. Carter, *Buffalo Bill Cody: The Man behind the Legend* (New York: John Wiley, 2000); Helen Cody Wetmore, *Buffalo Bill, Last of the Great Scouts: The Life Story of Colonel William F. Cody* (Lincoln: University of Nebraska Press, 1965); *Buffalo Bill and His Wild West Companions*, a work with no author designated (Chicago: Henneberry Company, 1893); John M. Burke, *Buffalo Bill from Prairie to Palace: The Papers of William F. "Buffalo Bill" Cody* (Lincoln: Bison Books, 2012); Joseph G. Rosa and Robin May, *Buffalo Bill and His Wild West: A Pictorial Biography* (Lawrence: University of Kansas Press, 1989); Stella Foote, ed., *Letters from Buffalo Bill*

(El Segundo, CA: Upton and Sons, 1991); Dan Cody Muller, *My Life with Buffalo Bill* (Whitefish, MT: Literary Licensing, 2011); William F. Cody, *The Wild West in England* (Lincoln: University of Nebraska Press, 2012); William F. Cody, *The Life of Hon. William F. Cody, Known as Buffalo Bill* (Lincoln: University of Nebraska Press, 2011); Judy Alter, *Wild West Shows* (New York: Franklin Watts, 1997); James Monaghan, "The Stage Career of Buffalo Bill," *Journal of the Illinois State Historical Society* (December 1938): 411–22; Sandra K. Sagala, "Buffalo Bill v. Doc Carver: The Battle over the Wild West," *Nebraska History* (March 2004): 2–15; Nate Salsbury, "The Origin of the Wild West Show," *Colorado* (July 1955): 204–14; William S. E. Coleman, "Buffalo Bill on Stage," *Players* (January 1972): 80–91; Dorothy Wagner, "Buffalo Bill, Showman," *Palimpsest* (December 1930): 522–40; and W. B. "Bat" Masterson, "Colonel Cody—Hunter, Scout, Indian Fighter," *Human Life* (March 1908): 135–46.

My great thanks also go to the staff and archives at the Buffalo Bill Center of the West in Cody, Wyoming.

The Last Chance mining camp encounter appears in a Buffalo Bill dime novel by Colonel Prentiss Ingraham, *Buffalo Bill's Sweepstake; or the Wipe-Out at Last Chance* (New York: Beadle and Adams, 1893). It was rushed out just as Cody pronounced the winner of the Great Cowboy Race.

The *Charlotte (NC) Daily Observer* reported the Wild West train wreck on October 30, 1901. More can be found in Caron Myers, "Buffalo Bill Derailed in Davidson County," *Our State* (October 2011): 56–58, 60, 62.

Cody's letter to his sister Julia can be found in Carter, *Buffalo Bill Cody*. Julia's further personal recollections and correspondence with her famous brother are in Don Russell, ed., "Julia Cody Goodman's Memoirs of Buffalo Bill," *Kansas Historical Quarterly* (Winter 1962): 442–96.

To venture further into Cody's affair with Mrs. Gould, as well as his attractions to other women, see Carter, *Buffalo Bill Cody*, 388; and Chris Enss, *The Many Loves of Buffalo Bill: The True Story of Life on the Wild West Show* (Guilford, CT: TwoDot, 2010), 75–93. The Gould scandal electrified the daily newspapers, including the courtroom accounts of her divorce and her connection to Cody. For a sampling, try the *Nebraska State Journal*, April 22, 1894, 13; "Mrs. Gould's Libel Action," *New York Times*, April 14, 1899, 14; "Says Howard Gould Was Won by Fraud," *New York Times*, November 15, 1907, 5; "Sordid Troubles of the Married Rich," *Covington (NY) Sun*, April 16, 1908, 1; and "Mrs. Gould's Jaunts with Dustin Parnum," *New York Times*, June 12, 1909, 3.

The episode of an enraged Lulu returning home after realizing someone else was sharing her husband's hotel bed in Chicago is told in Carter, *Buffalo Bill Cody*, 374; Enss, *Many Loves of Buffalo Bill*, 76; and Foote, *Letters from Buffalo Bill*, 114–15.

Warren K. Moorehead's recollections of the day Buffalo Bill came to Newark, Ohio, appear in his *The American Indian in the United States: Period 1850–1914* (Andover, MA: Andover Press, 1914), 303.

Frank C. Huss delighting in sharing drinks with Cody is drawn from an oral history taken by his daughter, Mrs. Frank Wilsey, and published in Bert L. Hall, *Roundup Years: Old Muddy to Black Hills* (Pierre, SD: State Publishing, 1954), 133.

Cody's earliest plans to haul his Wild West train to Chicago in hopes of joining the world's fair began in early 1982. See *Richmond (VA) Dispatch*, February 21, 1892, 5; *Omaha Daily Bee*, March 17, 1892, 4, and June 19, 1892, 12; *Lincoln County (NE) Tribune*, June 29, 1892, 3; *New York Sun*, July 1, 1892, 2; *Omaha Daily Bee*, July 24, 1892, 15; *New York Evening World*, October 27, 1892; *Columbus (NE) Journal*, November 2, 1892, 3; *Omaha Daily Bee*, November 3, 1892; *McCook (NE) Tribune*, November 4, 1892, 6; and *San Francisco Morning Call*, December 4, 1892, 11.

Buffalo Bill's extensive remarks in Europe regarding long-distance racing—a prelude to the Great Cowboy Race in America and his initial plans to park his Wild West show next to the fair in Chicago—were carried in the *St. Paul Daily Globe*, November 13, 1892, 8.

Cody's hopes to open a federal nature preserve are described in the *Asheville (NC) Daily Citizen*, April 8, 1893, 3.

Cody's plans and meetings in Washington, D.C., are described in the *Washington Evening Star*, January 16, 1893, 7, and January 17, 1893, 4; the *St. Paul Globe*, January 24, 1893, 4; and the *Omaha Daily Bee*, January 25, 1893, 5, and March 6, 1893, 1.

Buffalo Bill's lengthy interview with an *Omaha Daily Bee* reporter ran March 22, 1893, 2, describing his decision to "leave for North Platte tonight" and prepare for opening his Wild West show next to the Chicago fair.

Cody's complaint about Chicago real estate men is quoted in Steve Friesen, *Buffalo Bill: Scout, Showman, Visionary* (Golden, CO: Fulcrum, 2010), 89.

The arrival of Cody's train cars, cowboys, and wildlife was showcased in the *Chicago Tribune*, April 14, 1893, 2.

The archives are rich with stories of Buffalo Bill's triumphant 1893 Wild West season in Chicago. In addition to the Cody biographies, other works include Nellie Snyder Yost, *Buffalo Bill: His Family, Friends, Fame, Failures, and Fortunes* (Chicago: Sage Books, 1979), 236–74; Joy S. Kasson, *Buffalo Bill's Wild West: Celebrity, Memory, and Popular History* (New York: Hill and Wang, 2000), 93–121; Foote, *Letters from Buffalo Bill*, 20–35; Rosa and May, *Buffalo Bill and His Wild West*, 66–96; Richard J. Walsh, *The Making of Buffalo Bill: A Study in Heroics* (Indianapolis: Bobbs-Merrill, 1928), 293–304; Robert W. Rydell and Rob Kroes, *Buffalo Bill in Bologna: The Americanization of the World, 1869–1922* (Chicago: University of Chicago Press, 2005); Richard Slotkin, *Gunfighter Nation: The Myth of the Frontier in Twentieth-Century America* (New York: Atheneum, 1992), 63–87; Hickey, Wunder, and Wunder, *Nebraska Moments*, 102–9; Henry Blackman Sell and Victor Weybright, *Buffalo Bill and the Wild West* (New York: Oxford University Press, 1955), 192–202; Judy Alter, *Wild West Shows* (New York: Franklin Watts, 1997); Corbett, *Orphans Preferred*, 161–71; Walter Havighurst, *Annie Oakley of the Wild West* (New York: Macmillan, 1994), 165–82; Warren, *Buffalo Bill's America*, 419–21; Friesen, *Buffalo Bill*, 89–98; Sarah J. Blackstone, *Buckskins, Bullets, and Business: A History of Buffalo Bill's Wild West* (New York: Greenwood Press, 1986), 24–27; Daniel Justin Herman, "God Bless Buffalo Bill," *American History* (June 2001): 228–37; Louis S. Warren, "Cody's Last Stand: Masculine Anxiety, the Custer Myth, and the Frontier of Domesticity in Buffalo Bill's Wild West," *Western Historical Quarterly* (Spring 2003): 49–69; Louis E.

Cooke, "Origin of the Wild West," *Billboard*, October 2, 1915; and Kathryn White, "'Through Their Eyes': Buffalo Bill's Wild West as a Drawing Table for American Identity," *Constructing the Past* 7, no. 1 (2006): 35–50.

Cody's introduction of his Indian actors for his Wild West performances appeared in the *Chicago Inter Ocean*, April 20, 1893, 7, and the *Chicago Record*, April 20, 1893, 1. Subsequent features ran in the *Chicago Herald* over the next several days.

Many useful histories have been written about the experiences of Indian peoples at the World's Columbian Exposition and other fairs and expositions. They include L. G. Moses, *Wild West Shows and the Images of American Indians, 1883–1933* (Albuquerque: University of New Mexico Press, 1999); Linda Scarangella McNenly, *Native Performers in Wild West Shows: From Buffalo Bill to Euro Disney* (Norman: University of Oklahoma Press, 2012), 44, 50–52; Raymond D. Fogelson, "Red Man in the White City," in *Columbian Consequences: The Spanish Borderlands in Pan-American Perspective,* vol. 3, ed. David Hurst Thomas (Washington, DC: Smithsonian Institution Press, 1991), 73–90; Francis Paul Prucha, *American Indian Policy in Crisis: Christian Reformers and the Indian, 1865–1900* (Norman: University of Oklahoma Press, 1976), 319–26; Philip Burnham, *Song of Dewey Beard: Last Survivor of the Little Bighorn* (Lincoln: University of Nebraska Press, 2014), 88–107; Chauncey Yellow Robe, "The Menace of the Wild West Show," a speech he gave to the Fourth Annual Conference of the Society of American Indians, Madison, WI, October 6–11, 1914; Robert A. Trennert Jr., "Selling Indian Education and World's Fairs and Expositions, 1893–1904," *American Indian Quarterly* (Summer 1987): 203–20; L. G. Moses, "Wild West Shows, Reformers, and the Image of the American Indian, 1887–1914," *South Dakota History* (Fall 1984): 193–221; Robert W. Rydell, "The Trans-Mississippi and International Exposition: 'To Work Out the Problem of Universal Civilization,'" *American Quarterly* (Winter 1981): 587–607; and L. G. Moses, "Indians on the Midway: Wild West Shows and the Indian Bureau at World's Fairs, 1893–1904," *South Dakota History* (Fall 1991): 205–29.

The opening day of Buffalo Bill's Wild West show in Chicago drew rave reviews—found April 27, 1893, in the *Chicago Record, Chicago Times, Chicago Inter Ocean, Chicago Post,* and *Chicago Dispatch,* among many others.

5. A Cowboy Race

Amy Leslie was quite the newspaperwoman of her day, and her column written after visiting Cody at the fair ran on June 26, 1893, in the *Chicago Daily News.* Her impressions of Cody and his Wild West show were later expanded upon and incorporated into her book, a collection of her columns from the Columbian Exposition, called simply *Amy Leslie at the Fair* (Chicago: W. B. Conkey, 1893), 20–25, 134–39, 148, 151–52, 165–72. She is profiled in Ishbel Ross, *Ladies of the Press: The Story of Women in Journalism by an Insider* (New York: Harper and Brothers, 1936), 408–9; Alma J. Bennett, *American Woman Theatre Critics: Biographies and Selected Writings of Twelve Reviewers, 1753–1919* (Jefferson, NC: McFarland, 2010), 103–9; Edward T. James, ed., *Notable American Women, 1607–1905* (Cambridge, MA: Belknap Press, 1971), 389–90; Charles Yanikoski, "Stephen Crane's Inamorata: The Real Amy Leslie," *Syracuse University Library Associates Courier* 33 (1998–2001): 117–33; Kathryn Hilt and Stanley Wertheim, "Stephen Crane and Amy Leslie:

A Rereading of the Evidence," *American Literary Realism* (Spring 2000): 256–69; and Joseph Katz, "Some Light on the Stephen Crane–Amy Leslie Affair," *Mad River Review* (Winter 1964–65): 43–62. Alma J. Bennett further discusses Leslie in "Traces of Resistance: Displacement, Contradiction, and Appropriation in the Criticism of Amy Leslie, 1895–1915," PhD diss., Kent State University, 1993.

Chadron is pitched far out on the northern rim of the Nebraska Panhandle and remains today steeped in Western lore. The local Dawes County Historical Museum houses old newspapers, town diaries, photographs, and other regional artifacts and vividly tells the story of this nearly 135-year-old community. Here, too, is the largest reservoir of items from the Great Cowboy Race, including the golden Colt revolver. My thanks for the museum's generous hospitality and willingness to share materials on both the city of Chadron and the cowboy race itself.

Other prime sources for Chadron include A. B. Wood, *Pioneer Tales of the North Platte Valley and Nebraska Panhandle* (Gering, NE: Courier Press, 1938), 198–204; *Chadron Centennial History*; George D. Watson Jr., *Prairie Justice: A 100 Year Legal Study of Chadron and Dawes County* (self-published, 1985), 1–37; Minnie Alice Rhoads, *A Stream Called Deadhorse* (Chadron, NE: Chadron Printing, 1957); Grant L. Shumway, *History of Western Nebraska and Its People* (Gage County, NE: Western Publishing and Engraving, 1921), esp. the Dawes County chapter; *Chadron: A Chronological View of the Early History of the Old-Home-Town*, a pamphlet compiled by H. D. Mead in 1925; *Nebraska: A Guide to the Cornhusker State*, comp. by the Federal Writers' Project of the Works Progress Administration for the state of Nebraska (New York: Viking Press, 1939), 320–21; Addison E. Sheldon, "Life on the Frontier," an address to the Lincoln, NE, Kiwanis Club, August 11, 1939; Tammi Deines, "Old Chadron before, during and after White Settlement," a personal history, May 14, 1980, 1–7; "The Heroic-Classic Age of Chadron," an unpublished type-written history, author unknown, on file at the Dawes County Historical Museum; "Chadron's Namesake Was Obscure Trader," *TCR Fur Trader*, July 2, 1993, 11; Leslie D. Ricker, "Early Years in Dawes County," *Nebraska History* (July–September 1932): 206–8; and E. E. Egan, "Old Town Story of the Trials and Hardships of the Pioneering Days in Old Chadron, and Incidents Otherwise," repr. in the *Chadron Record*, September 1, 2014.

W. W. Wilson's success at farming was chronicled in the *Omaha Daily Bee*, March 11, 1892, 6.

The Dawes County Courthouse is profiled in Watson, *Prairie Justice*, 8–9.

Orlan Carty's day in court is memorialized in Watson, *Prairie Justice*, 15.

Bill Malone's antics and those of other cowboy upstarts are recorded in Watson, *Prairie Justice*, 2. For more of the adventures inside Angel's Place, see Rhoads, *Stream Called Deadhorse*, chap. 5.

Red Jacket is profiled in Watson, *Prairie Justice*, 35–37.

The *Omaha Daily Bee*'s description of "cowboys, horse thieves and bad men" circulating through Chadron was published on June 13, 1893, 6.

The sturdy old Blaine Hotel building stands today, and more can be learned in "Blaine Motel Still Making History," *Crawford (NE) Clipper* (Summer 1993): 26.

Fannie O'Linn was Chadron's "first lady." An amazing woman, she helped establish the community before the railroad pushed west and the O'Linn settlement moved to the new Chadron town site. Details of her story can be found in Watson, *Prairie Justice*, 24; *Compendium of History, Reminiscence, and Biography of Western Nebraska*, 150–51; and Radcliffe, *Chadron to Chicago Cowboy Horse Race*, 4–5.

The Chadron settlement's relocation to a new site next to the train tracks is beautifully described in Egan, "Old Town Story."

Much of the lifelong endurance of Louis John Frederick Iaeger, known as "Billy the Bear," is intimately told by the man himself in his valuable *Man of Many Frontiers: The Diaries of "Billy the Bear" Iaeger* (Omaha: Working History, 1994). He also lives on in Marianne Brinda Beel, ed., *A Sandhill Century, Book I: The Land, a History of Cherry County, Nebraska* (Cherry County, NE: Centennial Committee, 1989), 217; *Compendium of History, Reminiscence, and Biography of Western Nebraska*, 130–32; James E. Potter, "A Peculiar Set of Men: Nebraska Cowboys of the Open Range," *Nebraska History* (Fall 2013): 137–38; "Billy the Bear," *Nebraska History* (April–June 1933): 98–99; Don Huls, "Billy the Bear," in *Chadron Centennial History*, 36–37; and "Nebraskan Has No Feet, No Hands," *Omaha Daily News Magazine*, November 16, 1919, 5.

Billy the Bear's wedding announcement to a niece of one of the cowboy riders appeared in the *Dawes County Journal*, April 15, 1892, 1. On July 11, 1893, just after the cowboy race was run, the *Omaha Daily Bee*, 4, reported that Buffalo Bill had presented Billy with a new "pair of artificial legs."

Billy's death in March 1930 made the local papers in Chadron, as well as p. 1 of the *Omaha World-Herald*, March 7, 1930. On March 14, 1930, the *World-Herald* reported on p. 10 that one of the last acts of this indomitable man was to pick out the Bible reading for his funeral.

John Maher, Chadron newspaper correspondent, Army officer, and business executive, died in June 1939, and his death was reported widely around the state of Nebraska, including in the *Lincoln Star*, June 10, 1939, 1, and the *Lincoln Evening Journal*, June 10, 1939, 3, as well as in the *Omaha World-Herald*, June 10, 1939, 1. The papers duly noted his lively wit and his knack for spinning preposterous stories and often entire fabrications. But Maher could rise to the demands of a correspondent for major Eastern papers. His coverage of the Wounded Knee massacre, the last of the great Indian conflicts, for the *New York Herald* appeared on the paper's front pages from December 30, 1890, through January 3, 1891. His "Farmer John at the Fair" column from the Chicago World's Fair ran in the *Chadron Signal*, August 26, 1893, 1.

Maher's lively times in Nebraska are recorded in Louise Pound, *Nebraska Folklore* (Lincoln: University of Nebraska Press, 1959), 104–21, which includes the embarrassing interview with Mari Sandoz; Addison E. Sheldon, *Nebraska: The Land and the People* (Chicago: Lewis Publishing, 1931), 197–98; David Dary, *Red Blood & Black Ink: Journalism of the Old West* (New York: Alfred A. Knopf, 1998), 235–37; "Tall Tales," *Nebraska Folklore Pamphlets*, from the Federal Writers Project in Nebraska, July 1938, 1–10; Welsch, *Treasury of Nebraska Pioneer Folklore*, 151–54; Patricia C. Gaster, "A Celestial Visitor Revisited: A Nebraska Newspaper Hoax from

1884," *Nebraska History* (Summer 2013): 90–100; and Austin E. Fife, "The Bear Lake Monsters," *Utah Humanities Review* (April 1948), 99–106. Maher also is mentioned quite often throughout Billy the Bear's diaries, *Man of Many Frontiers*.

On November 29, 1892, the *Arizona Republic* reported that cowboys in Nebraska and the Dakotas were hoping to raise $1,000 and a gold medal to spur interest in a race from Chadron to Chicago.

The *New York Sun*'s boast that American Western horses could stand more hardship than those that had raced a year earlier between Germany and Austria ran on November 28, 1892, 6.

As early as the first weeks of 1893, *Chadron Citizen* newspaper editorials questioned the idea of a cross-country cowboy race, deriding it as something that "originated in the fertile brain" of John Maher.

McGinley called for a meeting to lay out the race plans in the *Dawes County Journal* on December 16, 1892. Doc Middleton planned to ride, as did Emmett Albright.

Ed Lemmon's log books can be found in Lemmon, "Developing the West," 6.

The *Omaha Daily Bee* announced on December 25, 1892, 2, that talk of a long-distance cowboy race was sweeping the West.

On February 23, 1893, the *Chadron Citizen* reported on its front page that as many as three hundred cowboys from Nebraska alone might enter the race and that advertising for the endeavor was spreading around the region.

The first meeting of race committee officials was held March 18, 1893, at the Chadron Opera House, as reported in the *Dawes County Journal*, March 24, 1893, 1, and the *Chadron Citizen*, March 23, 1893, 1. Here the preliminary set of rules was announced.

Buffalo Bill agreed to help sponsor the race and to place the finish line at his Wild West show tent grounds in Chicago, as reported in the *Chicago Inter Ocean*, March 19, 1893, 13. The text of Cody's telegram to Sheriff Dahlman announcing his cosponsorship was published in Walter Livingston, "Riders East," *Adventure* (December 1941): 66.

George Angell's initial protest against the race appeared in his column, "Our Dumb Animals," on April 1, 1893, in the newsletter of the Massachusetts Society for the Prevention of Cruelty to Animals.

Clabe Young surfaced as a potential rider in the *Chadron Signal*, April 1, 1893, and the *Dawes County Journal*, April 7, 1890, 1. Jeptha Sweat, as reported in the *Chadron Signal*, April 15, 1893, was prepared to race. The *Helena (MT) Independent*, April 5, 1893, 3, reported that Narcisse Valleaux Jr. would ride.

Updated race rules were reported in the *Chicago Inter Ocean*, April 6, 1893.

"Texas Ben" and Jim Murray were likely riders, according the *Chicago Inter Ocean*, April 12, 1893. The *New York Sun*, May 14, 1893, 4, reported that Indian tribal horsemen might join the race, as well as Jack Flagg of the Big Horn Basin, Emma Hutchinson of Colorado, and others. The contestants from Kearney, Nebraska, were identified in the *Kearney Daily Hub*, April 20, 1893, 3.

The *Chadron Citizen,* April 27, 1893, 1, reported that John Berry, the railroad man, had been slipping in and out of town recently and that Paul Fontaine of the Minnesota Humane Society had fired off a letter encouraging his colleagues around the country to join him in protesting the race.

Special gifts for some of the riders—the saddle and the bridles—were noted in the *Dawes County Journal,* June 9, 1893, 1.

The judge in Lincoln submitted his letter of protest to the *Lincoln State Journal,* and the *Chadron Signal* reproduced it on April 29, 1893, 1.

More details on Buffalo Bill's involvement in the race, and the news that he would donate $500 of his own money and award the golden Colt revolver, appeared in the *Chadron Signal,* April 29, 1893, 1.

The letters from Barron, Wisconsin, and from Caroline Earle White and the Women's Branch of the Pennsylvania Society for the Prevention of Cruelty to Animals, sent to Iowa Governor Boies, were retrieved from the Iowa state archives. White also wrote a separate letter of complaint on May 25, 1893, to Nebraska Governor Crounse, included in the Nebraska state archives.

The meeting of the Illinois Humane Society was held May 6, 1893, and reported in the *Chicago Daily Tribune,* May 7, 1893, 11. On p. 2 the same day, the paper reported that Nebraska Governor Crounse had been invited to kick off the race in Chadron by firing the pistol to send the cowboys to Chicago.

Reverend David Swing's sermon was reprinted in the *Chicago Inter Ocean,* May 22, 1893.

Two separate protest letters from the Wisconsin Humane Society, May 9, 1893, were obtained from the Iowa and Nebraska state archives.

Nate Salsbury's extraordinary May 19, 1893, letter to race committee secretary Harvey Weir was printed in full in the *Chicago Inter Ocean,* July 2, 1893, 5, after the Humane Society officials publicly released it as part of their final report on the Great Cowboy Race.

Paul Fontaine's May 15, 1893, letter of protest to the *Chadron Signal* appeared in the paper on May 20. That day, the paper also reported that the Colt was on display at the jewelry store in downtown Chadron. The *Dawes County Journal* further cited the Fontaine letter on May 19, 1893, 1.

The Aurora, Illinois, Humane Society entered the protest against the race in a letter to the editor, run on May 23, 1893, 7, in the *Omaha Daily Bee* and in the *Chadron Citizen* on June 1, 1893.

Shortall, head of the Illinois Humane Society, announced on May 24 that he was encouraging Buffalo Bill to drop his sponsorship of the race. This comes from an unnamed newspaper source included in the files of the Buffalo Bill Center of the West in Cody, Wyoming. In a May 27 letter to the race committee and secretary Harvey Weir, Shortall wrote "I beg you" to cancel the race. The letter was obtained from the Dawes County Historical Museum. The letter also was published in the *Chicago Inter Ocean,* the *Chicago Tribune,* and the *Chicago Herald,* all on June 4, 1893.

The Salsbury correspondence and Cody's misgivings about the race once it received a flurry of national protests are discussed in Bernard Schuessler, "Great Chadron to Chicago Horse Race," 1.

Governor Altgeld's proclamation warning against any cruelty to the horses and threatening arrests appeared in newspapers throughout the nation. See the *Chicago Herald*, June 14, 1893, 1, and the *Sioux City (IA) Journal*, June 14, 1893, 1. For more, see Harry Barnard, *"Eagle Forgotten": The Life of John Peter Altgeld* (Indianapolis: Bobbs-Merrill, 1938), 178–79.

The *Intelligencer* in Wheeling, WV, editorialized against the race on June 6, 1893, 4.

Angell's reward of $100 and/or a gold medal to stop the race was reported around the country, including in the *Freeport (IL) Bulletin*, May 29, 1893, 1.

The so-called Dalton Gang letter threatening harm if the race were stopped was printed widely, including in the *Shenandoah (PA) Evening Herald*, June 6, 1893, 3.

Doc Middleton was quoted that he would ride—come hell or high water—and his determination was reported in the *Iowa City Daily Citizen*, June 3, 1893, 3.

Sheriff Dahlman vowed not to shut down the race, in comments quoted in the *Dawes County Journal*, June 2, 1893, 1.

Efforts to organize humane society officials in Dubuque, Iowa, were reported in the *Omaha Daily Bee*, June 4, 1893, 2.

The Shortall letter to Iowa Governor Boies is dated June 3, 1893. It is included in the Iowa state archives. The governor's request for Iowa county sheriffs to be on the lookout for animal cruelty was printed in the *Algona Upper Des Moines* newspaper, June 14, 1893, 4, and again, once the race had started and the cowboys were approaching Iowa, in the *La Porte City (IA) Progress-Review*, June 17, 1893.

The story of Rattlesnake Pete and his drinking buddies chasing after the circus parade was reported in the *Chadron Signal,* June 10, 1893.

The *Chicago Inter Ocean*'s call urging Buffalo Bill to "exercise his influence" and halt the race was reported in the *Lincoln County (NE) Tribune*, June 7, 1893, 2.

Broncho Harry's defense of Buffalo Bill and the cowboy race was printed in the *Chicago Daily Tribune*, June 9, 1893, 7.

Reverend Swing's objections to the race ran in the *Chicago Inter Ocean* and the *Chicago Daily Tribune* on June 9, 1893, both on p. 7.

The *Chadron Citizen*'s boast that there were "plenty of men in the West" who could ride over 100 miles a day, even for two or three days in a row, appeared on June 8, 1893, 1.

Shortall's complaint that "horseflesh is cheap" out on the Western Plains was reprinted in the *Sioux City (IA) Journal*, June 11, 1893.

6. Race Day

Details about the women's meeting in Chadron on the eve of the Great Cowboy Race can be found in Sly, "1000 Mile Horse Race," 3. It also was detailed in the Chadron newspapers. See esp. the *Dawes County Journal*, June 16, 1893, 1.

For more on Mary E. Smith Hayward, see the *Chadron Journal*, February 11, 1938, 1.

Harry Rutter's cowboy life and times are chronicled in his personal recollections, taken down by Georgia Rechert and written up as "Cow Tales" in 1931. I found this document at the Montana Historical Society. See also Pat Hill, "Harry Rutter Was a Cowboy: He Drove Cattle to Montana, Put Away Outlaws, and Got the Girl," *Montana Pioneer* (March 2010): 9. In 2009, Rutter was posthumously inducted into the Montana Cowboy Hall of Fame; his profile is at www.montanacowboyfame.com/151001/212712.html.

Rutter's distaste for seeing Cowboy Annie's drawers hanging in a friend's cabin is documented in Tinkle and Maxwell, *Cowboy Reader*, 193–201, and Abbott and Smith, *We Pointed Them North*, 105–13.

Emma Hutchinson's wandering ride from Denver to Chadron was followed closely by the nation's press. See the *Chicago Evening Journal*, June 13, 1893, 1; *New York Sun*, June 13, 1893, 5; *Salt Lake Herald*, June 13, 1893, 1; *Wichita Daily Eagle*, June 22, 1893, 6; *Dawes County Journal*, June 21, 1893, 1; *Kearney (NE) Daily Hub*, May 8, 1893, 1; *Salt Lake Tribune*, June 11, 1893, 11; and *Charlotte (NC) Democrat*, June 30, 1893, 3.

Achievements of other horsewomen were recorded in the *Du Quoin (IL) Tribune*, June 1, 1893. Broncho Kate Chapman's abilities were showcased in the *St. Paul Daily Globe*, July 10, 1892, 11.

The W. B. Lower missive blasting the "human cranks" who opposed the race appeared in the *O'Neill (NE) Frontier*, June 15, 1893, 1.

T. H. McPherson was interviewed by a reporter in Sioux City, Iowa, and the story ran in the *Sioux City Journal*, June 13, 1893, 1.

E. C. Walker's letter from Boston to Nebraska Governor Crounse is included in the governor's correspondence file at the Nebraska state archives.

The letter from "the Rustler" criticizing the race was published in the *Omaha Daily Bee*, June 3, 1893, 8.

Army Captain E. L. Huggins's thoughts about the stamina and strength of horses in a cross-country race were published in the *Chicago Post*, June 13, 1893, 1. Also quoted was the Reverend F. M. Bristol, decrying the racing cowboys. The story further detailed Shortall's determination to continue protesting the race and waving off any "implied threats" that humane society officials might be harmed.

Newspaper coverage of the Blaine Hotel meeting was extensive. Of note are the *Chicago Record*, June 14, 1893; *Chicago Times*, June 14, 1893, 1; *Chicago Herald*, June 14, 1893, 1; *Chicago Times*, June 14, 1893; 1; *Chicago Tribune*, June 14, 1893, 2; *Omaha Daily Bee*, June 14, 1893, 1; *New York World*, June 14, 1893; 3; *Sioux City (IA) Journal*, June 14, 1893, 1; *Chadron Citizen*, June 15, 1893, 1; *Dawes*

County Journal, June 16, 1893, 1; *Chadron Signal*, June 17, 1893, 1; and *Rushville (NE) Standard*, June 23, 1893, 1.

Jack Hale is profiled in Bob Lee and Dick Williams, *Last Grass Frontier: The South Dakota Stock Grower Heritage* (Rapid City, SD: Black Hills Publishers, 1964), 58–59.

Sheriff Dahlman, a town leader in Chadron and later across the state of Nebraska, came to embody the "cowboy mayor." The best sources on him are Fred Carey, *Mayor Jim: An Epic of the West* (Omaha: Omaha Printing, 1930); "Recollections of Cowboy Life in Western Nebraska," an address that Dahlman delivered January 10, 1922, to the annual meeting of the Nebraska State Historical Society, later published in *Nebraska History* (October–December 1927): 334–39; J. R. Johnson, *Representative Nebraskans* (Lincoln: Johnsen Publishing, 1954), 60–64; Sandoz, *Cattlemen*, 407–17; Minnie Alice Rhoads, "Ol' Jim Dahlman a Real Cowboy," *Chadron Record*, August 1, 1960; Watson, *Prairie Justice*, 30–31; and *Chadron Centennial History*, 25.

7. Post Time

Many local and national newspapers covered the crowds and the excitement of the start of the cowboy race. They included the *Chicago Times*, June 14, 1893, 1; *Chicago Herald*, June 14, 1893, 1; *Chicago Tribune*, June 14, 1893, 2; *Omaha Daily Bee*, June 14, 1893, 1; *New York World*, June 14, 1893, 3; *Sioux City (IA) Journal*, June 14, 1893, 1; *Chadron Citizen*, June 15, 1893, 1; *Dawes County Journal*, June 16, 1893, 1; *Chadron Signal*, June 17, 1893, 1; and *Rushville (NE) Standard*, June 23, 1893, 1.

Bill McDowell of Casper, Wyoming, a descendant of John Berry, pulled together various family materials, historical accounts, and photographs. These sources included newspaper clippings and family letters as well as Wyoming stories that chronicled Berry's life. Equally valuable were old newspaper obituaries from Newcastle, Wyoming, beginning April 3, 1913. I thank Bill for sharing his time and collections.

Berry's work as a railroad man is cited in Albert Watkins, *History of Nebraska: From the Earliest Explorations to the Present Time* (Lincoln, NE: Western Publishing and Engraving, 1913), 455; and *Nebraska: A Guide to the Cornhusker State*, 313, 320.

One of the best descriptions of Berry comes from the *Chicago Herald*, June 26, 1893. Doris Bowker Bennett mentions her uncle John Berry in *A Girl in Wyoming*, 26–27. David Howell, a nephew of John Berry, was interviewed by the author on December 8, 2013.

Berry's wife, Winifred, recalled the race and her life with John in "Cowboy Race Winner Called at Last Minute," *Lincoln (NE) Star*, July 27, 1960, 17. See also Dolly Donlin, "Chadron to Chicago Race," *Casper (WY) Tribune-Herald and Star*, September 30, 1962; and an undated, unnamed newspaper article titled "Berry Never Got His Purse—Sheriff Gambled."

Doc Middleton's life on both sides of the law is told best in Hutton, *Doc Middleton*. Hutton further deals with Middleton in *Vigilante Days: Frontier Justice along the Niobrara* (Chicago: Sage Books, 1978), 15–30. No one better captures the man, the outlaw, and the reformed thief. Middleton also rides again in John Carson's thirty-three-page pamphlet *The Unwickedest Outlaw* (Santa Fe, NM: Press of the Territories, 1966). He also can be found in I. S. Bartlett, ed., *History of Wyoming* (Chicago: S. J.

Clarke, 1918), 622–23; Butcher, *Pioneer History of Custer County*, 119–33, 172–76; Laurence J. Yadon and Robert Barr Smith, *Outlaws with Badges* (Gretna, LA: Pelican Publishing, 2013), 203–27; Faulkner, *Roundup*, 86–90; Sandoz, *Cattlemen*, 128–29, 200, 226–27; T. D. Griffith, *Outlaw Tales of Nebraska* (Helena, MT: TwoDot, 2010), 33–42; Bob Rybolt, "Even a New Name and State Couldn't Save Doc Middleton," *Omaha World-Herald Magazine of the Midlands*, November 18, 1984, 14–15; Alan J. Bartels, "On the Trail of Doc Middleton," *Nebraska Life* (May–June 2011): 122–31; James H. Cook, "Early Days in Ogallala," *Nebraska History* (April–June 1933): 89–92; Barbara E. Andre, "Doc Middleton: Horsethief or Lawman?" *Golden West* (May 1968): 15, 51–52; Elizabeth Parker, "Doc Middleton, Nebraska's 'Gentleman Outlaw,' Eventually Reformed and Even Became a Lawman," *Wild West* (February 1999): 12, 14, 66; *Omaha Daily Bee*, May 24, 1893, 5; and *Chicago Evening Journal*, June 24, 1893, 1. Further, he is repeatedly mentioned in Iaeger, *Man of Many Frontiers*.

For background on Joe Gillespie, I thank Clay Comer of Calumet, Oklahoma, and his work in pulling together family history, letters, photographs, and memoirs about his great-grandfather. "I always knew he was a famous cowboy and thought I knew him well," Clay told me as we researched the old man. "But it has been amazing how time can change your memories."

Harold Comer's comments are drawn from his personal writings as well as interviews he gave to others, including Chadron reporters in the summer of 1993 to mark the hundredth anniversary of the Great Cowboy Race. Also of help was great-grandson Daniel Gillespie of Shady Cove, Oregon.

For more on Joe Gillespie, see Watson, *Prairie Justice*, 31–33; and *Voices of the Sandhills*, Tryon, NE (Winter 2004–2005): 1.

The *Cedar Rapids (IA) Journal* article on favorite son Joe Gillespie was published during the cowboy race on June 25, 1893.

The quotation regarding Gillespie's "glib manner" is from the *Chicago Daily News*, June 26, 1893, 1.

Gillespie's dustup with Chadron town marshal Timothy Morrissey comes from Iaeger, *Man of Many Frontiers*, 241. For more about Morrissey, see *Compendium of History, Reminiscence, and Biography of Western Nebraska*, 140–41.

Ora Niegel's reminiscences about her grandfather appeared in *True West* (September–October 1959): 10–11.

Also of great value is the travel diary of Gillespie's wife, Anna, documenting their trip from the Nebraska Panhandle to west central Oklahoma. It is included in "Coxville, Nebraska, to Fay, Oklahoma, by Wagon (1893): The Journal of Anna Gillespie," *Nebraska History* (Fall 1984): 344–65.

James "Rattlesnake Pete" Stephens eventually returned to the middle of Kansas, and it was there that I discovered much about his long life as a cowboy–turned–town barber who often regaled boys and newspaper reporters with tales of the Great Cowboy Race. Family member Joan Pivonka was of great help in learning more about Rattlesnake Pete, as was Jack S. Gellerstedt of Forest, Virginia, one of the boys who long ago came crashing into Pete's barbershop.

Of special interest is Ed Tolle, "Rattlesnake Pete and the Great 1,000 Mile Horse Race," in the Reno County Historical Society's journal, *Legacy* (Fall 1995): 2–11. Stephens was periodically quoted in the *Hutchinson (KS) News* and the *Hutchinson News-Herald*, generally describing the race and complaining about false stories that occasionally popped up, such as allegations that he had served whiskey to his horse General Grant. The dates of these stories are July 7, 1927; June 6, 1930; March 10, 1932; June 13, 1933, 1; April 17, 1942; June 13, 1943, 1; June 6, 1944; April 26, 1946; June 16, 1946; May 16, 1948, 18; and June 19, 1957. A good description of Stephens during the race ran in the *Chicago Herald*, June 16, 1893, 1.

In the dying days of the Old West, a number of "Rattlesnake Petes" rode in off the prairie. Buffalo Bill's aide William Liddiard, for instance, is mentioned in the *Columbus (NE) Journal*, March 14, 1900, 1.

The imposter bursting into Deadwood, South Dakota, was unmasked in the *New Orleans Times-Picayune*, August 9, 1935, 8.

August "Gus" Robson claimed that he had hunted in Africa with Theodore Roosevelt and served as the former president's personal barber, according to the *Lincoln (NE) Star*, January 9, 1932, 1. Robson also showed up in the *Waterloo (IA) Press*, February 2, 1939, 3; and in Laura Trowbridge, "The Fabulous Cowboy Race," *West* (April 1968): 16–17, 48–50, where Robson is confused with the Rattlesnake Pete of Kansas.

"Rattlesnake Pete" Gruber of Pennsylvania can be found in the *Los Angeles Herald*, September 19, 1897; *New Orleans Times-Picayune*, July 31, 1893, 8; *Columbia (TN) Herald,* June 9, 1893, 6; and *Reading (PA) Times*, July 15, 1901, 5.

Stephens's position on the local barbers' union strike was reported in the *Hutchinson (KS) News*, October 25, 1916, 2.

Emmett Albright is featured in Iaeger, *Man of Many Frontiers*, 106, 110–11, 115, 120, 129, 137, 144. See also *Chadron Citizen*, February 23, 1893, 1.

Joe Campbell is highlighted in the *Chadron Signal*, May 27, 1893, 1.

All that could be found regarding "Little Davy" Douglas came from a story in the *Philadelphia Times*, August 20, 1893, 5, relating that he was being mistaken for a stockman named Dave Douglass from Montana.

George "Stub" Jones, also sometimes called "Abe" or "Eb," is mentioned in Lemmon, "Developing the West," 6–7.

Charley "C. W." Smith appears in Lee and Williams, *Last Grass Frontier*, 244; and the *Hot Springs (SD) Daily Star*, June 8 and October 27, 1893.

Meg van Asselt of McPherson, Kansas, the granddaughter of the man who donated Smith's boots to the Dawes County Historical Museum, was interviewed by the author on January 25, 2015.

8. So Long, Nebraska

The nation's newspapers recorded the crack of the pistol shot fired high above the Blaine Hotel and the launch of the cowboys to Chicago. Stories were published in the *Chicago Times*, June 14, 1893, 1; *Chicago Herald*, June 14, 1893, 1; *Chicago Tribune*, June 14, 1893, 2; *Omaha Daily Bee*, June 14, 1893, 1; *New York World*, June 14, 1893, 3; *Sioux City (IA) Journal*, June 14, 1893, 1; *Chadron Citizen*, June 15, 1893, 1; *Dawes County Journal*, June 16, 1893, 1; *Chadron Signal*, June 17, 1893, 1; and *Rushville (NE) Standard*, June 23, 1893, 1.

The Buck letter to Governor Crounse is in the Nebraska state archives.

Governor Boies's letter to Iowa county sheriffs was reported by the *Sioux Valley News* in Correctionville, Iowa, June 15, 1893, 1; and the *Helena (MT) Independent*, June 14, 1893, 1.

The Altgeld pardons, as well as the Illinois lynching, are discussed at length in Barnard, *"Eagle Forgotten,"* 178–79. See also *Omaha World Herald*, June 27, 1893, 1.

Governor Altgeld's proclamation warning against any cruelty to the horses is included in Barnard, *"Eagle Forgotten,"* 178–79. See also *Chicago Herald*, June 14, 1893, 1; and *Sioux City (IA) Journal*, June 14, 1893, 1.

John Shortall's prediction that "there must be cruelty" appeared in the *Omaha Daily Bee*, June 15, 1893; and the *Columbus (NE) Journal*, June 21, 1893, 1.

Oscar Little's work in alerting Iowa county sheriffs was covered by the *North Platte (NE) Tribune*, June 14, 1893, 1; and the *Cedar Rapids (IA) Gazette*, June 13, 1893.

Buffalo Bill Cody's sudden insistence that "I knew nothing about the race" ran in the *New York World*, June 17, 1893, 4; and the *New York Evening World*, June 17, 1893, 3.

Cody's lengthy comments decrying the "Eastern people" who "don't understand what our western prairie horses are like" appeared in the *Chicago Evening Post*, June 17, 1893, 1.

As the cowboys tore off for Chicago, the nation's newspapers and magazines followed them with daily and weekly coverage across three states to the world's fair. But often the most comprehensive coverage came from local newspapers along the route, while the larger papers in Omaha and Chicago hired correspondents and stringers in Nebraska, Iowa, and Illinois for updates.

Coverage highlights included the following:

Hay Springs, Nebraska—*Chadron Citizen*, June 15, 1893, 1; *Chadron Signal*, June 17, 1893, 1; *Chicago Herald*, June 15, 1893, 1.

Rushville, Nebraska—*Rushville Standard*, June 17, 1893; *Chicago Herald*, June 15, 1893, 1; *Omaha Daily Bee*, June 15, 1893, 1.

Gordon, Nebraska—*Chadron Citizen*, June 15, 1893, 1; *Chadron Signal*, June 17, 1893, 1; *St. Paul Daily Globe*, June 15, 1893, 5; *Nebraska State Journal*, June 15, 1893, 1; *Decatur (IL) Republican*, June 15, 1893, 5; *Chicago Herald*, June 15, 1893, 1; *Quincy (IL) Daily Herald*, June 16, 1893, 1; *New York Evening World*, June 15, 1893, 3; *Omaha World Herald*, June 16, 1893, 1; *Chicago Record*, June 15, 1893; *Omaha Daily Bee*, June 15, 1893, 1; *Ainsworth (NE) Star-Journal*, June 29, 1893.

Valentine, Nebraska—*Chicago Daily Tribune*, June 16, 1893, 1; *Omaha Daily Bee*, June 16, 1893, 1; *New York Evening World*, June 16, 1893, 5; *Quincy (IL) Daily Journal*, June 16, 1893, 1; *Washington (DC) Evening Star*, June 16, 1993, 6.

Ainsworth, Nebraska—*Ainsworth Star Journal*, June 22, 1893, 1; *Dawes County Journal*, June 16, 1893, 1; *Chicago Herald*, June 17, 1893.

Long Pine, Nebraska—*Nebraska State Journal*, June 18, 1893, 1; *Chadron Signal*, June 17, 1893, 1; *Leavenworth (KS) Times*, June 17, 1893, 1; *Omaha Morning World-Herald*, June 17, 1893, 1; *Chicago Daily Tribune*, June 17, 1893; *Chicago Herald*, June 17, 1893; *Chicago Tribune*, June 18, 1893; *Chicago Post*, June 18, 1893; *Iowa City (IA) Daily Citizen*, June 17, 1893, 1; *Omaha World-Herald*, June 18, 1893, 1.

The *Omaha Daily Bee*'s column that began "Talk about circus day" was published June 17, 1893, 1.

The Harvey Weir telegram was reported by the *Chadron Signal*, June 17, 1893, 1.

Newspaper editorials from Toledo; Minneapolis; Milwaukee; Lawrence, Kansas; and New York were collected under the headline "Cowboy Cruelty" and published in the *Chicago Daily Tribune*, June 16, 1893, 13.

Newport, Nebraska—*Chicago Evening Post*, June 17, 1893; *Algona Upper Des Moines*, June 21, 1893, 1; *Norfolk (NE) Daily News*, June 19, 1893, 1; *Washington (DC) Evening Star*, June 17, 1893; *Omaha World-Herald*, June 18, 1893, 1. The *Chicago Evening Post*, June 17, 1893, described Rattlesnake Pete's headgear full of snake tails as a "hideous looking ornament."

O'Neill, Nebraska—*O'Neill Frontier*, June 22, 1983, 1; *Nebraska State Journal*, June 18 and 19, 1893, 1; *Quincy (IL) Daily Herald*, June 17, 1893; *Chicago Tribune*, June 18, 1893; *Chicago Herald*, June 18 and 19, 1893; *Chicago Post*, June 18, 1893; *Omaha World-Herald*, June 18, 1893, 1; *Sioux City (IA) Journal*, June 18, 1893, 1; *Springfield (IL) Sunday Journal*, June 18, 1893, 1.

"Little Davy" Douglas's decision to throw in the towel and quit the race was reported by the *Chicago Herald*, June 18, 1893; and the *Omaha World Herald*, June 19, 1893.

The *Cedar Rapids (IA) Evening Gazette* editorialized against "cowboy cruelty" in its June 17, 1893, edition.

Wausa, Nebraska—*Omaha Daily Bee*, June 19, 1893, 1; *Quincy (IL) Daily Herald*, June 17, 1893; *Algona Upper Des Moines*, June 21, 1893, 1; *Chicago Herald*, June 19, 1893; *Chicago Tribune*, June 19, 1893; *Sacramento (CA) Record-Union*, June 19, 1893; *Columbus (NE) Journal*, June 21, 1893; *Chicago Record*, June 19, 1893; *New Orleans Times-Picayune*, June 19, 1893, 2; *Omaha World Herald*, June 19, 1893; *Sioux City (IA) Journal*, June 19, 1893, 1.

The Missouri River crossing by the top three leaders in the race was reported by the *Sioux City (IA) Journal*, June 20, 1893, 1; *Omaha Daily Bee*, June 20, 1893; *Iowa City (IA) Daily Citizen*, June 20, 1893, 2; *Dubuque (IA) Daily Herald*, June 21, 1893, 1; *Chicago Inter Ocean*, June 20, 1893, 1; *Cedar Rapids (IA) Evening Gazette*, June 20, 1893; *New York Evening World*, June 20, 1893, 3; and *Chicago Post*, June 20, 1893, 1.

9. In God's Land

Sioux City, Iowa—The long night of excitement at the river shore and inside the Hotel Oxford, the saloon, and the horse barns was vividly told in the *Sioux City, Iowa, Journal*, June 20, 1893, 1; *Cedar Rapids (IA) Evening Gazette*, June 20, 1893; *Chicago Inter Ocean*, June 20, 1893, 1; *Chicago Herald*, June 20, 1893; *Dubuque (IA) Daily Herald*, June 21, 1893, 1; *Sioux Valley News*, Correctionville, Iowa, June 22, 1893, 1; *Norfolk (NE) Daily News*, June 21, 1893; *Madison (NE) Chronicle*, June 28, 1893; and *Iowa City (IA) Daily Citizen*, June 20, 1893, 2.

The response to George Angell's comments from an unidentified race committee member in Chadron appeared in the *Chicago Inter Ocean*, June 19, 1893.

Doc Middleton's internal struggles on whether to continue racing were discussed in the *Norfolk (NE) Daily News*, June 20, 1893; *Dubuque (IA) Daily Herald*, June 22, 1893; and *Chanute (KS) Daily Tribune*, June 23, 1893, 2.

Laura Penrod told of the overnight visit by Doc Middleton at her family home in Galva, Iowa, in a story in the *Ida County Courier*, June 26, 1985. The article includes a photograph of a smiling Penrod, ninety-one years old, holding up her family's prized quarter.

Correctionville, Iowa—*Sioux Valley News*, Correctionville, June 22, 1893, 2.

Galva, Iowa—*Sioux City (IA) Journal*, June 22, 1893, 1; *Omaha Daily Bee*, June 22, 1893, 1; *Chicago Herald*, June 22, 1893; *Dubuque (IA) Daily Herald*, June 23, 1893, 1.

The letter signed "J. H. B." ran in the *Chicago Inter Ocean*, June 21, 1893, 9.

The newspapers venting their opposition to the cowboy race—in Boston, Milwaukee, and Grand Rapids and Kalamazoo, Michigan—were cited in the *Chicago Inter Ocean*, June 21, 1893. Other editorials that weighed in against the race were published in Wheeling, WV; New York; Evansville, IN; St. Paul; Indianapolis; Washington, DC; Alton, IL; Springfield, IL; Detroit; and Bloomington, MN.

Joe Gillespie's recollections appear in Ora Niegel's profile in *True West* (September–October 1959): 10–11.

Fort Dodge, Iowa—*Fort Dodge Chronicle*, June 21, 22, and 24, 1893; *Marshalltown (IA) Evening Times Republican*, June 22, 1893, 1; *Omaha Daily Bee*, June 22, 1893; *Dubuque (IA) Daily Herald*, June 23, 1893, 1; *Iowa City (IA) Daily Citizen*, June 23, 1893, 3; *Chicago Inter Ocean*, June 23, 1893, 2; *Nebraska State Journal*, June 23, 1893.

Webster City, Iowa—*Chicago Herald*, June 22, 1893; *Lincoln (NE) Daily News*, June 23, 1893, 2; *St. Paul Daily Globe*, June 23, 1893, 5.

Iowa Falls—*Marshalltown (IA) Evening Times Republican*, June 24, 1893; *Cedar Rapids (IA) Evening Gazette*, June 24, 1893; *Chicago Tribune*, June 24, 1893; *Iowa State Register*, June 24, 1893.

The antics by Joe Gillespie and James Stephens at the Cedar Falls circus and Rattlesnake Pete's dream were reported in the *Dubuque (IA) Herald*, June 25, 1893, 1.

Manchester, Iowa—*Manchester Herald*, June 26, 1893; *Chicago Inter Ocean*, June 25, 1893.

Waterloo, Iowa—*Chicago Herald*, June 24, 1893; *Iowa City (IA) Herald*, June 28, 1893, 2.

Cody's involvement in the race, and the suggestion by the *Omaha World Herald* that he "could put himself at a very much better enterprise," was picked up by other newspapers around the nation, including in small papers out west such as the *Red Lodge (MT) Picket*, June 17, 1893; and the *Nevada State Journal*, June 23, 1893.

Oscar Little's encouraging of sheriffs along the Mississippi River to stop the cowboys was reported in the *Freeport (IL) Bulletin*, June 24, 1893; *Chicago Herald*, June 22, 1893; *Marshalltown (IA) Evening Times Republican*, June 26, 1893; and *Chicago Mail*, June 23, 1893.

10. Across the River and into Illinois

Dubuque and the Mississippi River bridge—*Dubuque Daily Times*, June 25, 1893, 1; *Dubuque Daily Herald*, June 27, 1893; *Chicago Herald*, June 26, 1893; *Chicago Times*, June 26, 1893; *Chicago Inter Ocean*, June 26, 1893; *Marshalltown (IA) Evening Times Republican*, June 27, 1893.

The *Sioux City (IA) Journal* noted that Doc Middleton rode the train to Dubuque, and the *Omaha Daily Bee*, June 27, 1893, reported that Doc shipped his horse from there to Chicago.

Galena, Illinois—*Chicago Record*, June 26, 1893, 1; *Quincy (IL) Daily Journal*, June 16, 1893; *Lincoln (NE) Daily News*, June 26, 1893, 2; *Davenport (IA) Daily Republican*, June 27, 1893, 1.

Freeport, Illinois—*Freeport Bulletin*, June 26 and 27, 1893, both 1; *Chicago Record*, June 27, 1893, 1; *Chicago Daily News*, June 27, 1893, 1; *Chicago Evening Journal*, June 2, 1893; *Rockford (IL) Register*, June 26, 1893; *Chicago Inter Ocean*, June 27, 1893, 1.

Rattlesnake Pete's complaints that other cowboys had secretly passed him in wagons and buddies appeared in the *Chicago Herald*, June 27, 1893.

Byron, Illinois—*Chicago Record*, June 27, 1893, 1.

DeKalb, Illinois—*Chicago Tribune*, June 27, 1893; *New York Evening World*, June 27, 1893; *Chicago Herald*, June 27, 1893.

The final two routes to Chicago, including the shortcut, were detailed by the *Freeport (IL) Bulletin*, June 27, 1893, 1; and the *Chicago Tribune*, June 27, 1893.

11. Chicago

Additional sources about Chicago and its years leading up the fair include Edgar Lee Masters, *The Tale of Chicago* (New York: G. P. Putnam's Sons, 1933); Bessie Louise Pierce, *A History of Chicago: The Ride of a Modern City, 1871–1893*, vol. 3 (Chicago: University of Chicago Press, 1957); Donald L. Miller, *City of the Century:*

The Epic of Chicago and the Making of America (New York: Simon & Schuster, 1996); Bessie Louise Pierce, ed., *As Others See Chicago: Impressions of Visitors, 1673–1933* (Chicago: University of Chicago Press, 1933), esp. 369–517; Perry R. Duis, *Challenging Chicago: Coping with Everyday Life, 1837–1920* (Urbana: University of Illinois Press, 1998); Chaim M. Rosenberg, *America at the Fair: Chicago's 1893 World's Columbian Exposition* (Mount Pleasant, SC: Arcadia Publishing, 2008); Dennis B. Downey, *A Season of Renewal: The Columbian Exposition and Victorian America* (Westport, CT: Praeger, 2002); Erik Larson, *The Devil in the White City: Murder, Magic, and Madness at the Fair That Changed America* (New York: Crown, 2003); and Emmett Dedmon, *Fabulous Chicago* (New York: Random House, 1953).

For more on the 1893 World's Columbian Exposition itself, see Larson, *Devil in the White City*; David F. Burg, *Chicago's White City* (Louisville: University of Kentucky Press, 1976); Robert W. Rydell, *All the World's a Fair: Visions of Empire at American International Expositions, 1876–1916* (Chicago: University of Chicago Press, 1984), 38–71; Dave Walter, *Today Then: America's Best Minds Look 100 Years into the Future on the Occasion of the 1893 World's Columbian Exposition* (Helena, MT: American & World Geographic Publishing, 1992); and Stanley Appelbaum, *The Chicago World's Fair of 1893: A Photographic Record* (New York: Dover, 1980).

Mable L. Treseder's personal journal, "A Visitor's Trip to Chicago in 1893," edited for publication by her son, Sheldon T. Gardner, in 1943, is available at the Chicago History Museum.

Julian Ralph's "Chicago—The Main Exhibit," a spot-on essay describing a noisy, growing, feisty city on the shores of Lake Michigan, appeared in *Harper's Monthly* (February 1892): 425–35.

Edith Ogden Harrison, the mayor's wife, and her fascination with "wheel mania" are described in Duis, *Challenging Chicago*, 178.

British editor William T. Stead's comments on Chicago and the fair are included in Pierce, *As Others See Chicago*, 355–65.

Giuseppe Giacosa's observations appear in Pierce, *As Others See Chicago*, 275–86.

Lucille Rodney's journey by foot to the Chicago fair was traced by the *Galveston (TX) Daily News*, June 7, 1893, 6; *San Francisco Chronicle*, June 11, 1893, 13; *Rock Island (IL) Daily Argus*, June 13, 1893; *Galveston Daily News*, June 23, 1893, 2; *Kansas City Star*, July 4, 1893, 2; *Decatur (IL) Herald-Dispatch*, July 29, 1893, 3; *Brooklyn (NY) Daily Eagle*, July 31, 1893, 2; *Kansas City (KS) Daily Gazette*, August 1, 1893, 1; and *Galveston Daily News*, August 6, 1893, 14.

Comments on Chicago and the fair by Mulji Devji Vedant appeared in the *Asiatic Quarterly Review* (January 1894): 190–96; and *Littell's Living Age*, February 17, 1894, 435–41.

For more about the Illinois governor, see Barnard, *"Eagle Forgotten"*; for the pardons controversy in particular, see 178–79.

Chicago May is profiled in Nuala O'Faolain, *The Story of Chicago May* (New York: Riverhead, 2005).

Frederick Jackson Turner's classic *The Frontier in American History* is available in numerous editions. Another understanding of Turner as a historian can be found in Gerald D. Nash, *Creating the West: Historical Interpretations, 1890–1990* (Albuquerque: University of New Mexico Press, 1991).

12. The Finish Line

All the nation's major newspapers, especially those in Chicago and the smaller ones in Omaha, Lincoln, and Chadron, splashed headlines across their front pages once the tired, spent, and nearly broken riders stumbled across the finish line outside Buffalo Bill's tent door. For the next several days, journalists closely followed the accounts of some of the riders who had raced for fourteen days; the arguments over who had won, who had lost, and who had cheated; the closed-door meetings between Cody and the race committee; the analyses by the humane society inspectors; and the triumphant parade of cowboys and horses around the Wild West show arena.

For an example of Cody's newspaper ads promoting the Wild West show's parade of racing cowboys, see *Chicago Daily Tribune*, June 29, 1893, 3.

Over the years since the race was run, a few books and magazine stories (cited in detail at the beginning of this sources section) have fleshed out additional details on those several days of indecision in Chicago about how to award the prize money and the golden Colt revolver. Otherwise, few personal stories told by the cowboys themselves survive today. One is Ora Niegel's recounting of tales by her grandfather Joe Gillespie in *True West* (September–October 1959): 10–11. After he returned to central Kansas, James "Rattlesnake Pete" Stephens occasionally reflected on his glory days of racing across the middle of America. These stories ran in the *Hutchinson (KS) News* and the *Hutchinson News-Herald* on July 7, 1927; June 6, 1930; March 10, 1932; June 13, 1933, 1; April 17, 1942; June 13, 1943, 1; June 6, 1944; April 26, 1946; June 16, 1946; and May 16, 1948, 18.

There remains also the reporting of the determined (but uncredited) newsman who pedaled a bicycle after the mounted cowboys along the race's home stretch. His accounts were published in the *Chicago Inter Ocean* as "They Rode Hacks," June 28, 1893, 1, and "How They Got There," June 29, 1893, 1.

13. The Agony Is Over

"The agony is over," proclaimed the *Chadron Citizen*, June 29, 1893, 1.

The proposed new race featuring Emma Hutchinson was reported by the *Chadron Citizen*, June 29, 1893, 1, including a copy of her telegram to Chadron; *Lincoln County Tribune*, July 12, 1893, 2; *Omaha Daily Bee*, July 16, 1893, 5; *Chadron Citizen*, July 20, 1893, 1; *Dawes County Journal*, July 21, 1893; *South Dakota Farmers' Leader*, July 28, 1893; and *Red Cloud (NE) Chief*, July 28, 1893, 7.

The *Chicago Inter Ocean* pronouncement describing the cowboy race as "dishonest" ran as an editorial on June 30, 1893, 6.

The findings of the humane society officials were reported by the *Chicago Inter Ocean*, July 2, 1893, 5; *Chicago Herald*, July 2, 1893; *Lincoln Daily News*, June 30, 1893, 3; and *Brooklyn (NY) Daily Eagle*, June 30, 1893, 1. The officials later formally presented their updated findings at a Minneapolis Humane Society meeting, as reported in the *Minneapolis Tribune*, September 6, 1893, and the *St. Paul Daily Globe*, September 6, 1893, 3.

Race secretary Weir's tribute that "you cannot speak too highly" of the humane society inspectors appeared in the *Dawes County Journal*, July 7, 1893.

Cody sought input from Billy the Bear about the race and promised to send him a new pair of artificial legs, as reported in the *Dawes County Journal*, July 7, 1893. The paper therefore declared Billy the "only big winner" in the race. See also the *Omaha Daily Bee*, July 11, 1893, 4.

The *Dawes County Journal*, July 7, 1893, reported that Joe Campbell had been hired at $60 a month by Buffalo Bill. The *Chadron Citizen* mentioned it on August 10, 1893, as did the *Humboldt (IA) Republican* on September 21, 1893, 6.

Emmett Albright's stolen horse was reported in the *Lincoln (NE) Daily News*, July 6, 1893, 1.

John Berry's comments looking back at the race, calling it a "success outside of the frauds that were practiced," appeared in the *Dawes County Journal*, July 7, 1893.

Middleton's efforts to stage his own Wild West show are covered in Hutton, *Doc Middleton*. They were further reported in the *Chadron Signal*, July 8, 1893; *Omaha Daily Bee*, July 11, 1893, 4; *Chadron Citizen*, July 20, 1893; *Chadron Signal*, July 22, 1893, 1; *Oshkosh (WI) Daily Northwestern*, August 17, 1893, 1; *Sundance (WY) Reform*, September 9, 1893; *Dawes County Journal*, September 15, 1893; and *Sundance (WY) Gazette*, December 1, 1893.

For more on Jerky Bill, see Miles Edwards, "Jerky Bill—This Cowboy Could Stick to a Horse Like a Shadow at Noon," *Casper (WY) Journal,* December 9, 2012.

For more on Opportunity Hank, see Shumway, *History of Western Nebraska*, vol. 2, 564. Hank's mantra: "I'm a fighter, I am; I can lick any man in Chadron."

The William Moore Gillespie letter is courtesy of Clay Comer. It was dated August 1, 1893, and was written from Cotesfield, Nebraska.

The story of the stolen and later pawned golden Colt revolver appeared in the *Chicago Journal*, July 14, 1893.

The antics of the boys playing cowboy in Buffalo, New York, were told in the *Roanoke (VA) Times*, July 12, 1893, 12.

The drunken cowboys hauled into city court in Chadron made the *Dawes County Journal*, September 1, 1893.

Doc Middleton's arrest, conviction, and death in the county jail are recorded in Hutton, *Doc Middleton*, 206–21.

David Howell, a nephew of John Berry, spoke with the author on December 8, 2013.

John Berry's sudden death at the local debate was reported in the *Newcastle (WY) News-Journal*, April 3, 1913; and the *Johnstown (NE) Enterprise Supplement*, April 18, 1913.

Joe Gillespie's seven-hundred-mile wagon trek to Fay, Oklahoma, was documented en route by his wife and later published as "Coxville, Nebraska, to Fay, Oklahoma, by Wagon (1893): The Journal of Anna Gillespie," *Nebraska History* (Fall 1984): 344–65.

When Old Joe died, the local Oklahoma newspapers made no mention that he had run the fabulous cowboy race four decades earlier. But family clippings of his obituary, dated December 1933, noted that he was eighty-three years, eleven months, and twenty-three days old, and still so strong that he had outlived all nine of his siblings.

James "Rattlesnake Pete" Stephens's obituary ran in the *Hutchinson (KS) News*, June 19, 1957.

Postscript

Feisty Broncho Charlie Miller's coast-to-coast ride toward the Western sunset at age eighty-one remains an enormous feat of endurance. He is memorialized in Gladys Shaw Erskine, *Broncho Charlie: A Saga of the Saddle* (New York: Thomas Y. Crowell, 1934), esp. 301–16; Corbett, *Orphans Preferred*, 231–45; Warren, *Buffalo Bill's America*, 340–43; and Sam Henderson, "Broncho Charlie Miller," *Golden West* (July 1996): 20–23, 50–52. His triumphant arrival at the Golden Gate was recorded by the *San Francisco Chronicle*, May 14, 1932.

Index

Note: Page numbers followed by *f* indicate figures.

prizes and prize money, 4, 78, 81,
109, 134, 204–5
Pullman, George Mortimer, 182
Pullman Palace Car Company,
182

railroad, 34, 35, 64
Rain-in-the-Face, 54
rainmaker. *See* Pawnee rainmaker
Ralph, Julian, 29, 31, 180–81
ranges, 30–31, 35–36
rats, 19
"Rattlesnake Bill," 79
"Rattlesnake Dick," 80
"Rattlesnake Pete." *See* Stephens,
James Harold ("Rattlesnake
Pete")
Raymond, Henry H., 17
Raymond, Nebraska, 20
Record, Augustine A., 101, 104
Red Cloud (Chief), 5, 29, 32, 60,
71*f*
Red Cloud, Jack, 54
Red Front Saloon (Chadron,
Nebraska), 62
"Red Jacket," 62
Red Wing (horse), 200
Reynolds, William Henry, 207–8
Richards, Ed, 29
Riley, James, 114–15
Robb, J. S., 115
Robertson, Emma, 19
Robson, August "Gus," 124
Rock Creek, Wyoming, 66
Rockford, Illinois, 202
Rocky Bear, 54
Rodney, G. B., 184
Rodney, Lucille, 184–85
Rome, New York, 207
Romeo (horse), 126, 147, 148,
154
Roosevelt, Teddy, 124
Root, Amos Ives, 34–35
Rousiers, Paul de, 37

Royce, Lois, 18–19
Ruede, Howard, 19
Russell, Charles M., 26
Rutter, H. J. ("Harry"), 92–94, 97

salary of cowboys, 28
Salsbury, Nate, 48, 52, 53, 80,
83–84, 134
Sanders, Mike, 80
Sand Hills, Nebraska:
Buffalo Bill Cody's ranch in, 66
frontier life in, 7–8, 21
in Great Cowboy Race, 2, 78,
121, 140, 152
James "Rattlesnake Pete"
Stephens in, 215
Sandoz, Mari, 8–10, 73–74
Sandy (horse), 194
Satterlee, E. D., 77
Satterlee, Winn, 76
Scout's Rest Ranch, 45, 66
Sears, Richard, 186
Shakespeare, New Mexico, 25
Sheridan, Philip "Little Phil," 40,
46, 51
Sherman, William Tecumseh, 36,
37
Shortall, John G.:
criticism prior to race by, 82, 83,
84, 86, 87–88, 100
final report after race by,
209–10
at finish line, 197, 198
on inspection stations, 133
sickness, 13–14
Sioux City, Iowa, 98, 147–56
Sioux County, Nebraska, 80
Sitting Bull, 31–32, 47
slang, 28
Smith, Charley "C. W.":
at banquet at end of race, 201
bridle given to, 81
at finish line of race, 200, 200*f*,
211*f*